UNDERGROUND RAILWAYS
OF THE WORLD

O. S. Nock

B.Sc., C.Eng., F.I.C.E., F.I.Mech.E.
Past President, Institution of
Railway Signal Engineers

ADAM & CHARLES BLACK · LONDON

FIRST PUBLISHED 1973
A & C BLACK LTD.,
4, 5 AND 6 SOHO SQUARE, LONDON W1V 6AD

© 1973 O. S. NOCK

Reprinted 1974

ISBN 0 7136 1304 1

Phototypeset by Filmtype Services Limited, Scarborough
Printed in Great Britain by BAS Printers Limited,
Wallop, Hampshire

CONTENTS

ACKNOWLEDGEMENTS

The author and publishers are pleased to acknowledge the assistance rendered, both with technical information and illustrations, from the managements of the underground railway systems of Madrid, Milan, Montreal, Paris, Rome, Stockholm and Toronto, also from the Bay Area Rapid Transit system of San Francisco. We are also indebted to the Glasgow Corporation for permission to reproduce certain photographs, and to the Post Office, for much valuable information about the Post Office Tube in London. The Victorian Railways have furnished us with much data concerning the projected Underground Loop in Melbourne, while we are deeply indebted to London Transport for supplying a very large number of photographs.

Reference has been made to extensive published material on various underground railways in 'The Engineer', the 'Railway Gazette', the 'Railway Engineer' and the 'Railway Magazine' and we are indebted to the present publication director of 'The Railway Gazette', Mr. B. W. C. Cooke, for permission to reproduce certain maps and diagrams that have appeared at various times in that journal and its associated contemporaries. We are indebted to the Councils of the Institution of Civil Engineers, and of the Institution of Railway Signal Engineers for permission to reproduce diagrams from their proceedings, and finally to the Westinghouse Brake and Signal Company for the use of certain photographs.

PREFACE

Street traffic congestion and atmospheric pollution are no new things in the great cities of the world. In the latter part of the nineteenth century the rapid growth of urban population, the slowness of road haulage by horse, and the almost complete dependence upon coal fires for heating made the problem every bit as acute as in this modern age, albeit in a different form. The construction of railways running beneath city streets provided an interesting, if no more than an interim solution, and it is a fascinating study to trace the history of the earliest railways in London, Paris and elsewhere, in their varying approaches to the same problem. While in London the first steps towards the creation of the present network were the results of several independent, and to some extent competing companies, in Paris the 'Metro' was planned as a whole, from the outset.

The scientific engineering practices of tunnelling as revealed in the underground railways of the world form a fascinating study in themselves, from the original 'cut and cover' method in London, to deep-level boring by shield, and the ingenious laying of tubes in specially prepared canals in Rotterdam and Stockholm. Equally absorbing is the development of traction methods from steam on the earliest London lines, and cable-traction in Glasgow, to the automatically driven electric trains of the Victoria Line, and the equally novel high-speed trains of BART in San Francisco. Attempts to provide greater amenities by reduction of the noise of travel can be seen in the rubber-tyred trains of one line on the Paris-Metro, and on its counterpart in Montreal.

I have written this book on the basis of personal acquaintance with the underground systems concerned, and this explains why I have not otherwise mentioned the suburban underground lines in Japan. But in other directions I have been concerned throughout my professional life with the design and manufacture of equipment for underground railways, principally in London, but also for Toronto, Rotterdam, and Montreal. In my younger days I had the honour of serving under three men who, perhaps more than, any others, laid the foundations of that impeccable standard of safety in travel that one has come to take for granted on the London Underground: H. G. Brown, who came from the Boston Elevated to be the signal engineer of the Westinghouse Brake Company, in London; Bernard H. Peter, signal engineer of the Metropolitan District Railway, and later General Manager and Chief Engineer of Westinghouse Brake and Signal Company, and eventually succeeding H. G. Brown as Managing Director, and finally there was Walter Allan Pearce, a most talented design engineer.

In later years in London, the policy of Lord Ashfield in constructing long feeder lines into the country from the central network brought its problems of intense utilisation of the innermost tube lines, and gave signal engineers and their contractors an opportunity to develop some of the most sophisticated systems of control to be found anywhere in the world. At the same time one noted with much interest how other large cities were planning and developing their networks—in particular the remarkable Regional Express Metro, in Paris. In writing this book I have naturally recalled the careers of many eminent engineers, of different nationalities and outlooks, and it has been a pleasure to pay tribute, even though it is anonymously in many cases, to their work in difficult and very often hazardous circumstances—underground.

My warmest thanks are due to the managements of the various overseas railways described in this book for supplementing my own observations by much additional information, and a wealth of fine photographs; but of course my most patent obligation is to London Transport, for so generously putting at my disposal a magnificent selection of pictures from their extensive photographic library.

Lastly I am, as always, most grateful to Olivia my wife for her care and skill in typing the MSS, and for the recollections it brought to us both of 'adventures' on the Paris and Rome Metros, and to recall equally that one does not need to journey out of Central London to have the occasional experience of boarding trains that 'go the wrong way'!

Silver Cedars   O. S. NOCK
High Bannerdown   July 1972
Batheaston
Bath

CHAPTER ONE

Genesis of Underground Railways

To anyone familiar with the vast conurbation of modern London, with its ever-increasing population and its critical traffic problems it could seem almost incredible that little more than a hundred years ago the main line railways striking north and westwards entered open country in little more than a mile from their respective termini. Names like Old Oak Common, Primrose Hill, and Hackney Downs gave a good indication of the kind of landscape that one would see, on journeying 3, $1\frac{1}{2}$ or 3 miles out of Paddington, Euston or Shoreditch respectively. At the same time it must be recalled that the new railways had built their terminal stations on the very outskirts of the crowded centre of business and population. Coming in from the south and east the railways had stopped short on the Surrey side, at the south end of London Bridge, and at Vauxhall. The Great Western came no further eastwards than Paddington Green, while the London and Birmingham, enshrined behind the splendours of the Doric Arch in Euston Grove, was on the very threshold of open country when it opened for business in 1838. Euston became known as the 'Gateway to the North'. At first it was as much a gateway to the country of early Victorian times as the mediaeval gates of the City of London, Moorgate, Aldgate, Ludgate had been centuries earlier.

The second trunk line to the north began operation from London in 1850. This was the Great Northern, and with their well-established rival flourishing at Euston it can well be imagined that the new competitor would not wish to incur the great costs of a penetration nearer to the heart of London, however advantageous the eventual business might be. And so the Great Northern terminus was planned at a point less than a mile eastwards from Euston, and at the same distance northward of the City. Threshold of the open country it may have been, but it seems to have been little more than a rubbish tip, to which site, above all places, had been moved the London small-pox hospital in 1793! Pictures of this establishment—a stately enough building in itself and wholly in the Georgian style—show it standing in open fields like some country mansion. Beside it ran the northbound road known as Maiden Lane, reaching in less than a mile to the Copenhagen Fields. With the coming of the Great Northern the rubbish dumps were cleared away, and the smallpox hospital moved to Highgate. Another ill-starred monument, but one nevertheless that gave its name to the district, had been pulled down some four years earlier—the extraordinary 'Kings Cross'. This was not, as sometimes thought, one of the chain of exquisite crosses to Queen Eleanor, wife of Edward I, of which Waltham Cross and Charing Cross are two, but a hideous affair put up in 1830 in memory of George IV, which ended its short existence as a beer shop!

1

The establishment of the railway terminus at Kings Cross, together with the Euston Station near at hand, invested this northern fringe of London with a greatly added importance, and a new road—'The New Road'—was constructed from Kings Cross to connect with the Edgware Road, which of course followed the line of the Roman Watling Street. Already however business interests were beginning to feel the inconvenience of having the main line stations so far from the centre of things, and even before the Great Northern had opened their fine station at Kings Cross, Charles Pearson, solicitor to the Corporation of the City of London, began to propound a proposal for one grand central station to serve all routes out of the metropolis. He suggested that a site either in Holborn or the Haymarket would be ideal, and that all existing railways should extend their lines into this one central point. In 1852, the Eastern Counties Railway was still bogged down, impecuniously, at High Street, Shoreditch, and the cost of extending this line through the heart of the City would, even in those days, have been astronomical. The South Eastern, the Brighton and the South Western would all have had to cross the Thames, and the Great Western had no particular inclinations to move from its palatial Brunel-designed station at Paddington. Euston and Kings Cross were nearest at hand, but neither company showed any desire to extend further.

Charles Pearson was an eloquent advocate, and he tried to impress upon the Great Northern management in particular the rewards they would reap from a 'cheap, rapid and frequent service' to the northern suburbs. But in 1852 the 'northern suburbs' just did not exist. The Great Northern had no more than four stations in the $17\frac{3}{4}$ miles between Kings Cross and Hatfield, located at Hornsey, Southgate, Barnet and Potters Bar. Adjacent to those stations there was nothing approaching a commuter population. In fact the only dwellings were a few country mansions of the aristocracy and 'merchant princes', and no advocacy from Charles Pearson could persuade the Great Northern Board to indulge in further capital expenditure. There was argument and criticism enough when a new 'station' was opened at Seven Sisters Road, Holloway, in 1861—the present Finsbury Park—and irate shareholders, mindful of their diminishing dividends, declared it an incubus. So Pearson got no further with his idea of a central London station. Instead a Bill was deposited with Parliament for the session of 1853 for a 'North Metropolitan Railway' to run *beneath* the New Road, from Kings Cross to Edgware Road. This also got no further. At that stage in railway history tunnels, in the view of the travelling public, were things to be avoided wherever possible, and the idea of a wholly underground railway beneath the streets of London was quite abhorrent.

Nevertheless, with the rapid development of the railway network in Great Britain some link up between the lines running north and south of the Thames was becoming increasingly necessary, though the tightly-packed agglomeration of warehouses, overcrowded dwellings, churches and public buildings that lay between the New Road and the River Thames constituted an obstacle that would require a great deal more than mere money to surmount, or pierce a way through. Strangely enough it was one of the most unlikely financial propositions that actually came to fruition, though it proved in part responsible for bankrupting the railway company that was the principal instigator. But before referring in any detail to the audacious extension of the London Chatham and Dover Railway northbound from Herne Hill, across the River, to Ludgate Hill, I must return once again to the Underground proper, the outcome of the almost still-born North Metropolitan Railway Company authorised by the Act of Parliament dated 1853. This latter provided for a line only between Kings Cross and Edgware Road, and without any connection with, or backing from the main line companies would have been of little value. The fact that it was to be entirely underground prejudiced public opinion against it. At that early stage it was the interest of the Great Western Railway that eventually got the scheme under way in a more practical form, though the Great Western interest like that of the Great Northern was quite unconnected with purely local passenger travel in London itself.

In 1852 the Great Western had extended the broad gauge main line network to Birmingham, and was entering into direct competition with the London and North Western for the inter-city traffic. The broad gauge people, feeling that they were at a disadvantage in respect of London terminal stations to the North Western at Euston Square, welcomed the idea of a connecting link to the City, and they offered to subscribe the then substantial sum of £175,000 to the North Metropolitan Scheme if it could be extended westwards to form a physical link with their own line at Paddington, and eastwards from Kings Cross into the City. A terminus near the General Post Office at St. Martins le-Grand was recommended. On August 7, 1854, a new Act was passed, authorising these extensions, but it proved very difficult to raise the necessary capital. The outbreak of war in the Crimea later that year, and deep public concern at news of the extreme privations suffered by our troops during the terrible winter of 1854–5

Building the Metropolitan; a striking contemporary sketch from the 'Illustrated London News' of January 1862, showing work at Coppice Road, Clerkenwell.

put a damper upon investment of any kind, and the end of a not-very-glorious war was followed by the financial crisis of 1856. So the Metropolitan Railway project hung fire for some years. Both the Great Western and the Great Northern Railways were interested to the extent of securing the authorisation of capital investment, but despite this the capital could still not be raised. This difficulty was of course accentuated by the lack of interest by the general public, and the openly expressed aversion to the prospect of riding on a railway that was entirely underground. There could be no doubt that the interest of the Great Western and of the Great Northern was far greater in respect of goods than of passenger traffic. It was not, indeed, until April 1859, five years after the passage of the amended Bill through Parliament, that Charles Pearson's efforts were crowned finally with success. Then he persuaded the Corporation of the City of London to subscribe £200,000, and the required capital of a million pounds was completely raised.

As finally agreed the City terminus was located at Farringdon Street, within easy walking distance of Ludgate Circus, and the scheme provided for junctions with the Great Western at Paddington, and with the Great Northern at Kings Cross. The 'main line' was laid throughout with mixed gauge tracks, so as to permit through working to and from the Great Western broad gauge system, though naturally the connections to the Great Northern at Kings Cross were laid only with the standard gauge. As planned there were short sections of daylight at Edgware Road, Portland Road, and east of Kings Cross, while the final approach to the Farringdon Street terminus was in the open for the last quarter of a mile; otherwise the total of $3\frac{3}{4}$ miles from the terminus to its junction with the Great Western was entirely in tunnel. Such was the plan for the world's pioneer underground railway. Sir John Fowler was appointed Engineer, he, who with Sir Benjamin Baker, was jointly responsible for design of the Forth Bridge; and the contracts for the construction were placed in December 1859. The interest of the two major railways in the scheme was enhanced when, in 1860, the City Corporation decided to establish a central meat market at Smithfield, and the two companies secured a lease of the basement under the market for use as a goods station. Still the major interest remained in goods traffic, and Charles Pearson's optimistic thoughts about the new line enabling the working classes of London to live in the surrounding country districts were generally considered to be mere 'pie in the sky'.

The great merit of any form of Underground railway, as a means of avoiding congestion in busy city streets, scarcely applied at all in the case of the first section of the Metropolitan; for it ran through districts well removed from the crowded thoroughfares of the City itself. By its very design however it had to be carried beneath streets. It was located only just below the surface, and construction was by what is known as 'cut and cover' methods. A deep cutting was excavated, and then the top of this was covered in. As most of this had to be done along the line of the New Road—now Euston Road and Marylebone Road—the inconvenience during the constructional period must have been considerable. Much thought was evidently given to means of rapid progressing of the work, and to provide immediate access to the line, both for removal of earth excavated from the cuttings and supply of materials, the section linking up with the Great Western was completed first. As might be imagined there were many incidental troubles during the construction. During May and June 1861 some of the cuttings between Euston and Baker Street caved in. The engineers had to use extreme care in avoiding damage to underground sewers, despite which the Fleet Ditch Sewer

Work in progress at Kings Cross. The clock tower of the Great Northern terminus can be seen, and the then-narrow thoroughfare of Euston Road, straight ahead.

burst into the works near Farringdon Street and flooded the tunnels for nearly a mile in the direction of Kings Cross. The connections to the Great Northern Railway involved some steep gradients and sharp curves, each line running in a separate single-line tunnel, and the down line running beneath the Great Northern Hotel and being known accordingly as the 'hotel curve'. At Paddington no steep gradients were involved in the connection. Rail level in the Great Western terminus is a considerable depth below that of the neighbouring streets, as travellers will appreciate from the inclined ramps by which cars now enter and leave the station.

The line was not ready for opening until 1863, but long prior to this there had been much consideration given to the question of motive power. The Metropolitan Railway had been authorised on the strict instruction that any form of locomotives used must emit no smoke, nor exhaust steam when running through the tunnels. At that period steam was the only form of motive power to have attained any degree of reliability, and as the exhausting of the steam to atmosphere through the blastpipe and chimney was virtually a fundamental necessity for maintaining steam pressure in the boiler, it certainly seemed that a pretty little problem faced those responsible for providing locomotives for the new line. Sir John Fowler conceived the idea of a hot-brick engine. It was proposed to have arrangements for boiling water at each end of the line, in the open air so as not to contravene the tunnel restrictions; the engine boiler was to be

5

filled and steam raised by piling red hot bricks around the boiler. A locomotive to this extraordinary specification was actually built, by Robert Stephenson & Co. and a trial made between Paddington and Edgware Road, on November 28, 1861. It was set to haul a few open trucks, and a contemporary report said that 'a cloud of smoke, dust and steam soon covered the train and continued until it emerged from the tunnel into the open air.' Apparently it was at its last gasp for steam on reaching Edgware Road; but quite apart from that, the indescribable 'atmosphere' created in the tunnel was enough to damn the project for good and all. It is not without significance that not a whisper of this weird thing occurs in that famous work *A Century of Locomotive Building*, which describes so comprehensively the products of Robert Stephenson & Co. As usual, E. L. Ahrons put the outcome in a light-hearted nut-shell: 'Like King Alfred's hot cakes, Sir John's hot bricks were a failure.'

In the meantime Daniel Gooch had not been idle. In view of their interest and large investment in the Metropolitan Railway it was agreed that the Great Western should work the line. While Sir John Fowler was inadvertently doing his best to asphyxiate his associates with a mixture of steam and brick dust in the tunnels, Gooch was carrying out trials to see how far an orthodox locomotive would run without any blast on the fire, and the outcome was the production of a class of 22 broad gauge tank engines of the 2-4-0 type which consumed their own exhaust steam, by means of condensing apparatus. They were notable in being the only broad gauge engines ever built which had the cylinders outside. This was necessary in order to provide space beneath the boiler and between the frames for the water tanks and condensing equipment. These locomotives were fitted with a valve by means of which the driver could direct the exhaust up the chimney in the normal way, or into the condensing tanks when working through the tunnels. Although these locomotives were something of 'a box of tricks' Gooch contrived to give them a very neat and compact appearance, quite in keeping with his main line Great Western engines, except for the unusual provision of outside cylinders. The water tanks and condensing pipes were all discreetly hidden away— too discreetly, as it turned out!

The condensing pipes were below the water level in the tanks, and the natural suction created in the cylinders when the locomotives were running with steam shut off would have drawn water into the cylinders. To avoid this, automatic flap valves were fitted in the exhaust pipes. These valves proved an unmitigated nuisance. They could not be kept tight, and when the pipes and connections were not sucking air in from outside they were allowing water to leak out from inside! Added to this, the tanks themselves were not large enough, and with the discharge of exhaust steam into them when working in the tunnels they got overheated, and prejudiced the condensing arrangements. When they eventually reached Farringdon Street the hot water from the tanks was emptied out and a fresh supply of cold water put in. The time taken in thus servicing the engines at Farringdon Street was considerable. Many a time, one would imagine, the drivers would have been glad to have used that diverting flap valve, and when no one was looking put the exhaust through the chimney and liven up the fire. In any case an intermittent dose of exhaust steam in the tunnels was better than coming ignominiously to a stand in the darkness through shortage of steam—Acts of Parliament notwithstanding! But, as the very first condensing locomotives ever to be put into service, they were a notable achievement on Gooch's part. Had they not been required in such a hurry one feels that some careful experimenting with a prototype

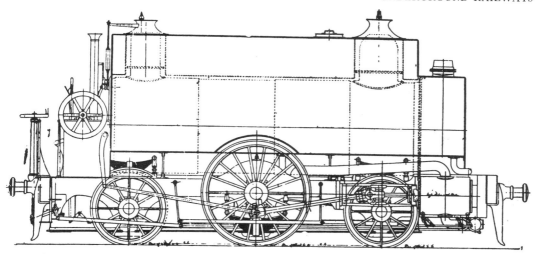

'Hot-brick' broad-gauge locomotive, Metropolitan Railway.

Baker Street station, from an early coloured print.

would have ironed out most of the difficulties. As it was, construction of them had to be divided between three works: six from the Vulcan Foundry; six from Kitsons of Leeds and the remainder at Swindon.

Their first sojourn on the Metropolitan turned out to be unexpectedly brief. The passenger service between Paddington (Bishops Road) and Farringdon Street was inaugurated on January 10, 1863, with four trains an hour each way, and proving very popular the Metropolitan wished to increase the frequency. This was however only one matter upon which friction very soon began to develop between the owners and the Great Western. An eastward extension from Farringdon Street to Moorgate was projected, and as the new stock raised by the Metropolitan to provide capital for this new extension was selling at a premium the Great Western Board asked for an allocation. This the Metropolitan refused, on the grounds that the G.W.R. had no statutory authority to subscribe more than that already contributed. The folks at Paddington were so annoyed that they went to law over it, and lost. All this naturally did not contribute much to the harmonious working of the line, and when the Metropolitan continued to press for more trains they were met with a solid refusal. It is fair to say that the Great Western was then experiencing some distinctly hard times, and there seems to have been a genuine feeling among their senior officers that an increased service would not pay. But the insistence of the Metropolitan, coupled with the 'atmosphere' that had developed at Board level over the Moorgate extension stock led

The 'Bellmouth' junction, Praed Street, showing a broad gauge train hauled by a 'Gooch' 2-4-0 tank engine, in 1863.

to an announcement by the Great Western that they would cease to work the line after September 30, 1863.

Now it so happened that the standard gauge connection to the Great Northern, at Kings Cross, with a service of trains to Farringdon Street, was to open on the very next day, October 1, so that the Metropolitan merely acknowledged the Great Western statement, and advised them that they would take over the working from October 1. This was not in the least what the Great Western expected. So far as was known at Paddington the Metropolitan had no locomotives of their own, and while it could be inferred that the Great Northern would be providing some condensing locomotives to work its own service through the tunnels between Kings Cross and Farringdon Street it was not imagined that any would be available for the existing service of four trains an hour from Bishops Road, let alone for the more intensive working that the Metropolitan was demanding. Charles Saunders, the great secretary of the Great Western, felt sure he had the Metropolitan in the hollow of his hand, and incensed by the apparently calm acceptance of the notice of withdrawal from September 30, he replied that all Great Western locomotives and carriages would be withdrawn after August 9. This savage ultimatum once again did not have the desired effect, for Myles Fenton, the General Manager of the Metropolitan, was the last person to be intimidated by bullying. Instead of replying to Saunders he went straight to Kings Cross.

He knew, of course, that the Great Northern were getting locomotives ready for their own service to Farringdon Street, to commence on October 1, but the date was then July 31, and there were only ten days to go before the Great Western withdrawal. Fortunately for Fenton the whole attitude of the Great Northern management was the very antithesis of that of the Great Western. While the latter had developed a dignified aloofness, as befitted so senior and long established a company, the Great Northern was essentially a fighter, ready to take any difficult situation on a challenge, and at Doncaster Works they had a locomotive superintendent in Archibald Sturrock who was the living embodiment of that spirit. For some·time previously to the opening of the passenger service he had been converting some of the oldest locomotives of the Great Northern into tank engines. This was not originally in view of any possible use on the Metropolitan, but to provide some light power for branch line service. The engines concerned were a class of 50 pretty little 2-2-2s built by Sharp Brothers, and delivered to the G.N.R. between 1847 and 1849. They were the first locomotives the company possessed, and were appropriately numbered 1 to 50. They were tiny little things, and by the year 1862 were quite outclassed for main line traffic. It was, in fact, no less than 10 years previously that Sturrock had converted 11 of them into tank engines. This had been done by lengthening the frames to the rear of the driving wheels, and placing the trailing wheels 3ft. 1in. farther back. This gave space for the addition of a water tank and coal bunker, and by July 1852 all eleven of them had been thus converted.

In readiness for the service to Farringdon Street, from October 1, 1863, Sturrock was adapting some of these little engines to condensing; but it was one thing to provide power for a short length of line, little more than a mile long, and quite another to take over the entire service from Paddington to Farringdon Street. There was no difficulty over carriages. Fenton obtained offers of help from both the Great Northern and the London and North Western, though just how carriages from the latter would have been conveyed to the Metropolitan was not so obvious; but so far as locomotives were concerned once the situation was put to Sturrock he rose to the challenge with the

9

Interior of Kings Cross station, showing broad gauge trains, 1863.

Junction of the Great Northern with the Metropolitan at Kings Cross.

utmost zest. All Doncaster was put on to conversion of the remaining 2-2-2 well tank engines. Those already prepared for the Kings Cross–Farringdon Street run, from October 1, were tried out. Those sharply-graded single-line tunnels at Kings Cross were already finished, and in those breathless first days of August 1863, when Saunders was confidently expecting a surrender from Fenton, the Great Northern waited each night until the last Great Western train had gone westwards to Paddington, and then down the Kings Cross junction came the Sturrock condensing 2-2-2 tanks for extensive trials in the secrecy of the night! The outcome was that Saunders waited in vain, and that after the Great Western withdrawal the Great Northern took up the working on the very next morning, sharp on time, without any interruption whatever. So far as local passenger working on the Metropolitan was concerned the Great Western was out—for ever!

Despite their rebuff however, and the strained relations that resulted from it, the Great Western was on too good a thing to withdraw entirely from the Metropolitan passenger service and they continued to work the outer residential trains, some from Ealing, and some from as far out as Windsor through to Farringdon Street, with broad gauge locomotives and stock. In the years 1863 to 1869 that original section of under-ground railway—the very patriarch of all underground, tube and 'rapid transit' systems the world over—presented an astonishing appearance. On some trains would come the broad-based outside cylindered 2-4-0 tanks of Daniel Gooch's design, with those incredible broad gauge dogboxes of carriages seating nine a side (!), and then a dainty little Sharp 2-2-2, with Sturrock's condensing apparatus, with always the chance that the flexible pipes between smokebox and condensing tanks would burst. Exquisite though the little Sharp 2-2-2s were to look upon, they were hardly ideal for the underground traffic, and a number of coupled engines of various types were adapted by Sturrock to Metropolitan conditions. Among these may be mentioned certain 0-4-2 and 0-6-0 tender engines of Hawthorn build. All these were nevertheless in the way of makeshifts, and the drivers became expert in the way of 'fiddling' them along to maintain steam pressure in the tunnels without exhausting through the chimney in the normal way.

The whole locomotive stock working over the Underground in that first year of operation, standard gauge and broad gauge alike could not be regarded as other than makeshifts, and in the meantime the Metropolitan Railway had on order from Beyer, Peacock & Co. 18 engines of the famous 4-4-0 tank design. Although so very distinc-tive in appearance, and creating quite a sensation when the first of them arrived from Manchester in 1864, they did not represent a truly original design. Two years previously the firm had built 8 very similar engines for the Tudela and Bilbao Railway in Northern Spain, and the only essential difference other than of dimensions was that the Metro-politan engines had condensing apparatus. They deserve much more than a passing mention, because they became virtually a standard type for London underground working, not only on the Metropolitan, but on other railways the services of which took them through the tunnels. Their remarkable appearance, which will be appre-ciated from various illustrations, stemmed particularly from the large side-tanks, and the very short wheel-based bogie. The latter was not a bogie in the usual understanding of the term, which pivoted about a central pin. The Metropolitan bogie had an action like that of model locomotives designed to negotiate very sharp radiused curves. It was a swivelling truck carried on a long arm pivoted near the leading driving axle.

11

The first 18 of these engines had Beyer's ornamental chimney, and a huge dome with the Salter type of spring-loaded safety valves mounted on the top of it. The *ensemble* looked all the more striking from the dome being mounted cheek by jowl with the chimney. The engines had no cabs, and there was just a plain weather-board to give the driver and fireman a little protection. Of course, at that time, cabs were the exception rather than the rule; but when they became general on the ordinary surface railways no such concession was made on the Underground. Perhaps the absence of cabs was deliberate, to give every inducement to the drivers to make their engines condense in the tunnels and not to take the occasional 'luxury' of exhausting through the chimney when they thought no one was looking! These splendid engines saw steam out on the Underground lines, and the last survivor, though much modernised, is preserved in the Museum of Transport at Clapham.

Despite the uncertainties of the earliest motive power the popularity which the Metropolitan quickly attained led to early extensions of great importance. I have mentioned already the projected extension eastwards from Farringdon Street to Moorgate, which precipitated the row with the Great Western. With this extension was associated the connection with the London, Chatham and Dover Railway, at Snow Hill. When the latter company projected its northward extension from Penge to cross the river at Blackfriars and make a city terminus at Ludgate Hill, two of the major railways, the London and South Western and the Great Northern were so impressed with the facilities this line would offer, if extended still further north to intersect the Farringdon Street–Moorgate extension of the Metropolitan, that they invested heavily in it, in return for running powers. The London and South Western trains did not

The original City terminus: Farringdon Road, with westbound trains hauled by the standard 4-4-0 tank engines preparing to depart: 1868.

12

penetrate beyond Ludgate Hill, but the Great Northern began working freight trains from Kings Cross through to Herne Hill, while the Chatham began a remarkable series of 'round London' local passenger trains. These originated at their new station at Victoria, crossed the Thames and went meandering off through Brixton and Herne Hill; recrossed the Thames, called at Ludgate Hill, and then pounded up Snow Hill and on to the Metropolitan. Thence through the underground tunnels to Kings Cross, and then, believe it or not, on to the Great Northern main line to terminate at Wood Green!

The 'Chatham' was also determined to get its money's worth out of the eastward connection on to the Metropolitan at Smithfield. The line coming up from Ludgate Hill made a triangle junction with the Underground, and the Chatham ran a service of trains into Moorgate. This service, I regret to say, was something of a joke with City men. It seemed that everything conceivable that could get in their way did so. The line was much used by both Great Northern and Great Western freights to and from Smithfield, and the unfortunate London, Chatham and Dover locals were the shuttle-cocks of the line. Persons who wanted to get from Ludgate Hill to Moorgate found it much quicker to walk! From all this it will be apparent that the original Underground railway was rapidly becoming a 'free-for-all', and this situation was much accentuated when the Midland Railway completed its London Extension and St. Pancras station was opened in 1868. For the Midland also had its connection to the Underground, though in their case the tunnel underneath St. Pancras station came to the surface nearly a mile to the north and not adjacent to the main line terminus as with the Great

Eastward extension: heavy excavation work at Smithfield, in the shadow of St. Paul's 1865.

Farringdon Road station
in 1866: 'Widened Lines'
tracks in the foreground

Northern, at Kings Cross. With the prospect of increased congestion on its line east of
Kings Cross, with the Midland joining the Great Northern and the Chatham in the
use of running powers, the Metropolitan built, at tremendous expense, a second pair
of tracks for use of the 'foreigners'. It kept the original line for its own trains, of which
there were an increasing number, while Great Northern, Midland, and Chatham
trains—passenger and goods—used the City Widened Lines. It is indeed an eloquent
testimony to the rapid increase in traffic over this pioneer underground railways that
its track capacity over its busiest section had to be doubled in three years from its first
operating.

The 'City Widened Lines'!—what memories they bring of my own early professional
work as an engineer. They began in the tunnels leading to the Great Northern and to
the Midland, under Kings Cross and St. Pancras. Then they ran parallel to the old
Metropolitan line until approaching Farringdon Street. There the new tunnel dived
deep under the old one so as to bring the Widened Lines on to the south side. The

On the City Widened Lines:
the burrowing junction just
to the west of Farringdon
Road, with a westbound
train passing into the
original tunnel, and an eastbound train, on the
Widened Lines, emerging
from the deeper-level
tunnel.

connections, to Smithfield goods station, to the Chatham line, and to the terminal platforms at Moorgate became completely clear of the purely Metropolitan trains. Just before I joined the Westinghouse Brake and Signal Company in 1925, the firm had secured a contract for re-signalling the Widened Lines. Although it is briefly bringing their story forward more than 50 years it is of conditions in the tunnels that I now write. Although the old Metropolitan line had long previously been electrified the Widened Lines were still steam worked, and even with locomotives condensing the atmosphere was at times indescribable. Working in those tunnels had their moments, as when a train would come along with an occasional carriage door swinging open, or when lying prone between the tracks adjusting an electric train stop, and a locomotive passed with its injector overflowing! Twenty years after steam working had ceased the tunnels of the old line were still smoke blackened, but that was nothing to the sight of that grisly lower tunnel near Farringdon Street, where the Widened Lines burrowed underneath the older Underground line.

CHAPTER TWO

The Network Spreads

The initial, and almost sensational success of the Metropolitan Railway in its first limited extent, led to a whole crop of schemes for underground transport systems in London, and in 1864 a Joint Committee of both Houses of Parliament evolved certain proposals for a circular system of communication in central London. From among these proposals there emerged the Metropolitan District Railway, authorised under three Acts of Parliament passed on July 29, 1864, to provide in the first place an underground line from South Kensington to Westminster Bridge. Concurrently, plans were in hand for the extension of the Metropolitan itself, from a junction in the tunnel half-way between Edgware Road and Paddington to run southwards through Notting Hill and Kensington High Street, to Gloucester Road. The Metropolitan Railway had a large share in the promotion of the new company, to such an extent indeed, that few people outside financial circles realised that it *was* a separate company at all. From the outset the 'District', to give it the name by which it became familiarly known afterwards, had the Chairman and three other directors of the Metropolitan on its board; it employed the same contractors in its construction, and had the same engineers.

The Metropolitan extension from the tunnel junction under Praed Street to Gloucester Road was opened in October 1868; the District Line from South Kensington to Westminster Bridge was planned to open on Christmas Eve of the same year. Obviously it was essential to link the two, if for no other reason than that Metropolitan locomotives and carriages were to be used for operating the District Line. This eventuality had apparently not been foreseen at the time the Praed Street Junction–Gloucester Road extension had been programmed, and the result was that the short continuing link to South Kensington, entirely in tunnels, had to be constructed in a shipwreck hurry, employing a force of 3000 men working night and day. But it was completed on time, and on Christmas Eve a continuous line of Underground railway extended from Moorgate Street westwards via Edgware Road and Gloucester Road, and so eastwards again to Victoria and Westminster Bridge. The new section of the Metropolitan included some stiff gradients, including a 1 in 70 bank from High Street, Kensington to Notting Hill; but it had not been a difficult line to construct. The 'District' section was far otherwise. It had been likened to a surgical operation in the care that had to be taken in avoiding the foundations of buildings, sewers and such like. At the eastern end it was close to the north bank of the Thames. No fewer than four pumping engines had to be installed at the outset to keep the tunnels clear of water, at Victoria, near to which a profuse underground spring was located; at Sloane

London, Chatham and Dover Railway: one of the 'Scotchmen' 0-4-2 tanks *Spey*, used for working the service to Moorgate Street.

Square, where the railway passed *under* a main sewer, while at South Kensington two pumping engines were necessary to maintain general drainage of the line. There was a westward extension from Gloucester Road to West Brompton, mostly in the open, brought into service in April 1869, and the very expensive extension eastwards from Westminster to Blackfriars, a little over 1¼ miles, opened in May 1870. This required yet another pumping engine, to keep out water from the Thames and which was installed at the Temple station.

So far as the Metropolitan was concerned the District, in those early years, was very much the poor relation. Its route mileage was only 5·7, and its traffic entirely passenger. It was isolated, having no connections with the main line railways except the distant and indirect ones reached over Metropolitan tracks, and there was thus no possibility of obtaining increased revenue by the granting of running powers, as the Metropolitan itself was so advantageously doing with no fewer than four main line companies. As for the District, a majority of its shareholders felt they could get on much better without Metropolitan assistance, and late in 1870 they gave notice of the intention to terminate the working agreement as from July 1871. In readiness for this they ordered their own locomotives and carriages. So far as engines were concerned they were on safe grounds in purchasing 4-4-0 condensing tank engines from Beyer, Peacock & Co., these were of almost identical design to those of the Metropolitan, but incorporating one or two small improvements, and a livery of deep olive green, instead of the chocolate brown of the Metropolitan. The carriages were compact little four-wheelers, close-coupled in sets of nine so as to occupy minimum platform space; and into these nine coaches they packed *seating* accommodation for 400 passengers. They were all of the ordinary

Building the District Railway: 'cut and cover' work in Parliament Square, Westminster, from the 'Illustrated London News', 1867.

19

compartment type, and with seats for 180 in a four-wheeled 'third' one would imagine that the seats were so close together that the knees of passengers touched those of their *vis-a-vis*, and that there would be literally no standing room. The second class carriages seated 140, and the 'firsts', 80. The standard make-up of a train was two 'firsts'; three 'seconds' and four 'thirds'. These little carriages weighed no more than 10 tons apiece, but a full 9-coach train would weigh something like 117 tons—27 tons of passengers to 90 tons of stock.

But the most significant point about the changes in administration of the District Railway that took place in 1871 was that the company appointed as Managing Director the tremendous personality of James Staats Forbes. Those with a taste for railway history in its most dramatic and colourful form will know something of his fantastic career in a similar post on the London, Chatham and Dover Railway; of how he personally weathered the effects of a catastrophic financial collapse, and carried the company along with him for another thirty years while paying next to nothing in dividends on the ordinary shares. He has been described, perhaps a little uncharitably, as 'a past master in the art of *bunkum* . . .' He was appointed General Manager of the Chatham in 1862; in June 1866 he, together with the Secretary of the company was appointed a Receiver in Chancery, and in the subsequent period of litigation he climbed to a position of undisputed eminence in control, from 1870 onwards. No one but a most forceful and dynamic character would ever have had the nerve to face out and *profit* from such a situation as developed on the Chatham in 1866, and this is the man to whom the District Railway turned when its proprietors decided to rid themselves of Metropolitan influence. He had a genius for the propagation of railways, for scenting new avenues for connections and train services. He propounded his ideas with such vigour and conviction as to carry his shareholders with them regardless of whether his ventures were likely to be profitable or not, and he led the luckless Chatham proprietors along the path of penury almost to the end of the century!

In Kent the London, Chatham and Dover Railway fought a continuous and ruinously competitive battle for traffic with the South Eastern Railway, over which there presided the formidable Sir Edward Watkin—'The Railway King'. In personality he was the very opposite of Forbes: a dour, hard-hitting promoter and financier, quite lacking in the light-hearted touches that made Forbes's most fantastical flights of bunkum seem plausible. But despite the financial vicissitudes in which he had been involved on the Chatham there is no doubt that the 'declaration of independence' by the District, and their appointment of Forbes as Managing Director much disturbed the Metropolitan, particularly as their own finances had begun to take a less favourable turn. So, who better to counter any subterranean activities of Forbes in London than Watkin. The Metropolitan invited him to take over the Chairmanship in 1872 and the running fight waged throughout the length and breadth of Kent between these two deadly rivals took on a new and more localised form in London itself. At the same time it had to be a more covert and subtle form of rivalry than in the Kentish 'fields'. The Metropolitan and the District were much interlinked, and before either Watkin or Forbes went 'underground' the Chatham, of Forbes, was closely associated with the Metropolitan at Ludgate Hill, Moorgate Street and on the City Widened Lines. Watkin on the other hand had no 'main line' stake in the underground fortunes. The South Eastern was one of the few companies that did not have some direct physical connection by the end of the century.

Extending the Metropolitan: excavation under residential property in Leinster Gardens, Bayswater, for the Inner Circle construction.

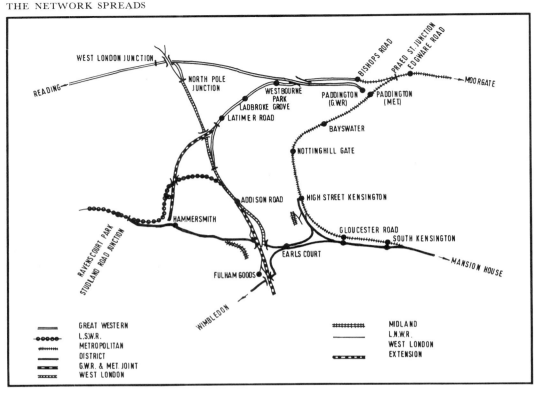

The Western connections to the Inner Circle.

Section	Main line connection	Date opened	
Gloucester Rd.–South Kensington (independent District line)	—	August	1870
Kensington High St.–Cromwell Rd. Jc.	—	July	1871
Cromwell Curve	—	July	1871
Earls Court (Warwick Rd. Jc.) to Addison Rd. (Earls Court Jc.)	L.N.W.R. G.W.R. L.S.W.R.	February	1872
West Kensington Jc. to Hammersmith	—	September	1874
Hammersmith to Studland Road Jc.	L.S.W.R.	June	1877

Forbes on the other hand immediately began to engineer extension lines at the Western extremity of the District, and in June 1877 it was directly linked with the London and North Western, the Great Western and the London and South Western, while the Midland had been granted running powers to goods stations of their own at Kensington High Street coal depot, and Lillie Bridge. The opposite sketch map shows how these were contrived while the following table gives the dates of opening. From this map it can be seen that all three main line companies could run on to the District line through Addison Road, and then over the spur from the West London line at Earls Court Junction to the Earls Court–West Brompton spur at Warwick Road Junction.

This connection was no sooner completed than two 'foreign' services began over the District line, and to distinguish these from the joint service operated with the Metropolitan from Mansion House to Moorgate Street, over the original underground line, they were referred to as the Outer and Middle Circles, the original service becoming known as the Inner Circle. At this time none of the three services made complete circuits; all were in the form of horseshoes. The 'Middle Circle', with a train every half-hour, was operated by the Great Western Railway. It ran from Paddington to Westbourne Park, and thence over the Hammersmith and City Line to Latimer Road Junction. Then the trains took the spur to Uxbridge Road Junction, on the West London Railway, calling at Addison Road, and thence on to the District Railway at Warwick Road Junction, continuing thence to Mansion House. The 'Outer Circle' which was operated by the London and North Western Railway originated at Broad

Sectional view on line of the District Railway on Thames Embankment, with Charing Cross South Eastern Railway station, at left. From the 'Illustrated London News', June 1867.

District Railway: one of the standard 4-4-0 tank locomotives used on all services.

Street, North London Railway, and followed the circuitous and sharply-graded line via Dalston, Camden Town, Hampstead Heath and Kensal Rise to Willesden Junction, and thence over the West London Railway to Addison Road to take up the same route as the 'Middle Circle' from that point onwards. The 'Outer Circle' also provided a half-hourly service.

It is certainly a tribute to the excellent reputation established from the outset by the special Metropolitan 4-4-0 tank locomotives that so highly individual a railway as the London and North Western should have adopted it for working the 'Outer Circle'. It is however fair to add that the service was inaugurated just at the time Francis W. Webb was taking up the reins as Chief Mechanical Engineer at Crewe. It is probable that he took the quickest way of getting some condensing locomotives of a well-tried type quickly rather than go to the trouble of designing something special. The 'specials' in L.N.W.R. motive power on the 'Outer Circle' came later. At first the coaches were painted in the standard North Western style, with white upper panels and chocolate brown bodies. Smart and distinctive though they looked however, those white upper panels were not ideal for the atmosphere of the Underground, however efficiently the locomotives of all types might condense! After a time the painting style was changed to one of plain teak. The Great Western trains on the 'Middle Circle' were, of course, standard and not broad gauge, and they were worked by the excellent little Armstrong 2-4-0 tank engines. They, like the Metropolitan and District 4-4-0s had no cabs. The carriages were tiny little things, close-coupled and with very cramped accommodation in the third class. It was sometimes said that the Great Western made these carriages deliberately cramped to emphasise the disadvantages of the narrow gauge! So far as outward appearances went however the Great Western trains on the 'Middle Circle' service were the smartest and most colourful of all running over the District line from Gloucester Road to Mansion House, with their Brunswick-green engines, with a pro-fusion of polished brass and copper work, and the chocolate and cream coaches.

It is extraordinary to recall that by the late 'seventies' of last century the District was running 20 trains an hour in each direction between South Kensington and Mansion House in the peak hours. Just think of it—a 3-minute headway, with steam traction,

Building the District Railway: 'cut and cover' work in front of Somerset House, in 1869. The line from Westminster to Blackfriars was opened in 1870.

Steam on the underground Metropolitan: a Hammersmith-bound train near Aldgate hauled by one of the standard 4-4-0 tank engines.

25

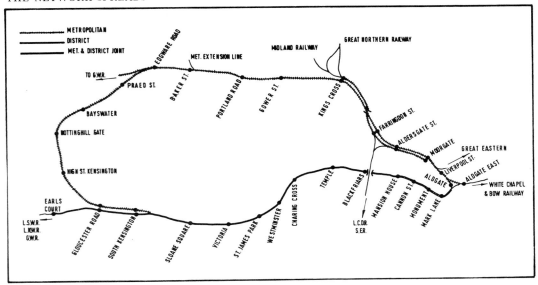

The completed Inner Circle.

mechanical signalling, and compartment-type carriages. In addition to the Inner, Middle and Outer Circle trains, the westward extensions beyond Hammersmith had enabled through trains from the City to run to Richmond by 1877, to Ealing by 1879, and to Fulham by 1880. All these trains terminated at Mansion House, and the scene there with engine changing, and the locomotives and stock of four different companies in evidence must have been a highly animated one in the peak hours. Even in the quieter periods there were never less than 14 trains an hour in each direction on the line between Mansion House and South Kensington. It will be realised that even at that early date in underground railway history extreme pressure was being put upon the purely underground part of the line, with services from no fewer than six different routes—Fulham, Richmond, Ealing and the three 'Circles'—all funnelling on to the single pair of tracks running eastward from South Kensington. On the north side of the Inner Circle the Metropolitan was much better off, because all its 'foreign' workings, with the exception of the Great Western, ran over the Widened Lines and did not disturb the Metropolitan's own passenger services.

With the District having arrived at Mansion House, and with the Metropolitan at Moorgate Street the logical thing was to make connection, and complete the Inner Circle. There were many difficulties, quite apart from the question of finance. The station on the District line bearing its name was actually some little distance from the Mansion House itself, and after prolonged negotiations between the many interests concerned a very useful circuitous route was decided on, linking up Cannon Street; Monument, a station at the North end of London Bridge; at Mark Lane—convenient for Fenchurch St., and the Tilbury line—and then round by Aldgate and Liverpool Street to Moorgate. There were to be five new stations, all within the City itself: and having regard to the benefits expected to result the Corporation of the City of London contributed no less than £800,000 towards the cost. The 'City Lines and Extensions', as the project was officially termed, were to be jointly owned by the Metropolitan and the District railways. All the constructional difficulties experienced in earlier underground lines in London were accentuated on this extraordinary 2¼ miles of railway, and the ultimate cost worked out at a million pounds a mile—*a million a mile* with the value of money standing as it was in 1880! It was opened for traffic in 1884. So far as the District was concerned this was not all. Knowing the personality and inclinations of James Staats Forbes one can hardly imagine him stopping once a way had been tunnelled through to the East End. He must open up connections with the railways running out into the Essex countryside, and into Kent through the Thames Tunnel at Wapping.

In the meantime the long-standing Watkin–Forbes confrontation that had bedevilled railway operation in Kent extended to underground railways in London. The Chatham penetration into the City, and its lavish and unremunerative services through Ludgate Hill to Moorgate Street on the one hand, and to both Great Northern and Midland lines via Kings Cross, has already been mentioned. Where the Chatham went so also had the South Eastern. A connecting line was built above the roof-tops of Southwark whereby the South Eastern trains from the Charing Cross extension line could join the Chatham line over Blackfriars bridge, and reach the Metropolitan through Ludgate Hill. And in 1878 the South Eastern began running trains between stations such as Woolwich and Greenwich to Muswell Hill and Enfield, via Ludgate Hill and Kings Cross. Naturally they called at all stations, but because of the Watkin–Forbes feud South Eastern tickets were not accepted at the two London, Chatham and Dover stations of Ludgate Hill and Snow Hill! Furthermore the enforcement of regulations thus arising was carried out with the utmost zeal and determination by the station staffs concerned, and woe betide the passenger with an L.C.D.R. ticket for Wood Green (G.N.R.) who attempted to make use of a South Eastern train that turned up at Ludgate Hill while he was waiting! At the height of this absurd competition the Chatham was actually running eighty trains a day in each direction between Ludgate Hill and Moorgate Street alone. Judging from contemporary accounts of their punctuality one can well imagine that the service extended far into the night before the last ones struggled their way home.

When Watkin resolved to link up his South Eastern and Metropolitan 'empires' with this strangely unproductive train service the South Eastern had no locomotives with the requisite condensing apparatus for working through the tunnels of the City Widened Lines between Farringdon Street and Kings Cross, and some of the standard 4-4-0 tank engines were hired from the Metropolitan to do the job. This brings me on to the subject of underground locomotives in general, of which there was an increasing variety working through the tunnels of the District and of the Metropolitan towards the end of the nineteenth century. The two owning companies remained faithful to the pioneer design of 4-4-0 tank. On both railways the locomotives underwent some detail modification such as changes in shapes of chimneys and dome covers, and styles of painting. By the end of the century the District had no fewer than 54 of these most reliable engines. It was the 'foreigners' however that introduced the variety. The Great Northern began using the handsome and powerful 0-4-4 tanks of Patrick Stirling's design, and the Midland changed also to the 0-4-4 type, with well tanks, and the characteristic Derby style of boiler mountings. The Great Western had no need to change from the efficient little Armstrong 2-4-0 tanks, but the Chatham began replacing the picturesque 'Scotchmen' 0-4-2 tanks by powerful black-painted 0-4-4 tanks of

Kirtley's design. During the nineteenth century these latter were probably the best locomotives to work through the underground tunnels of London.

For sheer *divertisement*, as the French might call it, one had to observe the locomotives of the Premier Line of all Britain, the princely London and North Western, and to ride the trains on the Outer Circle, as between Mansion House and South Kensington. Students of locomotive history will need no reminding that in the 'eighties' of last century the great compound era of Francis W. Webb was in full blast at Crewe. The 'great' man was not content with applying his precepts to main line express passenger locomotives; those precepts must also be tried out on heavy freight and suburban tank types. Now to all appearances the logical way to exploit the principle of two-stage expansion with three cylinders would have been to have one high pressure cylinder exhausting into two low-pressure. The ratio of expansion would have been easy to obtain. But for some reason that no one has ever really been able to explain Webb did exactly the opposite, with two high pressure cylinders exhausting into one low pressure. As a result, to obtain the requisite volume ratios, the high pressure cylinders were very small, and the single low pressure, located inside, was enormous. I need not have gone even to this extent in explaining the design of the Webb three-cylinder compound had it not been for the most peculiar effects they sometimes had in running. The fact that there was only one cylinder exhausting to atmosphere, and therefore only two 'puffs' for each revolution of the driving wheels, instead of the usual four, made the beat sound as though a very slow train was approaching, at half the speed than was actually the case. That however was the least of the peculiarities.

Passengers travelling by the main line express trains from Euston to the north were familiar with a pronounced fore and aft surging action when the three-cylinder compound engines were starting away from rest. This died away when the speed had reached about 25 m.p.h.; but then Webb applied his three-cylinder compound system, experimentally only it is true, on two locomotives working on the Outer Circle service. He first of all took one of the standard Metropolitan-type 4-4-0 tank engines, and rebuilt it as a compound with his usual layout of machinery: the high pressure cylinders, which were outside, driving the rear pair of coupled wheels, and the one inside cylinder driving the leading pair. Then to complete the conversion the coupling rods were taken off, leaving in effect two single-driver engines. Again, it can be appreciated that by having the two pairs of driving wheels uncoupled Webb hoped to get the freedom in running of a single-wheeler, but with the adhesion of a coupled engine; however, while such a feature, if it did actually exist, might have some slight advantage on an express locomotive, one cannot conceive it to be of the slightest use on a suburban tank engine, especially on a service like that of the Outer Circle, on which there were 31 stations to be stopped at in a distance of $19\frac{1}{2}$ miles. It seemed as though compounds were pre-ordained to be superior in performance to simples in that era on the London and North Western Railway, but for all Webb's enthusiasm only one engine of the Metropolitan was converted. Its appearances in traffic seem to have been somewhat sporadic, and no one at Crewe wrote a learned monograph on its behaviour.

The second compound tank engine came prominently, if briefly, into the limelight. Boiler and chassis-wise this engine, No. 687, was based on Webb's smart little 2-4-2 passenger tanks. These were straightforward two-cylinder simples, and although a little undersized for the work they were called upon to do were excellent engines. The 'convert' No. 687, had the usual layout of machinery of the three cylinder compounds, and for a time she put in a good deal of hard work on the 'Outer Circle' service. On her trains however it was hard work for the passengers as well as for the locomotive. For what reason I cannot say, but No. 687 displayed the fore and aft surging action, when starting, to a far greater extent than the main line express engines did, and as she was continually stopping and starting the effect on the passengers can be better imagined than described. With his usual eye for the funny side of railway operation E. L. Ahrons once wrote: 'On one occasion when leaving Victoria (underground) a carriage full of passengers were swinging backwards and forwards after the manner of a University "eight".' He added: 'Had the London and North Western tank engines had names, like the tender engines, I would have respectfully suggested the name *Fore and Aft*, for No. 687.' The *Fore and Aft* like the converted Metropolitan 4-4-0 tank

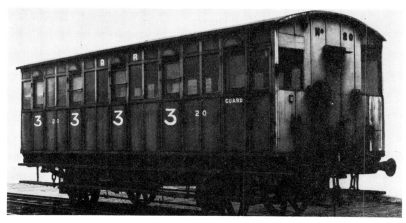

One of the standard 4-4-0 tank engines of the Metropolitan, with condensing gear and no cab, as used on the Inner Circle. (top)

District Railway: Third class carriage as used on the close-coupled trains until the line was electrified. The picture has been retouched to show the original lettering; but at the time the photograph was taken the carriage had been converted for use as an engineer's van.

remained the only one of her kind; and that, in view of Webb's enthusiasm for compounds, probably explains far more satisfactorily than pages of technical conjecture that the *Fore and Aft* was not very successful!

Turning from these curiosities to the hard work-a-day slogging of the standard 4-4-0 tank engines, the method of operating on the Inner Circle was interesting. It was jointly worked by the Metropolitan and the District with locomotives and stock in approximate proportion to the respective mileages of ownership. The distance round the Inner Circle was 15 miles, and of this 7 miles was owned by the Metropolitan, $5\frac{3}{4}$ miles by the District, leaving the $2\frac{1}{4}$ miles of the City extension between Mansion House and Moorgate Street jointly owned. The arrangement adopted was that all trains on the outer pair of rails, that is proceeding clockwise round the circuit were provided by the Metropolitan, and for the anti-clockwise circuit some were Metropolitan and some District. The stabling of locomotives working in Central London posed some problems, particularly as the traffic increased and more engines were needed. Until the country extension of the Metropolitan had reached as far out as Neasden, and there was space for an extensive works and locomotive depot, the 4-4-0 tank engines were parked in odd corners, at Aldgate, some at Farringdon Street, but most of them at Edgware Road. The present open space at the latter station accommodated no more than two platform roads and the rest was occupied by the engine shed. The locomotives of the District Railway were mostly shedded at Lillie Bridge, in the Vee between the Hammersmith and Fulham lines beyond Earls Court.

While the District, with the driving force of James Staats Forbes behind it was extending its tentacles into the outer suburban districts west of London, Sir Edward Watkin was playing a far more ambitious game with the Metropolitan. It must be recalled that he was Chairman not only of the latter railway, and of the South Eastern, but also of the Manchester, Sheffield and Lincolnshire. This latter was being extended southwards, little by little, from Sheffield towards Nottingham, and Watkin's grand strategy was to extend the M.S.&L. southwards, and the Metropolitan northwards till they met. Then, with running powers over the short section of the Chatham between Farringdon Street and Blackfriars Junction, a distance of precisely one mile, he would have control of a line of railway extending from Manchester to Dover, passing through the heart of London in the process. The criticisms that had been levelled at the location of the main line termini of the established northern companies, at Euston, St. Pancras and Kings Cross would be completely eliminated when trains on his route were able to run direct to Moorgate Street, or through Ludgate Hill to the South Eastern. Even this was not all, for Watkin, Member of Parliament for Hythe, was also sponsoring the first proposals for a Channel Tunnel: Manchester to Calais, entirely with Watkin! And so the Metropolitan was pushed further and further out into the country, reaching Rickmansworth by 1887, Aylesbury by 1892, while the incorporation of the Aylesbury and Verney Junction Railway in the Metropolitan took the pioneer 'underground' railway to a point nearly 51 miles from Baker Street.

By these country extensions both the Metropolitan and the District had of course greatly increased the complexity of their workings, and the connections with the main line railways brought all the complications of freight workings in the Metropolitan case. Though originally conceived as purely urban transport systems, for passengers, they had both become involved in the ordinary common-carrier business of the British railways. To the District in particular it brought little joy, and the very expensive

30

eastward extension of the Inner Circle from Mansion House to Aldgate had most disappointing financial results. It had been imagined that the construction of the underground line from Mansion House, serving Cannon Street, Monument, Mark Lane, Aldgate and Liverpool Street would have produced new traffic in the City itself, with passengers using the trains for purely local journeys. But it was the old story of the London, Chatham and Dover service between Ludgate Hill and Moorgate Street. Within the City boundary the 'Inner Circle' described an arc the centre of which was near to the Bank of England; the stations were located radially at roughly equal distances from this nodal point, and none of them were so much as half a mile distant from this centrum. With no more than a 10-minute service on the Inner Circle it was much quicker to walk! This is not to suggest that the completion of the Inner Circle was not appreciated; but season-ticket holders who had previously travelled to Mansion House extended their commuting to Cannon Street, or Mark Lane, or whichever station was nearest to their daily place of business. There was very little increase in the total number of originating passenger journeys.

London & North Western Railway: a Metropolitan type 4-4-0 tank converted to a three-cylinder compound, on F. W. Webb's system.

31

London & North Western Railway: the '*Fore and Aft*': three-cylinder compound 2-2-2-2 tank engine No. 687, originally used on the Outer Circle between Broad Street and Mansion House. The photograph was taken after the engine had been demoted, and relegated to the Manchester suburban service.

Great Northern Railway: One of the most modern steam locomotives to work over the City Widened Lines: a Gresley superheated 0-6-2 tank of Class 'N2'

CHAPTER THREE

Trials and Tribulations

This chapter can well begin with a study of the map on page 26, and of the numerous lines that fed into it. By the end of the nineteenth century, of the nine main line companies entering London only two, the London and South Western, and the London, Brighton and South Coast did not run over it at some part of the circuit, and of these the South Western connections in the Hammersmith area could have reacted to some extent on the running of District Railway trains. Of that crowded circuit only two short sections had more than two tracks, namely the stretch of the Widened Lines between Farringdon Street and Kings Cross, and the 36 chains between South Kensington and Gloucester Road. The Widened Lines proved an absolute godsend to the Metropolitan, while the quadruple tracks between South Kensington and Gloucester Road enabled the Circle trains to be run independently of the main stream of District Railway traffic, and to stand at South Kensington for engine changing, without delaying other trains. Note should be taken of the *goods* stations dotted around the Inner Circle with the Midland at Whitecross Street in the City, and at Kensington High Street, with the Great Northern at Farringdon Street, and the Great Western at Smithfield.

Blame for the poor return upon the huge capital investments represented by the City extension lines was laid partly upon road competition. This may seem strange at a time when all road transport was horse-drawn, and when the congestion in the narrow streets of the City made progress very slow. But competition between the rival companies, allowed to run where and when they liked, took the form of a drastic reduction in fares. By one company it was possible to travel from Putney to South Kensington, $3\frac{1}{2}$ miles, for one penny, and from Putney to Charing Cross for twopence! This naturally took some of the less urgent passenger traffic from the District Railway. That company estimated it had lost some £40,000 per annum from the competition of this one omnibus company. In an interview given to the Editor of *The Railway Magazine* in 1899, Mr. Alfred Powell, Manager of the District Railway said: 'The omnibuses are practically free from taxation; do absolutely nothing to maintain the roads over which they run; and while their expenses—large enough as they are in themselves in comparison with their earnings—are thereby kept down to the lowest figure, enabling them to charge fares out of all proportion to the service rendered, the District Railway is not only compelled to construct, at its own expense, the railways over which it runs, and to incur the enormous outlay which that construction involved, but is forced to contribute £32,000 per annum in rates and taxes towards the roads over which its competitors

—the omnibuses—run.' A present-day reader may smile at the tax bill, but the context is the same as that uttered by every railway management in many countries of the world ever since.

The District, and to a lesser extent, the Metropolitan were of course paying the penalty of being pioneers. Just as the British railway system as a whole has always suffered from the widespread use, from the earliest days, of little except four-wheeled wagons for freight, so the two original underground lines fell into the trap of organising surface connections that congested the central area, and prevented them really exploiting the great advantage that railways had over the horse-drawn omnibus, that of speed. As to fares, in that same interview with the Editor of *The Railway Magazine*, Mr. Powell revealed that in the year 1898 the average fare paid by each passenger, covering all distances and all passengers, first, second and third class included was only 2·18 pence. Of the total passengers carried more than 15 per cent enjoyed the very low fares of 'workmens' rates, by trains arriving before a certain hour in the morning. *The Railway Magazine* of that period once published an amusing photograph of the arrival of a 'workman's' train at one of the London stations, from which the majority of the passengers passing through the barrier were wearing the silk hats and morning coats that were then *de rigeur*, even among junior employees in City offices at that time, as my own father has often testified.

Of course Forbes, with his usual grandiose acumen, had an answer for lack of revenue on the District line, and that was to provide a high speed route to the heart of the City, independent of the Inner Circle. This was known as the 'Deep Level' route, and was to burrow below the existing District line from Earls Court, and to go straight through to the Mansion House beneath the Inner Circle line, with only one intermediate station—probably at Charing Cross. The idea was that outer residential trains would run to Earls Court, as they already did, exchange traffic there with the ordinary trains, and then run 'express' to Mansion House saving—it was hoped—about a quarter of an hour on the journey. In mentioning the 'Deep Level District' however, for which authorisation was actually obtained by Act of Parliament, I have drawn rather ahead of the chronological development of underground railways in London, though it is natural to follow the fortunes, or rather the misfortunes of the pioneers perhaps without due regard for what was happening elsewhere. It is nevertheless just as well that the long-suffering shareholders of the District Railway were spared the expense of the 'Deep Level' line, because in the meantime other factors had supervened. The most important of these was the development of electric traction, and to appreciate how this came to affect the pioneers I must turn aside briefly to consider the astonishing impact made upon the whole concept of transport within the confines of a great city by the successful opening of the City and South London Railway.

Apart from its location, as a deep-level 'tube', the essential difference between this new line and the Metropolitan and District Railways was that of electric, instead of steam traction. Yet strange though it may seem the use of electricity on the City and South London came almost as an after thought. As long previously as 1870 P. W. Barlow had obtained an Act authorising a cable-operated subway from the City to Southwark, having stations near the Monument on the one hand, and London Bridge Station on the other. Despite his reputation and eminence as a civil engineer he failed to raise the necessary funds. It was then in 1880 that J. H. Greathead, a pupil of Barlow's, developed the shield system of tunnelling, and he and his associates were anxious to

James Staats Forbes. A cartoon by 'Spy' published in *Vanity Fair* of 22nd February 1900 entitled simply 'L.C.D.R.'

find some project on which the potentialities of the shield could be demonstrated. A ready-made situation existed in South London. Although the London, Chatham and Dover line to Ludgate Hill ran through the heart of the busy Kennington district the trains were overcrowded and the lines congested. Even before the 1880s the Elephant and Castle Tavern had become known as a major road traffic junction, where streams of buses converged from several directions and whence others, together with horse-drawn trams continued to the river crossings at Westminster, Waterloo Bridge, Blackfriars and London Bridge. The situation was certainly ripe for the projection of a new underground railway, and so there was projected the 'City of London and South-wark Subway'. Using the Greathead shield, it was to burrow beneath the Thames, making a single circular bore for each track, and as it was rightly considered that steam traction was unthinkable in such circumstances, cable haulage was proposed.

While the idea of some form of conveyance that would be independent of road congestion was greatly welcomed in South London the proposals as first propounded were disappointing, as with cable traction they seemed to lack the essential ingredient of speed. The prospect of going deep underground merely to be hauled along by a rope did not prove attractive, and having in mind the failure of the Tower Subway the promoters discussed the whole project with Charles Grey Mott, a man of vision and influence, who was also a director of the Great Western Railway. He had been associated with both the Mersey and the Severn Tunnels. He at once showed great interest, and under his leadership the scheme was revived, but considering electric traction. The various systems that were being installed experimentally were all weighed up. There was no British railway experience to work upon. The City of London and South-wark Subway, if thus equipped, would not only be the first deep-level tube, but also the first British electric railway. The scheme was authorised by Act of Parliament in 1884 while still having cable traction in mind. It was to run from the Elephant and Castle deep below the Borough High Street to London Bridge, and thence by a curving tunnel under the river to a terminus near to the Monument, at the junction of King William Street and Cannon Street. Despite the interest of C. G. Mott, the 'advantages' of cable traction were still being strongly pressed in other quarters. The Cable Tram-ways Corporation was very active in its sales promotion, and the newly authorised Subway Company was induced to pay a considerable sum of money to secure the rights to use the cable system on its line, and on any extensions. Greathead was appointed engineer, with Sir John Fowler and Sir Benjamin Baker as consultants. The immense advantage of the deep-level shield system of construction over the methods that had to be adopted for the City extensions of the District Railway were shown in that the authorised capital of the Subway Company was only £300,000 for a line $1\frac{1}{4}$ miles long, against a million a mile for the District. At this stage however I am deferring detailed consideration of the civil engineering work involved in the construction of the line, while referring to the effect its inception had on the affairs of the District and on the Metropolitan. In the meantime proposals for cable traction on the Subway con-tinued. A large engine house was designed for installation at the Elephant and Castle, and with a further Act having been obtained in 1887 for a southbound extension from the Elephant and Castle to Stockwell two distinct speeds of operation were proposed—10 m.p.h. for the section between the Elephant and King William Street, and 12 m.p.h. cable. The average speeds of transit from station to station would be much less.

At first the new subway, and its proposed method of traction were treated with some disdain by established railway activities. Tunnelling under the river Thames proceeded however with strikingly little in the way of trouble; but when the subway company thought it would be a good idea to have an additional station at the south end of London Bridge, and connected to the existing terminus of the London, Brighton and South Coast Railway by a covered walking subway for passengers the 'Brighton' would have nothing of it. It was in 1888 that the subway company, under the strong influence of C. G. Mott as Chairman, was having serious second thoughts about the system of traction; and despite the financial involvement with the Cable Corporation and the contracts already placed for cable equipment, tenders were invited for an electric traction system that would provide for a train service at three-minute intervals. It was at this point again that the wide railway experience of C. G. Mott became of great value. It was second nature to such a man to appreciate that the utmost safety in operation was vital on a deep-level underground railway worked at such a high density of traffic. The most perfect signalling that could be devised was essential, and he called into consultation that remarkable man C. E. Spagnoletti, engineer in charge of telegraphs on the Great Western Railway. Unobtrusively, so far, he had made no small contribution to the successful operation of underground railways, but in his association with the new subway he was to play a major part in advancing new techniques of operation.

His unusual name, for a man in the employ of the Great Western Railway, was, in its origin, a good deal more unusual than might be imagined. He himself was a London Cockney, by birth, but he was descended from a once-famous Neapolitan family named Della Diana. They were extensive landowners in Southern Italy. His grandfather, Paulo Ludovico Della Diana was a child prodigy of a musician, and at a very young age made a highly successful tour of Spain. When he returned to Italy his success was acclaimed by the bequeathing upon him the affectionate nickname of 'Lo Spagnoletto' —the charming little one from Spain. The nickname stuck, and he liked it so much that he had it legally adopted as a family name in the plural form of Spagnoletti. He found the opportunities of advancement in his musical profession greater in England than in Italy, and settled permanently in London, where he achieved fame as an orchestral leader and composer. The grandson who came to have such an interesting railway career had the full name Charles Ernest Paulo Diana Spagnoletti (!) though in his engineering work he used only the initials 'C.E.'. His qualities can be appreciated from his appointment to take charge of telegraphs on the Great Western Railway at the early age of 23. That railway seemed to favour very young men in its engineering appointments; after all, Daniel Gooch was no more than 21 when he became locomotive superintendent.

Spagnoletti was of course well known to C. G. Mott, but even before the City of London and Southwark Subway was under construction he had been deeply concerned with the underground railways. From the early association of the Great Western with working on the Metropolitan line, apparatus designed by him had been used in the first underground signalling, and was subsequently adopted on the District Railway. Leaving signalling out of consideration for the moment Spagnoletti was a man of wide interests, including, incidentally, some of the musical talents of his grandfather; his railway interests were such that Mott took him into consultation over the traction system of the subway, a step that caused no little criticism in the engineering profession

C. E. Spagnoletti: engineer of telegraphs, Great Western Railway.
Consulting engineer to the City and South London Railway.

at the time. To established engineers it was abhorrent that a man whose known work was confined to telegraphs should be invited to specify methods of railway traction. But Mott knew his man, and Spagnoletti was largely instrumental in drawing up the specifications on which the contracts for the traction equipment were based. When it was finally announced, in 1889, that the company had settled for electric and not cable traction, more annoyance was caused to the 'establishment' of the engineering profession by the statement that the Board had taken the decision on the advice of C. E. Spagnoletti, 'an experienced electrical engineer'. It was pointed out by certain letters in the technical press that he was little better than a 'telegraph linesman'! It was the jealousy aroused by Stephenson all over again, and it availed as little as that of those who tried to stem the prowess of 'Old George'.

By the autumn of 1890 the line was fully equipped and ready for working, and the promoters mindful, perhaps better than they knew, of the epoch-marking nature of their achievement invited H.R.H. The Prince of Wales to perform the opening ceremony. This was a dignity neither of the pioneer underground railways had aspired to. But King Edward VII, as he afterwards became, was intensely transport minded, and on November 4, 1890, he duly declared the line open. The inspection on behalf of the Board of Trade was carried out by Major-General Hutchinson, Chief Inspecting Officer of Railways, and duly passed. But the company felt that in the case of so original a venture a little private running was desirable and it was not until Thursday, December 18, 1890, that the new line was opened to the public. By 7 p.m. on the first day 10,000 persons had passed the turnstiles at King William Street station. It was, in fact, an immediate and outstanding success, and a success moreover that began to bear heavily upon the fortunes and public goodwill of the Metropolitan and District Railways. In Chapter Four of this book I describe at some length the equipment and travelling

City and South London Railway: the Royal opening with the Prince of Wales, afterwards King Edward VII, arriving at Stockwell station, 1890.

conditions on the City and South London Railway as the line became known; but so far as the older underground lines were concerned it had the great feature of novelty. It made use of the latest techniques in railway traction and it had received the seal of Royal approval, from a man who was rapidly becoming one of the most popular members of the Royal family ever yet to live in England.

It is the merest platitude to suggest that generally there is no gratitude in business. The Metropolitan and District railways were to drink deep from this particular cup. The shareholders, and particularly those of the latter company had little reason to be satisfied, but like those of the British 'big four' during the 1930s they hung on, hoping that the enormous capital investment would eventually bring them some reasonable dividends. Some of those who looked further afield and studied the doleful record of the Chatham might have wondered whether things might have been better with a less adventurous chairman than Forbes; but by and large the two pioneer underground railways were doing a great job of transportation—a great job in every respect, save that of making money. While the steam-worked underground was the subject of gibes and cartoons from the public and the press they were for the most part friendly. The underground had become an institution in London life. But then, overnight as it were, everything was changed. The City and South London operating in the most austere and claustrophobic conditions suddenly set a new standard, by the simple adoption of electric traction. Overnight steam, in the eyes of the public and the press had become outdated for underground railways, and in a campaign that gathered crescendo as the years went by odium was heaped upon the pioneers for their seeming reluctance to change immediately to electric traction also. No one saw the advantage to be derived from such a change clearer than the astute managements of the Metropolitan and the District, but quite simply, where was the money coming from to finance such a change?

British industry was rather dragging its feet so far as electric railway traction was concerned. Foreign interests were quick to appreciate the atmosphere that was developing in London after the outstandingly successful inauguration of the City and South London 'tube', and the representatives of Continental and American firms began a campaign of propaganda every bit as sustained and subtle as that waged for the total abolition of steam traction on the British railways after World War II. A host of schemes for new tube railways grew up within months, all to be worked electrically, and all this activity had the effect of forcing the pace on the District. Now Forbes was not the kind of man to endure having the pace forced upon him. His normal rôle was that of pace-maker himself, and then the sudden and unexpected alliance between the age-old Kentish rivals—South Eastern and London, Chatham and Dover—set going a flood of rumours. This alliance saw Forbes relinquish his office as Chairman of the Chatham line and the rumour-mongers very quickly set to work to remove him from the District as well. In the meantime Watkin's great project of linking up the Metropolitan and the M.S.&L. had come to fruition in 1899 after his own retirement; the M.S.&L. of wholly north-country origin had become the Great Central. A rumour, quoted with approbation and seeming authority by *The Railway Magazine*, was that the Great Western, the Great Central, and the South Eastern were jointly to take over the District. *The Railway Magazine* went so far as to suggest that such a 'take over' would be of great advantage in the development of the suburban services of the Great Western, particularly if the takeover made available finance for the already authorised 'Deep Level' line of the District from Earls Court to Mansion House.

Forbes evidently had not the slightest intention of being taken over by any of the main line companies, and having been relieved of all the executive responsibility for the Chatham he threw all his energies and his remarkable talents of rhetoric into propagating schemes for the grandiose development of the District. He announced that the board proposed to go ahead immediately with electrification. He carried the shareholders with him, and when certain thoughtful souls with an eye to practical politics asked what would happen to the steam worked services operated over their line by the London and North Western and by the Great Western he tossed any thoughts of difficulty on one side. Once their line was electrified, he said, the 'proud and mighty' North Western—to use his own words!—and the equally proud and mighty Great Western would, in plain terms have to toe the line, and work their trains electrically. The District would no longer tolerate steam on their part of the Inner Circle. One can be amazed as well as amused at the chairman of an impoverished, if very busy local line in London talking thus to such a giant of the railway world as the London and North Western; but it was typical of Forbes. He had 'face' enough for anything.

The manufacturers of electric traction equipment were quick enough to weigh in upon the prospect of the District line electrification, and the issue seemed to narrow itself down to America, with direct-current propulsion, *versus* Continental Europe. It was appreciated that any electrification of the District would have to be done in conjunction with a similar move by the Metropolitan, because any question of changing the form of motive power in the course of perambulating round the Inner Circle was unthinkable. The rival forms of electric traction worked hard upon the respective managements of the Metropolitan and the District, and it was not very long before it was seen that matters were heading for a deadlock. It was perhaps typical of the way in which both companies were run, and of the antagonism between them, despite their fundamental partnership in the running of so essential a public service as the Inner Circle, that they should so quickly have come to loggerheads over the system of electrification to be employed. The Metropolitan came out firmly in favour of the alternating current system put forward by Ganz of Buda Pest, while the District was equally adamant for the simple direct current system of the Westinghouse Electric Company of the U.S.A. The situation was amusingly epitomised by a cartoon in *The Railway Magazine* reproduced on page 132, in which the initials representing the full title of the District Railway were neatly turned to indicate the M(onroe) D(octrine) Railway!

A joint committee of both companies was set up and this, strange to say, came out on the side of alternating current. Why the Metropolitan, and through its influence the joint committee should have been so strongly in favour of the Ganz system is difficult to appreciate at this distance in time. It used three-phase alternating current at 3000 volts, and had the feature of maintaining constant speed once the train was accelerated from rest. This had certain advantages on the main line services of the Italian State Railways and in other European instances where it was used; but I cannot for the life of me see any advantage from this feature on a service where every train was stopping and restarting every half mile! Until quite recently the three-phase system was used on the picturesque line along the Italian Riviera coast from the French frontier to Genoa. It was claimed to be more economical in power consumption, and this is probably the feature that outweighed all else with the management of the Metropolitan. A disadvantage that its rivals were loud in proclaiming, was its inconvenience in the event of a breakdown in power supply. It was not so much the modern risk of 'power cuts', because at that time electrified railways had to depend entirely upon their own generating stations; there was the risk of a breakdown of the machinery. The exponents of direct current claimed that in such an eventuality they could manage, on a reduced scale, by the use of storage batteries, whereas with the Ganz system it would mean a complete shut-down. The almost overwhelming advantage of the d.c. system was, of course, in its operating characteristics. The motors had a high starting torque, permitting of rapid acceleration from rest; and this is what the Inner Circle needed more than anything else, apart of course from the elimination of smoke and steam.

How the situation might have eventuated if Forbes had remained in control of the District one cannot say. Matters had reached the stage of the Metropolitan board accepting the recommendations of the joint committee; but then the entire situation was changed by the sudden appearance on the scene of a prominent American financier, Charles Tyson Yerkes. He was the moving spirit in a large syndicate that had recently re-organised and co-ordinated the transport system of Chicago. In London's traffic problems he saw an opportunity to do 'big business', and in a matter of weeks he had assumed virtual control of the District Railway by the simple process of purchasing large blocks of the shares. While the management, staff, and remaining shareholders were rubbing their eyes and wondering what had hit them Yerkes threw the whole question of electrification back into the open forum by flatly refusing to have anything to do with Ganz. The Metropolitan people were naturally furious, and having regard to the importance of electrification as a social necessity in Central London they appealed to the Board of Trade. Both companies thereupon agreed to refer the case to arbitration. The Hon. Alfred Lyttleton, was appointed arbitrator, with Messrs. Parker and Parshall representing the interests of the Metropolitan and of the District respectively. The Tribunal sat for two months during the year 1901, and eventually declared in favour of the direct current system—a triumph for C. T. Yerkes.

While it is probable that a majority of those British railwaymen who had given serious thoughts to electrification welcomed this decision, and particularly that the apparatus would be manufactured in England by the British offshoot of the Westinghouse Electric Company, instead of in Hungary, there were disturbing thoughts that high-powered American finance had turned the scale, and that Yerkes did not intend to stop with his acquisition of the District. It seemed that alien influences were assuming control of urban transport in the capital city of the British Empire. The air was soon rife with rumours of further American infiltration, into the main line railway managements of the country; though fortunately, with one or two exceptions, the financial position of these companies was strong enough to resist if any of the rumours circulating had foundation in fact. Nevertheless, it was not without significance that several of the largest English railway companies sent delegations of principal officers to the U.S.A. to study American railway methods on the spot. The outcome, so far as the present theme is concerned, did not materialise until some four years later; and in the meantime, at the close of 1901 the celebrated James Staats Forbes had disappeared from the District Railway scene, and in his place sat the stop-at-nothing Yankee tycoon Charles Tyson Yerkes.

CHAPTER FOUR

The Shield, and the City and South London

I must now take the story back to the mid-eighties, when construction of the 'City of London and Southwark Subway' began. From an engineering point of view the centre of interest was of course the Greathead shield. Like most notable inventions the shield was extremely simple in its conception. It was based on the principle of having a tunnel of completely circular cross-section, lined by a series of cast iron rings. These latter were of channel section, with the flanges inwards and providing a ready means of joining up adjacent sections of ring. As construction advanced the tunnel section was completed, and formed an integral part of the 'shield' mechanism. The shield itself could be likened to a cap, fitting over the last tunnel segmental ring placed in position, and having a strong diaphragm, as equivalent of the flat end of the 'cap'. Ahead of the diaphragm were a series of cutters, and in the diaphragm was a door through which the excavated material could be thrown out. Against the flange of the last cast-iron tunnel segment fixed in position were a series of hydraulic rams by which the shield was pressed forward, though at that time the actual excavation, within the circle of the shield was all done by hand.

The shield had necessarily to be somewhat larger than the outside diameter of the tunnel segmental rings, and thus there existed an annular space between the outside of the ring and the hole cut by the shield. This was filled with cement, thus forming a strong outer protection to the iron rings of the tunnel itself. The method of grouting was then novel, and devised by Greathead, as part of the shield form of construction. It is perhaps difficult for us to imagine a time when 'concrete' was a novel substance, and in contemporary descriptions the mixture is described as 'lime and water'. It was mixed in a cylindrical vessel, and then compressed air at a pressure of 50 lb. per sq. in. was admitted through what was termed the 'upper valve'. The lower valve of the grout mixing cylinder was connected by a short hose pipe to a hole in one of the tunnel segments, and when the valve was opened the grouting mixture was blown in to the annular space between the iron ring and the hole cut by the shield. The blowing in of the grouting mixture continued until the mixture began to appear at the upper hole in the segmental ring. Then blowing was ceased temporarily while the hose was removed, the hole plugged, and the hose connected to the upper hole. Thus the forcing in of the grout mixture, under air pressure, continued until the whole space was apparently filled up. In devising the mixing vessel Greathead designed what was probably one of the very first 'concrete mixers'. A spindle ran from end to end carrying a number of paddles. This spindle and its paddles were rotated by an external handle;

One of the original trailer cars—the 'padded cells'.

and a man was employed turning the handle continuously to prevent the mixture setting over the hose pipe from the lower valve.

Although the tunnels were bored so relatively deeply below the surface it was thought desirable to establish the line of railway below streets wherever possible to avoid any chance of interference with private property on the surface, or in basements immediately beneath. The stations platforms along most of the line are roughly 100ft. below street level, though there are some variations to meet the requirements of local conditions. From the original City terminus, where King William Street crossed to Arthur Street, the line curved sharply round to run beneath Arthur Street West, and it approached the river under Swan Lane. That thoroughfare was so narrow that the up line tunnel had to be located vertically above the down line so as to keep the railway within the width of the roadway. To achieve this, the down southbound tube had to be carried on a descending gradient of 1 in 14. Even though the terminus station was located so deeply it was still necessary to have gradients of 1 in 40 and 1 in 70 descending, to carry the tubes at a safe depth below the bed of the Thames. The complicated curves and gradients in this initial section from the City terminus provided a rare test of Greathead's skill in the deep-level manipulation of the shields. No difficulties were experienced. The less steeply graded northbound tunnel was commenced on October 28, 1886 and completed less than four months later. The more difficult southbound tunnel was commenced in March 1887.

Greathead was fortunate in that the whole of the northbound tube was bored in the London clay, an extraordinarily tough and homogenous strata that could be cut without any complications; but in driving the southbound tunnel, and going deeper to bring the second tube beneath the first under Swan Lane the lower limit of the clay was reached, and the tunnel entered less stable ground, including sand and underground water. To prevent water seeping into the workings the forward part of the tunnel was sealed and made into an airlock, at higher than atmospheric pressure. Workmen engaged on the shield, and in fitting the segmental rings as the shield

Interior of one of the 'padded cells' of the City and South London Railway.

City and South London Railway: one of the original electric locomotives hauling a train of modified coaches with large windows.

advanced passed into the working area through an airlock in the bulkhead, in which the air-pressure to which they were subjected was gradually raised from atmosphere, to the higher pressure of the workings. One very quickly gets used to the higher pressure, and work continued at the face of the shield, without any risk of water entering the 'tube'. On the Surrey side the work did not progress quite so rapidly as had been hoped for. Another belt of wet gravel was encountered near Stockwell, this time necessitating compressed air working in both tubes, and one tunnel was not through to Stockwell, the first terminus, until the beginning of 1890. On the face of it this was disappointing in view of the excellent progress made with the apparently difficult section under the river. The formal opening of the line, to be referred to later, did not take place until November 1890.

Having regard to the City and South London being a special railway, self-contained, and in no way connected originally to any other, the tunnels were made much smaller than standard to minimise the cost of construction. Whereas the standard dimensions for a single line tunnel on the ordinary railways called for a width of 12ft., and a height from rail level to the underside of the crown of about 14ft., some of the tubes of the City and South London were made no more than 10ft. 2in. diameter, and some 10ft. 6in. diameter. Very fortunately in view of later developments, the standard British rail gauge of 4ft. 8½in. was adopted. The rails were of the flat-bottom type resting on cross sleepers fitted into the tunnel segments. The diameter of the standard tubes of later days, 11ft. 8½in. was small enough in comparison with the size of a single-line tunnel on the main line railways; but the tube of the City and South London was still less by some 15 per cent. To provide the tractive power the 'third rail' system of electric traction was adopted. The original intention was to use an overhead wire; but there was insufficient height, and so a third rail was used, with return current passing through the running rails, as now standard on the electrified lines of British Railways, Southern Region. The third rail was fixed in the 'four-foot', but not centrally. The rolling stock was so low that the central couplings would have touched it.

It is extraordinary to recall the make-up of those first 'tube' trains. Each consisted of no more than three coaches of the bogie tramcar type, with longitudinal upholstered seats for 32 passengers. As there was no 'passing scene' to be enjoyed on the journey some genius decided that all that was needed in the way of windows was a series of narrow slits through which the station names might be read. Very soon these carriages earned the nickname of the 'padded cells'! They were drawn by tiny little four-wheeled electric locomotives which developed 100 horsepower at 25 m.p.h. The very short trains weighed no more than 40 tons loaded, and the little locomotives were powerful enough to maintain an average speed of $11\frac{1}{2}$ m.p.h. from end to end of the line, inclusive of intermediate stops. The total length of line, as originally opened was just over 3 miles, with intermediate stations at Borough, Elephant and Castle, Kennington and the Oval. The 'fare structure' was delightfully simple—twopence from anywhere to anywhere. You paid your money at a turnstile before entering a station, and could then travel to whatever destination you liked! No tickets, no other barriers were involved, and the accounting methods must have been just too easy. The stations were lit by gas, and the rather gloomy atmosphere, and those 'padded cells' of carriages led to the railway getting nicknamed 'The Drain'.

Gas lighting of the stations on a new electric railway may cause some surprise, but the power station at Stockwell was sufficient only to provide power for running the trains. There was nothing to spare for lighting. That power station was a tremendous affair. The great vertical-cylindered compound steam engines that drove the generators looked larger than the locomotives used for hauling the trains. There were three of these engines originally, each of 450 horsepower, and a fourth was added subsequently. While the railway itself, despite its claustrophobic atmosphere had the clinical air of all electric lines that power house was a steam man's dream, with huge belts from the engine fly-wheels driving the generators after the fashion of traction engines driving agricultural machinery, or the roundabouts at a country fair. Steam was provided from a battery of hand fired Lancashire boilers, at a pressure of 140 lb. per sq. in. The engines were built by John Fowler & Co. of Leeds, one of the most noted traction engine manufacturers of the day. It is of interest to recall, in view of the external pressure put later upon the managements of the District and Metropolitan Railways, that all the original suppliers were British. Mather & Platt supplied the locomotives; the carriages were built by the Ashbury Railway Carriage & Iron Co. Ltd., while the brake equipment, though of American design, came from the London Works of the Westinghouse Brake Co. A most unusual arrangement of the brake was adopted. To avoid carrying one of the large standard air pumps on each locomotive two reservoirs were mounted, one beneath each cab side. There was a single compressor plant at Stockwell, and each locomotive had its reservoirs re-charged after every round trip to King William Street and back. A fully-charged reservoir had capacity for 30 stops from full speed.

The signalling was installed to the requirements of C. E. Spagnoletti using a special form of his well-known 'lock and block' system. The actual working was mechanical,

47

Island platform at Stockwell Station, City and South London Railway.
'A contemporary sketch'.

but owing to the relatively low speed of the trains, and with the efficient air brakes it was not considered necessary to have any distant, or warning signals. The lowering of the starting signal at the leaving end of the station platform ensured a clear run into the next station, or up to the buffer stops at one or other of the termini. The only signals on the line were those at the leaving ends of each station platform. There had to be signal boxes at every station. At the City terminus of King William Street the mechanical interlocking frame had 9 levers; at Stockwell, with connections to the locomotive and carriage sheds a 24-lever frame was necessary. Reference has already been made to the tubes having to be at different levels on certain parts of the line to keep tunnels beneath the streets. This occurred at Borough, Kennington and the Oval; and so that the signalmen could see all the trains as they passed separate signal boxes had to be provided for each direction of running. The only station where one box controlled both directions was the Elephant and Castle. The original signalling equipment was supplied by Dutton & Co. of Worcester, a firm later absorbed by McKenzie & Holland Ltd.

The station layouts at the terminals differed. At King William Street there was originally only one platform, at which all trains arrived and departed. This hardly anticipated the growth of traffic that eventuated, and it proved the bottleneck of the whole line. Under the first signalling arrangements a train could not leave the Borough station until the line was clear up to the buffer stops at King William Street. As the time spent at the latter station included the detraining of all the passengers and the entraining of the return load, together with changing locomotives, northbound trains were frequently held up at Borough, waiting 'line clear', and this of course reacted back upon working over the whole line. At Stockwell, on the other hand, there was an island platform with running lines on each face. This made for much more expeditious working as a train could be accepted from Oval while another train was standing in the platform. It was of no avail for improving the frequency of service on the line as a whole while the bottleneck at King William Street existed. I should add, that the carriage and locomotive sheds at Stockwell were on the surface, connected with the tubes by a steeply graded tunnel, at 1 in $3\frac{1}{2}$, in which movement of locomotives was controlled by cable haulage.

However gloomy the atmosphere below ground might have been the exterior of the stations was in all cases magnificent, to judge from contemporary engravings in *The Railway Magazine*, and elsewhere. When the extension to Moorgate Street was built, and the first station near the Bank was sited in Lombard Street a most handsome classical facade was built in keeping with the Wren architecture of the church of St. Mary Woolnooth below which was the booking hall of the new station. Naturally space was at a premium in the City, but on the Surrey side the original stations at the Oval and Stockwell were crowned with grandiose domed cupolas after the style of St. Paul's Cathedral—or Bedlam lunatic asylum—whichever might be thought most appropriate to the pioneer tube railways! The interior of the lifts was also most ornate. All this preliminary ostentation was not exactly a fit prelude to a journey on the line. Some of the preliminary running was not without its diversions, as on March 7, 1890, when the Lord Mayor of London and other distinguished guests made a trip from King William Street to the Elephant and Castle, and back. The outward journey was

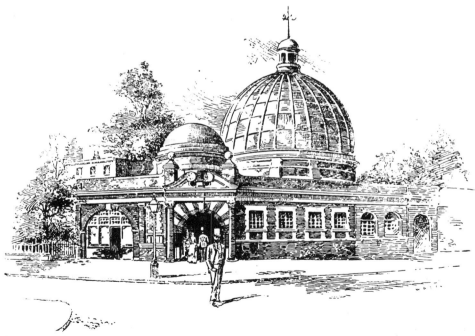

Exterior of the Oval Station, City and South London Railway.

accomplished without incident, but on the return there was a 'power cut', 1890-style! A turncock of the local water company shut off the water supply to the boilers at Stockwell; and down in 'The Drain' the Lord Mayor and his party waited an hour while someone sought out the local water 'authority' and got the supply restored. The line was formally opened by H.R.H. The Prince of Wales (afterwards King Edward VII) on November 4, 1890, and after some intensive preliminary running the public service began on Thursday, December 18, 1890.

The railway was an immediate success. On the first day more than 10,000 persons had passed through the turnstiles at King William Street by 7 p.m. Although not very rapid by modern underground standards it was immeasurably quicker than prevailing surface transport on the route from the Elephant and Castle to the City, and the regular travellers flocked to it. At first a five-minute service was run, and before long the company was carrying 15,000 persons a day. To what extent standing was permitted in the 'padded cells' I cannot say. There was plenty of standing room between the seats, but no pendant straps were provided as part of the original equipment. As could well be imagined King William Street station proved the bugbear of the whole opera-tion, and things were not improved by the steep gradients and sharp curves leading to it, in view of the modest power of the locomotives. It is somewhat significant that troubles due to the burning out of motor armatures on the locomotives was attributed to the carriages weighing more than was first calculated for. A fully loaded train was estimated to weigh 40 tons, but if in addition to the 96 seated passengers one added at least 100 more standing in the ample space between the seats, the loaded weight could be increased by 6 or 7 tons, or 17 to 18 per cent over the estimate. Unlike steam loco-motives their electrical confreres do not take kindly to overloading, and those on the City and South London appear to have burnt out in protest. At the time of the Board of Trade inspection of line the suggestion was made that the capacity of the Stockwell power station did not appear to have a sufficient margin in reserve; and at the sugges-tion of Major Cardew, the electrical expert assisting Major General Hutchinson, an additional generator and two more Lancashire boilers were added to the original Stockwell equipment.

The success of the line, and the near-embarrassment of the passenger traffic at King William Street led the management to consider a northward extension, whereby the City business could be spread more in relation to the location of business premises, rather than concentrated at the one station at the southward end of King William Street. The first application for authority to extend, from the existing terminus to the Bank, Moorgate Street and thence to the Angel, at Islington, was rejected by Parlia-ment. This was perhaps just as well, because it would have retained the severe inclines and curves in the approach to King William Street. In the meantime the welcome to the new line was rapidly becoming tempered with exasperation over the congestion and delays at King William Street. An entirely new approach to the City was therefore planned, with new tubes, on easy gradients, leaving the existing route near the Borough station, and proceeding on a fairly straight and easily graded route to Lombard Street, and continuing as before to Moorgate Street and to the Angel. Strange, that these old hostelries, the Angel and the Elephant, became as synonymous key points in London traffic working as Charing Cross, the Mansion House or Euston. What a pity it is that no one thought of christening an underground station 'Swan with Two Necks'—that great City departure point of horse-drawn mail traffic in the early days of the eighteenth century! It would have gone well with the Angel, and the Elephant and Castle. The Act of Parliament authorising the northward extension of the City and South London Railway was passed in 1893.

The company already had Parliamentary powers to extend their line southwards from Stockwell to Clapham, but they had feared to do it, for the remarkable reason that they expected the resulting traffic would be more than they could handle at King William Street. This was probably true enough, and it certainly hastened their intention to proceed with the northward extension as far as Islington. By proceeding as far as the Angel there is no doubt that they had intentions of further extensions to Kings Cross and Euston, which lay little more than a stone's throw westward of the Angel. But even now that the powers were obtained the board hesitated to go ahead and incur the heavy extra expense involved. To increase the capacity of the line, authority was obtained from the Board of Trade to instal outer home signals at each of the stations so that a second train could be accepted under the block regulations while another one was standing in the station platform. A further proposal was to increase the number of carriages on each train from three to four; but so parsimonious had the original layout at King William Street been conceived that there was literally no room to accommodate an extra coach. Although the locomotives themselves were so short, the one that had brought the train in standing close up to the buffer stops left only just enough space at the outer end for the fresh engine to back on, and just clear the points, so that these could be moved, and the train leave on the southbound line.

At King William Street the City and South London Railway was caught fairly in the embarrassment of its own prosperity, though why some room for expansion had not been built into the original layout is hard to imagine, with such an eminently practical man as Charles Grey Mott at the head of affairs. It is true that there had been a proposal in early days to use motor coaches instead of locomotives. This would have allowed the use of four-car trains; but the Board of Trade insisted on the use of locomotives once the company had decided against the installation of cable haulage. As it was, each train had a crew of four. The motorman was provided with a mate, in the person of a young lad who did the coupling and uncoupling at each terminus, and changed the lamps. There were two conductors on each train, each looking after the entrance gates, which were between the first and second, and the second and third cars respectively. Entry at the outer ends of the three-car sets, front and rear, was prohibited. There was an occasion when some inquisitive passenger, with suitable 'consideration', persuaded one of the conductors to let him ride on the front platform immediately behind the locomotive. The unfortunate man paid far more dearly than that 'consideration' to the conductor, for he fell off, and was killed.

The problem of the peak hours at King William Street remained the operational bugbear of the whole line. In 1894 an experimental four-car motor coach train was built and tried; but the space taken up by the electrical equipment prevented the full space of an additional carriage being available for passengers. Relief was finally sought in the conversion of the station to an island platform, with two tracks, and this killed the four-car train project stone dead. The platform faces had to be *shortened* to get in the scissors crossing at the outgoing end, and locomotive haulage continued right through to the time when the line was rebuilt as a standard-section tube. The alteration to the station took place in 1895, but although this improved the working there was still extreme congestion in the peak hours. It was then that the company tried to secure

51

some 'staggering' of the load by increasing the basic fare between the hours of 8 a.m. and 10 a.m. The howl of protest that greeted this manoeuvre took a long time to die down! For this was not a case of a company struggling to make both ends meet and attempting to charge a little more when it was deemed the demand would stand it, but the imposition of an artificial deterrent to travelling at the time the public most wanted the facilities. There was clearly nothing for it, but to construct the new line, for which Parliamentary powers had been obtained.

Late in 1895 work was commenced with a temporary shaft sunk near the Borough station to make the junctions with the existing tubes. At that point the tracks were arranged for right hand running, and over the new section the same configuration was maintained to a point somewhat north of the new station at the Bank. This station, and that at London Bridge was constructed with platforms on the same level, with cross passages, as usual in most of the later tube stations. Opportunity was taken however of crossing the tubes over between Bank and Moorgate Street to provide left hand running from the latter point onwards. Construction took a long time and while it was in progress another factor entered into the considerations of the company's expansion. A scheme for a large-size underground line of tube style, but capable of carrying standard main line railway stock, had been authorised for constructing a link between Finsbury Park and Moorgate Street. It is true that the Great Northern itself already provided a through service, via Kings Cross and the City Widened Lines; but the new line would take a short cut, and provide rapid electric transport through a new district in north-east London. It was to be carried down to tube level, and in 1899 the City and South London, realising that this line could be a source of further traffic to them, concluded an arrangement for a joint station at Old Street, the first one beyond Moorgate Street, and this of course was only the preliminary step to a running junction at some future time. Whether the possibility of this connection influenced the decision to switch the running on the City and South London from right to left hand between the Bank and Moorgate Street I cannot say; but it seems a likely explanation.

Work on the line to Moorgate Street had barely started before Greathead died, on October 21, 1896, at his home in Streatham. His contribution to the development of underground railways by his invention of the shield was a massive one. At the same time it must be remembered that the London Clay was an ideal medium for its use, and it was not suitable for universal application in the construction of deep level lines. It would have been practically useless in cutting rock. Nevertheless the problem of urban transport in London, at the turn of the century and afterwards, was infinitely more urgent than anywhere else in the world, except perhaps in Downtown New York; and Greathead provided the answer, constructional-wise at any rate. It is perhaps significant that in New York, which is built on rock, the earliest urban railways were built above, rather than below the streets. At this stage in the London story it remains for me to record that the City and South London service to King William Street ceased on February 24, 1900, and that the new line to Moorgate Street came into operation on the following day. Further extensions were to Clapham, in June 1900; and to the Angel in November 1901. On the latter line there were intermediate stations at Old Street and City Road.

CHAPTER FIVE

Cable Traction in Scotland

In view of the traffic problems that developed on the City and South London the reader may well be thinking how fortunate it was for the company that under the influence of Charles Grey Mott the idea of cable traction was abandoned, and that it became the first electric railway in Great Britain. In the meantime, however another cable haulage project was being pushed ahead to completion. This was the Glasgow District Subway, authorised by Parliament in 1890, and first opened to the public in 1896. In view of the change of policy by the City and South London the wisdom of the Scottish promoters in persisting with cable haulage might be questioned, particularly as the length of the projected subway was practically double that of the London 'tube' line. But cable haulage was not a novelty on railways in the Glasgow area at that time. The North British main line to Edinburgh left Glasgow on a very steep incline, extending from the Queen Street terminus for $1\frac{1}{4}$ miles on a gradient of 1 in 43–41 to Cowlairs; and up

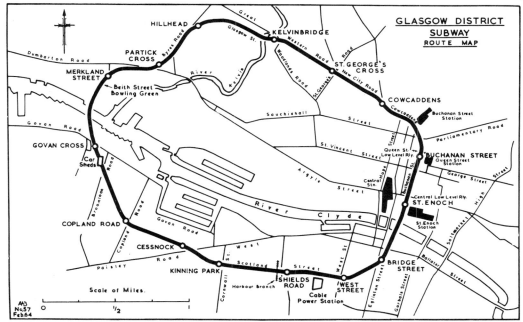

The Glasgow subway: route map.

this incline all trains were assisted by means of an endless rope, between the years 1847 and 1908. There was an ingenious arrangement whereby the locomotive hauling the train was disconnected from the cable, without having to stop, when the level track at the summit of the incline was reached.

The Glasgow District Subway was of course a very different proposition, and it differed not only in its method and circumstances of working the trains, but in its layout. In its general conception and geography one is met by the age-old 'chicken and egg' conundrum: was the layout dictated by the fact of the company having decided upon cable traction, or was cable traction adopted as a result of the route and layout decided upon? Whichever way one regards the proposition the two factors were indissoluably linked. First as to the route: this was a completely self-contained circuit of $6\frac{1}{2}$ miles. It passed through the heart of the business centre of the city, with stations near to the main line termini of the Caledonian and of the Glasgow and South Western Railways. The North British station at Queen Street however lay between the Subway stations of Buchanan Street and St. Enoch. From the latter, which was also relatively near to the Central station of the Caledonian the Subway passed under the River Clyde, and reached the teeming artisan-class district of the Gorbals. Then it turned west to Pollockshields, with stations at Shields Road and Kinning Park to touch the fringe of Bellahouston before turning north to pass under the Clyde again at Govan. After that it swung round north eastwards to serve the favoured residential district of Kelvingrove before joining the line of the Great Western Road and entering the northern part of the city centre via St. Georges Cross and Cowcaddens.

It was a highly cosmopolitan route, providing for a remarkably comprehensive cross-section of Glasgow life and activities. In the $6\frac{1}{2}$-mile circuit there were fifteen stations. No junctions nor extensions were contemplated with the system of traction proposed. The route was double-tracked, and with the arrangement adopted one group of trains orbited continuously in a clockwise direction, while another set went round anti-clockwise. Each line of rails had its separate tunnel, like the City and South London 'tubes', but at each station the tunnels were merged into a single opening, of which the approximate dimensions were, 28ft. wide, 16ft. high, and about 150ft. long. The platforms were of the island type, running the entire length of the station 'opening', and 10ft. wide. Only six of the stations were completely underground, namely those at Buchanan Street, Cowcaddens, St. Georges Cross, Kelvin Bridge, Govan, and Shields Road; the others, like most of the stations on the Inner Circle in London, had some daylight penetrating to their depths. The 'Subway' was not everywhere of 'tube' construction, and the engineer and his contractors had some anxious times when the tunnels were being bored.

The ground on both banks of the Clyde was very varied, including wet sand, river mud, sandstone, boulder clay, and solid rock. Furthermore, the country on the northern side rose to considerable heights, and the rail level was in places as deep as 114ft. below ground level. Work was commenced by sinking a large diameter shaft in St. Enoch Square, just in front of the large terminal station of the Glasgow and South Western Railway. From the bottom of the shaft four shields were set to work simultaneously—one for each tunnel in opposite directions. Where shields were employed, and at one time there were 16 of them in operation, the method of working differed somewhat from that pioneered by Greathead in the London clay in that an extensive timbered gallery was erected *ahead* of the shield. One would imagine that this procedure was adopted because the nature of the ground was so unpredictable and that the contractors never knew what they were going to strike next. From St. Enoch Square 'tube' type construction continued northwards to Buchanan Street, and thence, 40ft. beneath the ground in wet sand, sandstone and shale to Cowcaddens. It was near Kelvin Bridge that the maximum depth of 114ft. was reached. Then on the southward turn, and tunnelling under the Clyde they encountered mud, boulder clay and rock.

It was however at the second tunnel under the Clyde shortly after leaving southwards from St. Enoch working shaft that some of the greatest difficulties of all were encountered. The tunnel was planned to have 21ft. of cover in mid-stream. The ground was very bad, and to keep water out of the workings it was found necessary to introduce sealed sections with air pressure as high as 30 lb. per sq. in. above atmosphere. This meant that instead of the normal 15 lb. per sq. in. of the atmosphere the men were working under a total of 45 lb. per sq. in.—a bad thing in itself. This was also used on a short section in Govan, where the tunnels were being driven through wet sand. At the tunnel under the river near St. Enoch, the high pressure in the workings led to an extraordinary situation. At this point, of course, the Clyde is tidal, and there is no less than 11ft. difference between high and low watermark at normal times. That 21ft. of cover between the crown of the tunnel arches and the bed of the river consisted of loose, unstable ground, and on one dramatic occasion in February 1894 the weight of the river water at low tide was not enough to hold down the high pressure in the workings below, and a hole was blown from below and timber decking and other materials hurled up through the water and floated away. At such an occurrence, which formed the climax of a series of similar misfortunes, the contractor concerned threw in his hand. The engineer nevertheless tackled the job with immense resolution and resource, and by co-ordinating the use of 30 lb. per sq. in., below, with maximum depth of water in the river the tunnels were successfully completed, and the cast iron tube sections laid in behind the shield after the normal method of procedure.

For some distance on the line beneath the southern suburbs the tunnels were built just as in the District and Metropolitan lines in London, using the 'cut and cover' method of construction. Great care had to be exercised in many localities to avoid causing any damage to buildings, many of which were tall tenement blocks. The tunnels themselves were 11ft. diameter, normally with a distance of 3–6ft. between them, and the rail gauge was 4ft. Except where the line dipped down to pass under the Clyde the gradients were not severe; but at both St. Enoch and Govan gradients of 1 in 20 were used. Taken all round the Subway was a remarkable achievement, and reflected the greatest credit upon Alexander Simpson, the engineer. Special mention was also to be made of the contractor who he persuaded to take over the critical section under the river at St. Enoch, after the disastrous 'blow out' of February 1894; this was Mr. G. Talbot, of Glasgow.

The use of cable haulage was no freak, to be dispensed with as soon as any funds were available. It was a thoroughly sound proposition, and although the speed of transit was slow compared with later standards of underground travel, it served the City of Glasgow for no less than 38 years. Before describing the apparatus in detail—and very interesting it certainly was—the general principle of operation must be made clear. The cable was continuous round the inner and outer tracks of the complete circuit, and these two cables were maintained continuously moving at the running speeds of the trains. Each train was equipped with a clamping device, and when ready to start from a station the driver set this 'gadget', which gripped the cable. The train was thus carried away, until the next station was neared, whereupon the clamp was 'ungripped' and the train brought to rest in the platform. It will be realised that the power driving each cable had to be sufficient to haul simultaneously all the trains orbiting on the inner and outer circuits. The haulage capacity was provided by a single power station located on the south side of the river Clyde, between West Street and Shields Road stations. The cables for each circuit were continuous and kept in motion by a driving drum in the power house. Obviously the 'gripper' on the train could not go round the drum when this point was reached, and so an arrangement was made whereby the 'gripper' was disconnected for a short distance before and after reaching the drum, and the train 'coasted' in the interval. This interval was however no more than a few yards.

By the turn of the century the Subway was operating a three-minute service, and this required ten two-car trains to be orbiting continuously in each direction of circuit. Each train consisted of one gripper and one non-gripper car. The speed of running was 12 m.p.h. so that the maximum required from the power house was a haulage capacity sufficient, at a maximum, of keeping 20 cars travelling at 12 m.p.h. in each direction of circuit. In view of the lifelong association of Glasgow with shipbuilding on the Clyde and with marine engineering generally one might well have expected that the steam engines installed to provide power on the Subway would have been of the latest marine type: compound for a certainty, and very likely triple-expansion, condensing, in the bargain to ensure the utmost economy in working. On the contrary the engines in the Subway power house were single cylinder non-condensing. Preference was obviously

Kinning Park Station under construction in 1894. The gap for the stairway can be seen between the two tunnels.

given to the simplest conceivable form of power generating machinery, with the utmost reliability outweighing any considerations of extra economy due to refinements in design. The cylinder of each engine was 42in. diameter, with a stroke of 6ft. The fly-wheels were 25ft. in diameter and each weighed 50 tons. Each of the main engines was capable of developing 1500 horsepower.

In the ordinary way one of these huge engines was sufficient to haul the entire traffic on both lines, and only one was working at a time. When the Subway as a whole is considered it will be realised that the tension on the cable for each circuit can vary considerably. At any one moment some trains would be running, others standing at stations and thus putting no load at all on to the cable, while others might be in the act of starting, putting on a sudden load when the cable is called upon to start a train from rest. The variation in load, if not compensated for, could result in jerks or 'snatches' to trains in motion, and to undesirable variations in speed while on the run. It was to eliminate, as far as possible such inequalities that an apparatus called a tension regula-tor was installed. Varying tension on the cable resulted in the movement of a so-called tension carriage, and the consequent raising or lowering of some large weights. This device, which in this age of electronic computers might seem large, heavy and slightly primitive in its great length, and in the raising and lowering of heavy weights, was extraordinarily simple, and worked well, though it took up the space of a small factory in the process! The 'tension run', as the complete outfit was called, was included in the main power station. Its length was 138ft. and the three sections—engine house, boiler house and 'tension run' were accommodated in separate sections respectively 100ft., 88ft., and 30ft. wide.

Steam for the huge main engines was provided by a battery of eight Lancashire boilers, 8ft. in diameter, by 30ft. long. Today this type of boiler is completely outmoded in stationary steam plants, but as it was used in many power stations concerned with early underground railways it is worth referring to the design features of this once famous British engineering product. It was circular in cross-section, like a locomotive boiler, but had only two very large flues. On an 8ft. diameter boiler these flues would each be about 3ft. diameter. In these flues the fire grate extended for about one quarter of the length of the boiler, and to prevent the coal passing beyond the end of the grate into the purely circular part of the flue there was a firebrick wall. The fire door was about waist-high, and having fired one of these boilers myself I can testify to the knack necessary in giving a slightly upward throw to each shovelful to keep the firebars evenly covered. The two grates were fired alternately. In the power house on the Glasgow Subway, locally 'the poo-er-hoose', five of the eight boilers were continually in steam, with the remaining three in reserve. The plant was of an advanced design for the period in that the boilers were mechanically stoked, and that a degree of mechanisation was involved in the feeding of the coal to the various hoppers by means of an elevator and screw conveyors. At that time the great majority of Lancashire boilers were hand fired.

The two cables were each approximately 6·9 miles long—36,300ft. to be exact—and 1½in. diameter. They consisted of six strands each, containing 13 to 16 wires per strand, representing a total of about 600 miles of steel wire, and weighing some 57 tons. Reference was made earlier to the slipping gear whereby the cable was disconnected from each train as the latter approached the point where the cable briefly left the running tunnels and entered the power house to pass round the driving drums. This 'slip' mechanism was operated by the driver through a hand lever. Naturally however

57

the fullest consideration had to be given to the chance of a misjudgment on his part, or through inattention or failure to operate the slip lever at all. In such a case the same action of slipping was automatically brought about through a small roller on the forward end of the 'gripper' coming into contact with a ramp fixed between the rails. To demonstrate the effectiveness of this safety device the inventor, D. H. Morton, consultant mechanical engineer of the Subway, himself deliberately took a car into the area with the gripper still tightly clamped to the cable. The roller on the front of the gripper smoothly effected the disconnection.

The requirement that the driver himself normally carried out the disconnection emphasises an important point in railway operating psychology, that recurs many times in the history of evolution of safety devices on underground railways. The Glasgow Subway was constructed at a time when many forward-looking business personalities were making close studies of American methods. There was a disposition to regard things as good because they *were* new. Delegations from various British railways paid visits to the U.S.A.; but against all this there grew up an equally strong feeling that whatever novelties might be introduced the well-tried British traditions of railway operating must essentially remain. Of these there was nothing stronger than the sense of responsibility in engine drivers and signalmen that sixty years of railway working in the United Kingdom had built up. Nothing should be introduced, it was argued, that would make drivers or signalmen feel that their sense of responsibility was doubted. Safety devices of a 'long-stop' nature might be installed, but normally reliance continued to be placed on the 'wicket-keeper'. The Glasgow Subway was organised entirely on established railway practice, and so far as the 'slip gear' at the power station was concerned, its operation at the appropriate time and place was definitely laid down as one of the driver's duties. The roller fitted to the gripper was as much an emergency device as the 'dead man's handle', to be described later in connection with electrification projects in London.

Before leaving the question of the cable itself the task of its installation in the first place needs some mention. In operation it was continuous, but the splice, which joined the two ends, could not be made until the cable had been conducted round the $6\frac{1}{2}$ miles of the circuit. Through each tunnel the haulage cable was drawn by a messenger rope, and this was an operation needing the greatest care. When the circuit was completed, and the necessary tension obtained the splice, which was no less than 75ft. long, was made. Due to the curving nature of the line the cable had to be guided on curves, and in the two circuits there were no fewer than 3400 of these pulleys. At the power house each engine had two counter-shafts, each with a driving drum, and the incoming cable passed, first, to the further drum and then to the nearer one making in all four turns round the further drum and three round the nearest before passing to the tension regulator and so back to the line. Although the cable driving drums in their layout in the power house were associated respectively with the two separate steam engines there was a clutch mechanism that enabled both sets of cable driving drums to be driven by one engine. This was the normal method of working.

As the cars were gripped on to the cable, and all travelled at the same speed the chances of a collision were remote. But on a deep level 'tube' railway, and one passing at two places under the Clyde, nothing could be left to chance. There was always the possibility—very remote it is true—that a car might become 'de-gripped' in a tunnel, and consequently come to rest, and be struck by a succeeding car. Accordingly a

Trains in St. Enoch Station about the mid-nineteen-fifties showing the older cream and red livery. The train indicator panels are illuminated.

system of signalling was installed to ensure that an adequate space was at all times maintained between successive trains. This was the Saxby & Farmer semi-automatic block system. Each station had a semaphore starting signal, and it is of particular interest to recall that these were of the centre-balanced, or somersault type. They were, so far as can be traced, the only signals of this type ever to be installed in Scotland. The operating pull-wire was brought to a chain in the middle of the station platform, where it passed over a pulley and hung downwards. The lower end of this chain was high on the station wall, out of reach of the public. The official in charge of the station had a stick with a hook on the end by which he could pull down the chain and so lower the signal. Once it was pulled it was latched down. The action of lowering the signal was however not direct, but through a balance lever, and an electric 'slot' or interlock. Near to the chain there was a block indicator arm, which showed when the line was clear into the station ahead. Only when this was so was the somersault arm moved to the clear position to allow a train to go forward into the tunnel. The latch on the mechanism was released as the train left the station, so putting the signal to danger automatically.

This simple arrangement worked extremely well throughout the 28 years that cable operation was in use on the Subway. Two accidents, neither of them serious, were

59

nevertheless the subject of enquiries and reports by the Board of Trade. On the first of these, in June 1912, the gripper gear on a train became defective, and led to a train coming to a stop in the tunnel between Buchanan Street and Cowcaddens. The station master at the former place became anxious at the long delay in receiving the line-clear indication after the departure of the previous train and telephoned his colleague at Cowcaddens. It is curious that so often in cases of unusual circumstances messages on the telephone become garbled or misconstrued, and this certainly happened on this occasion. The driver of the second train was authorised, by written order, to proceed against the signal; he actuated the gripper mechanism, started away into the tunnel, and duly collided with the stranded train. Fortunately he was very much on the alert, and seeing lights ahead released his gripper mechanism in time to avoid anything but a minor 'pitch-in'. The second instance took place in April 1917 between Hillhead and Partick Cross in precisely similar circumstances, except that the stalling of the first train was due to the failure of the electric lighting skids, and the extinguishing of the lights of the train. This could potentially have been more dangerous as the stranded train was in darkness. Fortunately however, another safety precaution came into effect as the tail lamp of the train was oil lighted, and the driver of the second train saw it in time to avoid anything more than a minor collision.

Upon the use of oil-lit tail lamps on electricly-hauled underground trains there hangs an amusing tale of my own long association with the safety appliances for the London underground railways, and indeed for underground railways in a number of overseas cities. A casual lunch-table conversation in a senior officers mess referred to the use of oil-lit lamps on the underground trains, and a colleague with very modern 'all-electric' outlooks treated with withering scorn what he regarded as an archaic attitude, until some of us with longer experience of railway operation pointed out that electricity supplies could and *did* fail, and that the well-proved long-burning oil lamp was perhaps a better safeguard in cases of emergency.

Mention of carriage lighting on the Glasgow Subway leads on to the carriages themselves. These were a considerable advance upon the 'padded cells' of the City and South London Railway. They had vestibules at each end, with collapsible gates, and sliding doors to shut off the vestibules from the interior of the cars. At that stage in underground railway history passengers were not allowed to ride in the vestibules, and the experience of a friend of mine on the Hampstead 'tube' in London was yet to come. On this latter occasion the 'pack' on the open vestibule was so terrific one evening that having reached Golders Green and walked the quarter mile or so to his home, the pattern of the grille of the car gates was still imprinted on his overcoat when he arrived indoors! The Glasgow Subway cars gave seating accommodation for 42 passengers, 21 aside, allowing a width of 18in. each. The seat on each side was divided into three portions by partitions extending to the edge of the seats. Besides supporting the roof these partitions greatly improved the initial appearance of the cars. They were fitted with handsome stained glass panels, while the doors, ends and partitions themselves were of polished teak. Internally, the roof panels were of zinc, painted cream colour, and lined with gold and vermillion. Externally the cars were finished in a two-tone colour scheme of plum and cream.

This interior *décor* was of course a vast improvement upon the 'padded cell' technique, but nowadays we should consider the lighting excessively gloomy with no more than four 16 candle-power lamps per coach. The current for lighting was picked up from conductor wires running continuously on the inner side of the tunnels by means of contact brushes attached to the side of the cars. When released from the driving cable, by operation of the gripper mechanism to de-grip, the cars were normally brought to rest by hand brakes operated by the driver, but the two-car set trains were also equipped with the Westinghouse automatic air brake for use in emergency, or if a trailer car should become detached from the 'gripper'. Then, the parting of the couplings would cause the air brake to be applied automatically on each car. As on the City and South London Railway the Glasgow Subway trains were not fitted with individual compressed air equipment. The compressors were at the central power station, and the reservoirs on the trains could be pumped up to full pressure from a supply, 'on tap' as it were, at West Street station.

Another problem arising from the use of cable traction was that any form of points in the track was practically out of the question, and that some other means had to be devised for moving cars from the line for overhaul, stabling for the night, or removal if it were desired to run a less frequent service in the off-peak hours. After much discussion in the planning stages it was decided to build the car shed immediately over the tunnels. A large opening was provided, 55ft. long by 28ft. wide, known as the 'car pit', and over this was built a travelling crane by which cars could be lifted bodily off the track, hoisted 20ft. vertically to the surface, and then transferred to any part of the car sheds where they were required. The car shed itself was a large building capable of stabling all the cars on the system at night. In the car shed all repairs and maintenance work, together with day-to-day cleaning were carried out. By the turn of the century the Subway company owned a total of 60 cars, 30 grippers and 30 trailers, and of these 40 were needed for the daily service. This surplus of 20 not normally in use gave ample

Motor Coach 15, fitted with sliding doors in place of gates being lowered down the Car Sheds pit on to the Outer Circle track. One of the two removable doors in the front of the car has been taken off. Both doors are removed when trains are parked in the tunnels at night, thus giving access between trains.

opportunity for cleaning and maintenance, keeping the stock in the high standard of efficiency for which the Subway became noted.

From the outset it was intended to have a uniform fare throughout, as on the City and South London Railway, with the extraordinarily generous amount of one penny charged for any distance a passenger might like to go. Again the intention was that a penny was paid at the turnstiles, and that gave the freedom of the line. A passenger could travel around the whole circuit of 6½ miles if he so desired, or continue doing so, if he liked the experience, had the time, and was really determined to get his money's worth. But when the Subway was first opened on December 14, 1896, so great were the crowds that it was impossible to run any trains! At many of the stations, and particularly at St. Enoch Square long queues formed up, waiting patiently to pay their penny and have a ride, and the line had to be closed entirely while different ways of handling crowds and charging the fares were devised. The line was re-opened on January 21, 1897, with the issue of tickets. A penny ticket authorised a journey as far as the fourth station from the starting point, while a two-penny ticket gave one, as before, the freedom of the line. Tickets were collected as passengers left the cars. This arrangement worked well, and when statistics of passenger journeys were compared with those of the electrically operated City and South London, those who had adhered to the cable system for the Glasgow System could well feel satisfied. In the half-year ended on July 31, 1898, the Subway had carried a total of 5,779,119, whereas in the same period the City and South London had carried 3,478,977. To the latter figure had to be added 526 season ticket holders, who, if each made six return journeys a week would add another 164,000. Having regard to the greatly differing conditions of service the figures for Glasgow certainly underline the success and popularity that the cable worked subway attained.

St. Enoch Station, when built – in the background on the left is the St. Enoch main line station of the Glasgow & South Western Railway Co.

CHAPTER SIX

First Underground Railway
Overseas—the Paris Metro

France was early in the field of underground development, and a first study of transport and engineering literature published at the end of the nineteenth century could suggest that the suburban railway network of Paris was planned on a much more logical and comprehensive scale than that of London, where developments were the results of privately-enterprised individual companies. These were often in direct competition with one another, and resulted in a railway system that inevitably left a large number of loose ends that eventually had to be tied up. In Paris, as in many cities on the continent of Europe, strategic considerations dictated the form of railway development. Not thirty years before the opening of the first section of the 'Metro' Paris was completely surrounded by the besieging Prussian armies, and the spectacular contacts with the outside world by balloon may be recalled. The inner area of the city was encompassed by walled fortifications, maintained from far earlier times; at various strategic points round the perimeter were heavily protected and armed forts, and immediately inside the walls ran the Ceinture Railway—a means of furnishing supplies to the defence posts, and at the same time providing connection between some of the main lines that radiated from the centre of Paris to different parts. This 'circle' within the walls became known as the *Petite Ceinture* when the outer 'circle' or *Grande Ceinture* was opened in 1883 and provided connection, principally for freight between all the outgoing main lines.

The grievous experiences of the war of 1870–1 did nothing to diminish French faith in old style fortress-type defences, and the *Petite Ceinture* continued to exist in its strategic rôle. Although it provided Paris with a circular railway service, steam operated, its trains were too slow and infrequent, and the stations too far removed from the centre to make any contribution to the growing congestion in the heart of the city. In the last years of the nineteenth century a plan was drawn up for a complete network of underground lines to be operated as a co-ordinated whole, rather than as a series of individual competitive units. Their function was to be that of purely urban transport, exclusively passenger, and quite unconnected with the main line railways. Their extent was at first to be contained entirely within the fortifications and by frequency of service along well established routes, beneath the main thoroughfares, to *eliminate* the nuisance of proliferating omnibus services. It is important that this point is emphasised. The conception was to transfer underground the local traffic that was congesting the city streets and all within the walls.

The French engineers had no doubt watched with critical and discerning eyes the

The Paris Metro: 'cut and cover' work on the first line, in the Cours de Vincennes.

Paris: construction in the heart of the city, Place Saint André des Arts, and the Place Saint Michel.

pioneer British projects in underground railway construction, and noted the problems involved in the cut-and-cover methods used in building the Metropolitan and District Railways in London, and the first experiences in using the Greathead shield for deep level tunnelling. There is always a high prestige value in being pioneers; but unfortunately prestige does not pay for the cost of mistakes! It is left to others to profit by these later. This the builders of the Paris 'Metro' certainly did, but not in a very elegant way. In recalling the history of a very comprehensive piece of overall planning it is perhaps just admissible to draw well ahead of chronological sequence and to refer at the outset to the problem of crossing the river Seine. The Paris 'Metro' is not a deep level system, and very severe gradients would have been necessary to pass under the river. Furthermore, the French engineers were doubtless aware of the great troubles experienced in Glasgow where the 'cover' over the subway workings was not enough to prevent a blow-out, at low tide. The Seine is not tidal at Paris, but without any deep investigation tunnels under the river could well have landed the engineers in a great deal of trouble. There were no river crossings in the first underground lines built in Paris; but later, when a line was carried across to the left bank near to the Pont d'Austerlitz the line was brought from the tunnel, on a fairly steep gradient to cross the river on a bridge.

From the very outset it seemed that the engineers hesitated to employ anything but

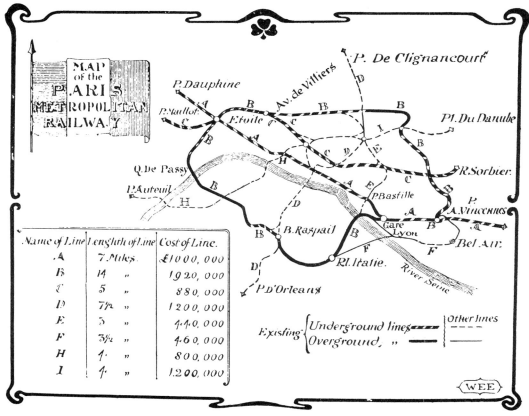

Name of Line	Length of Line	Cost of Line.
A	7 Miles.	£1000,000
B	14 "	1920,000
C	5 "	880,000
D	7½ "	1200,000
E	3 "	440,000
F	3½ "	460,000
H	1. "	800,000
I	1. "	1200,000

Paris Metro: sketch map of the first lines.

straightforward cut-and-cover work for the tunnels, and avoiding passing under any-thing except the streets. The first section of the line, which was brought into service in July 1900 had its easterly terminus beneath the very wide Cours de Vincennes, just short of the viaduct on which the *Petite Ceinture* crossed this major thoroughfare. It then proceeded westwards through the Place de la Nation and beneath the Boulevard Diderot to the Gare de Lyon. There it made almost a right-angle turn to the north to the Place de la Bastille. Beneath this wide square the 'Metro' resumed the westerly direction, beneath the Rue de Rivoli to pass the Louvre, the Tuilleries, and under the Place de la Concorde to reach the Champs-Elysées. Then past the Arc de Triomphe, and so to its western end at the Maillot-Gate, again stopping just short of the Petite Ceinture line. At neither terminating point however was there a 'dead end' as at King William Street on the City and South London. Instead there was a very sharply curved run-round, so that the trains had a continuous run. At the great squares, Nation, Bastille, Concorde and Etoile, the original tunnels did not penetrate directly across, and so pass beneath the huge central monuments, but instead made a deviation to pass round the outer confines of the square.

At an early stage in the history of the Paris 'Metro' the Place de l'Etoile became the general junction. While from the summit of the Arc de Triomphe the sightseer can delight in the spectacle of many gracious avenues and boulevards stretching away from the Place like the points of a star, giving rise to the beautiful name 'Etoile', as early as the year 1904 no fewer than five underground lines converged, unseen, from above, upon Etoile station. The original line from Vincennes to Maillot was an ideal route for sightseers—not of course from the train, which ran entirely in tunnel but from the numerous places of outstanding historical and cultural interest passed en route. It connected however with only one main line station, the Gare de Lyon. The second line built, and sometimes referred to as the Northern Circle, originated at the Porte Dauphine, again on the western walls, beyond which lay the world famous Bois de Boulogne. The Northern Circle made connection with the Maillot-Vincennes line at Etoile and thence by a chain of boulevards, and crossing three of the great main line railways. How this was done was a matter of some contention; but before coming to the Rue de Clignancourt the line has tunnelled under the main line of the former Etat system, about a quarter of a mile from its terminus at St. Lazare, and passed beneath the district famous in the night life of Paris. In the Boulevard de Clichy, under which the line of the 'Metro' runs, is the Moulin Rouge, and the Place Pigalle, at the foot of the hill crowned by Montmartre. Despite the proximity of the line to the Etat main line terminus the 'Metro' was hardly convenient for incoming travellers, as the nearest underground station, Rue de Rome, is half a mile from St. Lazare.

Continuing eastward beneath the Boulevard de Rochechouart the line comes to the surface at the Rue de Clignancourt, and climbs on to a viaduct above the street. This is preparatory to a high level crossing of the main lines of the Northern and then of the Eastern Railways. The single-span lattice girder viaduct over the former takes the 'Metro' trains in full sight of the great Gare du Nord terminus, starting point for the English boat trains. Reciprocally, many travellers have their first sight of the 'Metro' as its electric trains make their way across the many tracks of the Nord main line. As in the case of St. Lazare, however, proximity does not extend to convenience of ex-change. The 'Metro' station Place de la Chapelle is nearly half a mile from the Gare du Nord, while the Gare de l'Est is slightly further away. Clearly the 'Metro' was not

Paris: Construction of viaduct carrying the overhead section of the Metro, across the main line of the Northern Railway just outside the Gare du Nord.

Paris: the much criticised overhead section of Line 2 with the hill of Montmartre in the distant background.

planned to attract passengers wishing to interchange between the main line stations, or to use the 'Metro', on arrival, to reach their point of stay in the city. After crossing the two main lines the 'Metro' makes a wide circuit of the densely populated eastern suburbs, going underground again at Station du Combat, and terminating in a run-round beneath the Place de la Nation.

The elevated section came in for a great deal of criticism. While the Boulevard de Rochechouart was not one of the best known or most beautiful in Paris the railway viaduct looked horrible. But in referring to this part of the 'Metro', and its avoidance of immediate connection with the main line termini, I have drawn somewhat ahead of early history, which deeply influenced the form the whole 'Metro' system eventually took. Before the overall plan was drawn up there had been strong disagreement between the Government of the day and the Municipal Council of the City of Paris as to the nature of the railway. The Council wanted something completely independent of existing railways, contained, as previously mentioned entirely within the city walls. The Government wanted the most comprehensive series of connections with the main lines. For some time there was a complete deadlock of ideas. The Northern Railway was anxious to take advantage of the Government attitude, and offered to pay the entire cost of an underground connection from its own extensive yards at La Chapelle—eastwards of Montmartre—to the central markets of Paris. This was clearly in the pattern of the Great Western and Midland connections via the Inner Circle in London to the goods depots in the City at Smithfield and Whitecross Street. But the Municipal Council was implacable. The 'Metro' in Paris was to be a purely passenger line, quite separate from any other railway; and the Council won the day.

In March 1898 the entire project was authorised, covering the construction of no fewer than six lines. These were as follows:

1. Porte de Vincennes to the Porte Dauphine, along the central route already referred to. (A)
2. Circular route, following the line of the outer boulevards. (B)
3. Porte Maillot to Menilmontant, a point in the eastern suburbs on the Petite Ceinture line. (C)
4. A north–south route from Porte de Clignancourt, north of Montmartre, to the Porte d'Orleans, in the south. (D)
5. From the Boulevard Strasbourg to the Pont d'Austerlitz. (E)
6. From Porte de Vincennes to the Place d'Italie, (F) together with connecting lines from Auteuil station to the Opera, (H) and from the Palais Royal station to the Place du Danube. (I)

This historic network is shown on the map on page 65. To make sure that the main line railways were effectively excluded the Municipal Council decreed that the gauge should be narrower than standard; but when the folly of this decision was pointed out, in the restrictions it placed upon the transport of rolling stock from the manufacturers' works it was agreed to adopt the French standard gauge of 1·44 metres, which is near enough to the British standard of 4ft. 8½in. But having agreed to a common gauge the Paris Council were careful to make the tunnels too small to admit standard main line rolling stock!

The contractors seem to have had a high old time in building the original line. Although the tunnels were excavated at relatively shallow depth there was an attempt to use shields, and these appear to have worked well enough where the tunnels were in clay; but there were frequent intermissions of hard crystalline rock which played the very devil with mechanical cutters. In the wider thoroughfares the usual 'cut and cover' method was used, covering up the roadway once sufficient depth had been excavated to work underneath. Elsewhere there was much trouble with subsidence. At one time the main roadway over almost the entire length of the Champs Elysées sank several inches and had to be boarded off. This naturally caused something of an outcry from those who were inconvenienced by the consequent diversions of traffic, though actually from the public point of view—though not those of Council finances—this was no bad thing. The streets of Paris were then mostly in a very bad state of repair, and the damage caused by the construction made necessary at once the repairs that should have been done long previously! There was a working site at the Arc de Triomphe to which materials were at first brought by steam tractors. At a later stage a narrow gauge railway was laid down, and wagons hauled by hot water locomotives. There was a lot of trouble with the excavations near this area. There was a complete collapse of the tunnel for a distance of 20yd., and two people fell from the street into the cavity that had opened out.

The short branch line from the junctions at Etoile to the Porte Maillot, beneath the Avenue de la Grande Armée, gave immense trouble. Here again there was an alternation of clay and rock, and the whole of the work was done by hand. Pick-axes were used for the clay, and for the rock there was nothing more puissant than a hammer and chisel. Apparently there was a great reluctance to use explosives after the experience with subsidences that had been sustained elsewhere on the line. The cross-sections of the finished tunnels were of a composite shape, being quasi-elliptical at the top, and then tapering inwards to a little below rail level. The floor of the tunnel was a slight

Paris: a 'toboggan' section on Line 5, where the Metro climbs out of tunnel to cross the Seine near the Pont d'Austerlitz.

inverted arch. Most of the tunnels were double-tracked and had a maximum width inside of about 23ft. They were lined with masonry, and had a thick surround of concrete. The engineers were not clear of troubles even when the tunnels were nearly finished. On one section there was a collapse of the roof. This was attributed to severe frost following heavy rain, which had weakened the arch before the masonry had time to set properly. Generally speaking there was not a great deal of trouble with water, and no recourse had to be made with working with compressed air. Some flooding near the Tuilleries was overcome by construction of a temporary sump from which the water could be pumped. From such an expedient it will be appreciated that the ingress of water at this point was not very great.

At the stations a very elegant cross-sectional shape was adopted. The bore of the tunnel to include two tracks and the station platforms was elliptical, the transverse axis being 46ft. across, and the maximum vertical height about 21ft. The thickness of the masonry and concrete surround varied from 6ft. 6in. at the sides to 2ft. 3in. at the crown. It made a spacious layout for the station itself, with notably wide platforms. At the outset it was stipulated that on this first line, between the Vincennes and Dauphine gates there should be 135 trains a day each way, and that each train should be capable of carrying 100 passengers—a very modest estimate of what was to be required of the railway! Before leaving constructional days however no account would be complete without mention of the hazards experienced in dealing with underground water networks in the form of sewers and water mains. These were duly encountered and overcome beneath the streets of Paris, but an unusual problem had to be solved at the Place de la Bastille. There an underground canal existed. This could not be diverted, nor have its level altered; so the 'Metro' had to be built to cross the canal at a height that would not interfere with navigation, nor at the same time bring the crown of the railway tunnels too high to go beneath the level of the neighbouring boulevards. Fortunately there was just sufficient head room to build the railway to everyone's satisfaction.

Another very intricate task confronted the engineers at the Hotel de Ville station, beneath the Rue de Rivoli. The headroom here was very limited and the normal form of station construction previously described, with a solid masonry and concrete shell enveloping the entire tunnel, could not be applied. The roadway was first opened, in sections, and massive longitudinal girders inserted. Then, with these as a support, the roadway was restored, and excavation proceeded beneath. The roadway was not one of the wider thoroughfares, and the proximity of the Hotel de Ville itself necessitated some careful under-pinning while work was in progress. The roof of the finished tunnel through the length of the station was formed by a series of brick arches between the longtitudinal girders, there being seven arches in all running lengthwise, and parallel to each other throughout the length of the station. The walls and floor of the tunnel in the station area were formed in the usual way, with masonry lining to a thick concrete shell. The stations were designed to make them as inconspicuous as possible from the outside, in strong contrast to the flamboyant plastering of destinations served that characterised some of the District Line stations in London. The Parisians evidently had more feelings against the desecration of their city by crude advertisement than their contemporaries in London, though the practice of having no more than one entrance and exit at each station in the cause of inconspicuousness was to have disastrous results before the 'Metro' was three years old.

Paris: Modern rolling stock on the sections running on steel rails.

The line from the Porte de Vincennes to the Porte Dauphine was opened in 1900, and the first section of the circular route reference 2 on page 68 was opened in 1903. This was referred to as the 'Circulaire Nord', and ran from Etoile, via the outer boulevards on the northern and eastern side to the Place de la Nation. On this line there was some very awkward constructional work. It ran beneath the slopes of two isolated hills, that the French call *buttes* or humps, Chaumont and Montmartre, and it encountered some old gypsum quarries. Over the years all sorts of old rubbish had been tipped in, and the lowest 'strata', if one could call it such, had been solidified into an extraordinary agglomerate. And through some of these age-old rubbish pits the *Circulaire Nord* had to be tunnelled. Although it provided some difficulties in excavation, and some surprises at some of the choice items excavated, it was possible to build a satisfactory tunnel through it. But it was another matter when the line came to the surface and viaducts in the centre of the boulevards had to be constructed. The foundations had to be carried down very deep, to get to some solid ground beneath the strata of old junk. The engineers got little thanks for their efforts on this part of the line, and a strongly expressed contemporary comment in *The Engineer* said that the viaduct was 'utterly devoid of aesthetic lines as it had to follow the sinuosities of the boulevards'.

Despite all the various difficulties experienced these early sections of the Paris 'Metro' do not seem to have been very expensive to build. The viaduct section was criticised not only for its appearance, nor for its very existence in the centre of this chain of boulevards, but also for its high cost. *The Engineer* records that its cost per metre was roughly double that of a tunnel, and quotes the latter as costing on an average £56 per metre. This works out at roughly £100,000 a mile, which is 'a mere bagatelle' in comparison with the Inner Circle, some tunnel sections of which cost more than a *million* a mile! One cannot only think that the Parisians gained more than they really knew by coming to the surface at various points and bridging across obstacles like main line railways and the River Seine, rather than tunnelling beneath them. The cost of £56 per metre would appear to be that of 'easy' tunnelling and evading the more difficult tasks; but even so, when allowance is made for the much higher cost of the viaduct sections the overall cost of building the line remains quite moderate.

The line was equipped for direct current traction at 550 volts. The signalling was automatic using a system that was regarded with some scepticism by British railway engineers. I have already told in this book how the first electric underground railways in London were equipped with forms of well-tried mechanical signalling, in conjunction with lock and block; but on the Liverpool Overhead Railway, opened in 1893, a form of automatic signalling operated by treadle contacts actuated by the trains was installed. But because of the intermittent nature of the indications provided by the treadles the British Board of Trade insisted on having an ordinary bell-block system superimposed, and operated by the platform staff. French philosophy in ordinary railway signalling was in many ways opposed to well establish British ideas, and the Paris 'Metro' was originally signalled from treadle contracts operated by the trains themselves, and the signals were actuated by current from primary batteries, through circuits controlled by the treadle contacts. At first the signals stood normally clear. They were put to

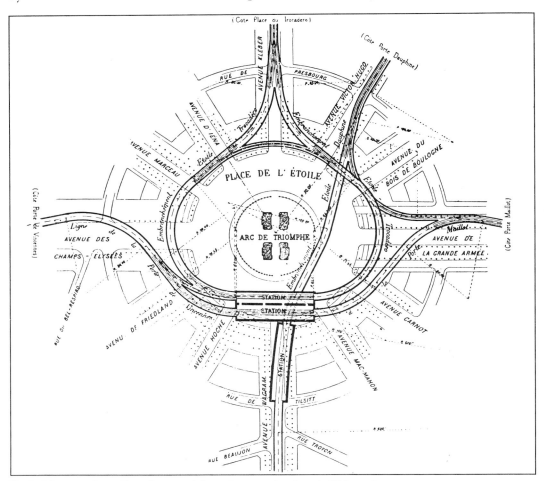

Paris Metro: plan of stations and junctions at the Arc de Triomphe.

danger by the passage of a train, and cleared when the train had travelled a stipulated distance ahead, as indicated by the passage over further treadles. Later the system was changed, to have the signals normally at danger, but cleared on the approach of a train if the line was clear for a sufficiently far distance ahead. This latter arrangement remained standard practice on the Paris 'Metro' until 1922 when a start was made with the installation of continuous track circuiting.

The inauguration of underground train working in Paris was in general well received, though Karl Baedecker in the 1904 edition of his handbook for Paris comments: 'This new electric railway begun in 1898, which runs mostly underground, now takes precedence of all other modes of locomotion in the interior of the city. The stations are below the level of the streets, like those of the "Tube" railway in London, but not so deep (no lift), and the atmosphere is similarly oppressive to susceptible people.' There was this difference however; whereas the prevailing odour on the Inner Circle in steam days was that of sulphur, on the Paris 'Metro' it was that of garlic! I have already referred to the policy adopted by the French of making their stations as inconspicuous as possible, and of having only one outlet to the street, whether underground or on viaducts. This policy was in part responsible for a terrible disaster in August 1903. It was ironic, too, that it did not arise primarily from the running of the trains.

A train proceeding eastwards on the Circulaire Nord, on reaching the station Boulevard Barbes, on the viaduct, and the nearest station to the Gare du Nord, was found to have a floor on fire in the leading motor coach. The passengers were instructed to get out, and under special instructions the following train was brought forward into the Boulevard Barbes station, with the object of using it to propel the disabled train to the car depot at Place de la Nation, eleven stations further on. At this stage the fire was not serious; but so that the propelling movement could be done without stopping at any stations the second train was also cleared of its passengers. The first train consisted of four cars, and the second of eight, and all passengers from both trains were left behind at Boulevard Barbes. Apparently power was shut off completely on the disabled train, and all stations were warned of the approach of the 'non-stop'. Naturally the men on this cortége wished to get through to Place de la Nation as quickly as possible, but progress was no more than moderate while the motors of an 8-car train were propelling 12 coaches on the viaduct section. Once the station Combat was passed, and they entered on the descent into the tunnels speed rose rapidly, and witnesses on Rue de Belleville station said afterwards that they passed at a very high speed.

The increased speed, and the intense draught caused on entering the tunnel fanned the fire, and the stationmaster at Rue des Couronnes stopped them, and said they must not proceed. An argument ensued with the train men, and it was only after much talk that he gave way. The train men were confident they could get through to 'Nation'. But before the train reached the very next station the Rue de Menilmontant, it 'went up' in a terrifying spontaneous combustion. The men managed to escape to Couronnes, but in a very few minutes the whole twelve coaches were blazing from end to end. In the meantime another train, conveying the passengers left behind at Boulevard Barbes, was proceeding normally, except of course that it was very crowded; and although the stationmaster at Couronnes had such misgivings as to the wisdom of allowing the burning train to proceed beyond his station he apparently took no steps to prevent this very crowded passenger train from coming forward from Rue de Belleville. The men of the burning train had scarcely got back to Couronnes and given the alarm when dense

F

acrid smoke came belching out of the tunnel; and at that very moment the heavily-loaded passenger train arrived. The situation was dramatic to say the least of it. Many of the passengers in that train were doubtless aware that a train ahead of them was on fire, and could well be uneasy on that score; but the sight of Couronnes station as they drew in was enough to strike terror into the staunchest heart. Naturally there was a rush to get out of that train, and in the midst of it all the lights went out. The fire in that tunnel had quickly developed into an absolute inferno, destroying electric cables, and the state of panic was now indescribable. The choking, suffocating smoke was bad enough; but in pitch darkness few people could find the only exit, and 84 people died of suffocation.

The disaster naturally caused a terrible outcry. All the inhibitions people had felt against underground railways rose in crescendo, and the 'Metro' suffered an immense reduction to traffic. For a time less than half the passengers previously travelling were using the underground system. The Police ordered the installation of an independent electric lighting system, supplied to the stations by surface lines from the Corporation mains. Critics rushed into print, writing of the dangers of electric traction, and with the examples then existing on the electric underground railways in London there was much talk of using separate locomotives instead of multiple unit trains. All stations were required to have a second exit. Other commentators drew attention to the potential dangers at Etoile, the largest exchange station on the Paris 'Metro'. The existence of conflicting streams of passengers was pointed out, and the hazards of what might occur if panic of a similar kind to that at Couronnes were emphasised. But apart from this one dreadful tragedy the Paris 'Metro' has sustained a remarkably good safety record, and in a later chapter reference is made to the many measures of modernisation carried out since 1930.

CHAPTER SEVEN

The Twopenny Tube

It was no more than natural that the almost embarrassing success of the City and South London Railway should spark off a crop of new tube railway schemes. It is however not generally appreciated that the idea of an underground railway beneath the teeming highways of Oxford Street and Holborn goes back to the time of the very inception of underground railways in London. The intensity of the street traffic, and the congestion from slow moving horse-drawn vehicles made this near-straight east-west route a natural one for railway development. But there were obstacles of a varied kind in the way. At the time of the Railway Mania in the mid-1840s a Royal Commission had recommended that no railway should penetrate into London between the Thames and the line of the New Road—now Marylebone, Euston and Pentonville Roads. The locations of Euston and Paddington had conformed to this recommendation likewise Waterloo and London Bridge; and when the Chatham and the South Eastern crossed the river their stations, with the exception of Ludgate Hill, did not constitute more than so many footholds on the north bank. But despite the recommendations of the Royal Commission independent railway promoters had their eyes upon the Oxford Street–Holborn route, and four schemes that for various reasons came to nought may be recalled:

1865: Oxford Street & City Railway
1868: Marble Arch & General Post Office
1872: Mid-London Railway: Marble Arch to Whitechapel
1884: London Central Railway: Trafalgar Square to St. Martins-le-Grand

It was not until the City and South London Railway was actually working from December 1890 that Parliament seemed ready to authorise further underground railways in London, and then, in August 1891 the Central London Railway obtained its Act, authorising a tube railway from Shepherds Bush Green to Cornhill. A further Act, passed in 1892, covered an extension both to the Bank, and to Liverpool Street, where it was at first intended to make a physical link up with the Great Eastern Railway. Although the project held out prospects of such a vast improvement in traffic handling public support from the financial viewpoint was markedly apathetic. Technically it had the highest backing with Sir John Fowler, Sir Benjamin Baker, and J. H. Greathead as engineers. It was announced that construction would be sponsored by a mining finance organisation known as the Exploration Co. Ltd., and after some preliminary manoeuvres the Central London Railway reconstituted its board to include directors of some of the main line railway companies, and secured the services of Henry Tennant, formerly General Manager of the North Eastern Railway as Chairman. A prospectus was issued in 1895 offering £2,850,000 capital in £10 shares, but public response was so poor that only 14 per cent of the capital was actually subscribed. The whole scheme therefore hung fire, until the Exploration Company came to the rescue, with a contribution of more than £2 million. It was then possible to go ahead.

Although the line was projected at deep level and entirely below streets, a good deal of trouble arose over the purchase of sites for the stations. The designs for these were modest enough, having relatively small entrances at street level. There was none of the grandiose dome-capped edifices that distinguished the City and South London. But where the latter Company displayed remarkable ostentation above ground, and the most dismal cramped conditions on the railway itself the Central London did almost exactly the reverse. The surface buildings were simple and business-like, but underground there was plenty of space and plenty of *light*. The cross-section of the tunnels was made larger, namely 11ft. 6in. internal diameter and that extra foot made all the difference. Because of the delays in settling preliminaries, both financial and in obtaining the necessary sites on the surface construction work did not begin until nearly five years after the passing of the original Act, but by September 1896 work was in progress in shafts at Chancery Lane, Shepherds Bush, British Museum, and a site at first known as Westbourne, but now Lancaster Gate. This station was originally the nearest the new tube came to a main line railway, being about five minutes walk from Paddington. Before the works had progressed to more than these very preliminary stages Greathead died, at the early age of 52. He was succeeded as resident engineer by Basil Mott, son of Charles Grey Mott, Chairman of the City and South London Railway.

As on the latter line the tracks had to be located vertically above each other in places to keep within the limits of street widths, and this was evident at three stations, namely Post Office, Chancery Lane and Notting Hill Gate. The first of these three was renamed 'St. Pauls' in recent years. It is perhaps difficult to appreciate the need for keeping strictly beneath the streets, as this imposed restrictions in layout that a really deep level line would seem to obviate; but there was a remarkable instance of this at the eastern end of Holborn where there is a reverse curve to enter Cheapside. This necessitated a curve of no more than 5 chain radius on the railway, and to provide clearance for the proposed bogie carriages on this curve the diameter of the tunnel was made 12ft. 5in. instead of the standard 11ft. 6in. It is particularly interesting that the contractor for the section from Post Office to the Bank, and for an elaborate series of subways and the sub-surface booking office beneath the large open space in front of the Royal Exchange, was George Talbot who had successfully carried the tube of the Glasgow Subway beneath the Clyde at St. Enoch, after the previous contractor had blown a hole in the river bed. Another interesting civil engineering feature of the Central London Railway, specified by Greathead in his original layout of the line, was the system of 'dipping' gradients from the stations. To secure rapid acceleration from each station stop the line was built on a descending gradient of 1 in 30 for 300ft. from the platform end, while to aid retardation, and lessen wear and tear on the braking equipment the approaches to the stations were made on a rising gradient of 1 in 60.

The actual boring of the tunnels did not involve any particular difficulties. For most of the distance the route was in the London clay. Air pressure had to be used only on two short lengths, beneath Threadneedle Street, at the original city terminus, and where the line passed beneath the Holborn Valley, and the line of the Old Fleet Ditch. The station tunnels lay at a depth of between 60 and 110ft. below the surface, typical examples being 60ft. at the Bank, 80ft. at Oxford Circus and 92ft. at Notting Hill Gate. The method of working with the shields consisted in the driving of a pilot heading 7 or 8ft. ahead of the shield. The clay was dug out to a depth of about 20in. ahead of the shield but not to the full diameter. When the cylindrical part excavated by the miners had reached a diameter about 6in. less than that of the shield hand digging stopped and the shield was driven forward by hydraulic rams, using the completed tunnel segments as an abutment, as on the City and South London Railway. The tube sections for the stations were 21ft. 6in. internal diameter. This, together with the brilliant electric lighting gave a spacious and cheerful air that was so noticeably absent down in 'The Drain'.

While construction was in progress some important changes took place in the top management of the company. Henry Tennant found that he had too many business responsibilities in the North of England to give the Central London the attention it needed, and the company was supremely fortunate in securing the services of Sir Henry Oakley, as Chairman. At the age of 75 he had, in 1898, just retired from the General Managership of the Great Northern Railway. He had held that office for no less than 28 years, and he had been in the service of the G.N.R. for well over 50 years. In coming to the Central London he brought all his vast experience of railway working to this small, but highly significant project; for with the civil engineering work advancing, and contracts let for locomotives, carriages and other equipment the company was nearing the time when the real 'crunch' would come. Put quite simply, they had got to run the railway, and Sir Henry Oakley was an ideal man to build up the necessary organisation. One of his most remarkable achievements was to get Charles Aldington

Central London Railway: one of the original locomotives, which were soon found unsatisfactory.

from the Great Western to fill the vital office of Traffic Manager. Now Aldington was no up-and-coming young man. He was an experienced officer with 23 years of excellent service behind him, and every indication of a still more distinguished career ahead of him. The inducement must have been attractive indeed for him to break into an experience with so solid and 'safe' a concern as the Great Western and join a yet unfinished tube railway not quite 6 miles long! He stayed with the Central London just long enough to get it well and truly going, and then returned to the Great Western. It is sufficient indication of his outstanding qualities to add that in 1910 he was appointed Superintendent of the Line, and in 1919 General Manager.

Another remarkable 'capture' so far as the Central London was concerned was that of Granville Cunningham, for General Manager. Cunningham was a Scot, born in Edinburgh and trained as a civil engineer, and at the age of 23 he went to Central America to engage in the survey of a projected new line in Spanish Honduras. In 1871 he went to Canada and took part in some of the exciting pioneer work on the Canadian Pacific. He was successively Chief Engineer to the Government railway of Prince Edward Island, then of the Canada Southern, in which capacity he selected the site for the bridge over the Niagara gorge at the Niagara Falls. He returned to the Canadian Pacific to become assistant engineer for construction of the Rocky Mountain Division. Then, at the age of 42, he became Assistant Engineer to the City of Toronto, and two years later he was appointed City Engineer. It was in this capacity that he first had to consider electric traction for urban transport. His services were however soon claimed by the sister city of Montreal, where he organised the conversion of the horse-drawn street tramways to electric traction. After that he returned to the United Kingdom in 1897 to carry out a similar task in Birmingham. It was unfinished when he was offered the post of General Manager of the Central London Railway. This then, was the man chosen by Sir Henry Oakley, and he came to the almost finished tube railway bringing a wealth of experience, not least in civic transport affairs from Toronto, Montreal and Birmingham.

There was certainly a galaxy of talent gathered in the management of the new railway. The civil engineers, consultants and contractors have already been mentioned, and I must now turn to the trains themselves. The consulting engineer and designer of the electrical power plant, all electrical equipment and of the electric locomotives was a brilliant young engineer of 34 years, Dr. H. F. Parshall. He recommended the use of 500 volts direct current for traction, using the third rail system, with return current through the running rails, as on the City and South London. The permanent way was unusual, with 'bridge' type rails, 100 lb. per yard, bolted direct to longitudinal timber sleepers. These were laid on the curve of the tube, embedded in concrete and connected only at intervals by the cross-ties used to support the centre current rail. One is inclined to wonder if Granville Cunningham had any part in deciding upon this unusual form of permanent way, because all previous experience both at home and abroad was such as to condemn it as unsatisfactory. Brunel's bridge rails and longitudinal sleepers on the broad gauge Great Western were extremely difficult to maintain and lacked the resilience of the usual transverse sleepered track. It was too rigid. Even so it was not so rigid as that of the Central London. The sleepers did rest in the ballast, whereas the new railway had the sleepers embedded in concrete. It was nearly as bad as the case of the early railway on which the rails were spiked direct to solid rock on one stretch of line!

On the Central London things were made much worse by the design of the electric

Central London Railway: trailer car in the original colours.

locomotives. The first 30 were of the so-called 'camel-backed' type, and built by the General Electric Company of Schenectady, U.S.A. They were of what we should now call the Bo–Bo type, running on two four-wheeled bogies. They were neatly and attractively styled, handsomely painted in purple-brown with yellow lining, and had a most distinguished air as they ran into the brightly lighted stations at the head of their six-car trains. The wheels were 3ft. 6in. diameter, and each bogie had a wheelbase of 5ft. 8in.; but the feature that proved so unsatisfactory in service was that the motors were mounted on the axles, and that of the total weight of the locomotive, 45 tons, a high proportion was completely unsprung. From the viewpoint of simplicity in design axle-mounted electric motors are an attractive proposition; but on British Railways today their damaging effect upon the track has been widely experienced. On the Central London it was many times worse because these powerful locomotives were running over a track that had practically no 'give' in it. Those longitudinal sleepers, bedded in concrete and resting on the solid rings of the tube were bad enough in themselves; but with the rails continuously supported there was not even the springiness of the rails that one gets on a track with transverse sleepers. Something had to go! Vibrations were set up, which were felt to a degree of unpleasantness in the carriages, but which were transmitted through the ground to surface buildings along the route. It was not long before the management was being deluged with complaints from irate householders, and owners of business premises.

I am to some extent anticipating, for there are other interesting features of the line to describe before coming to the actual inauguration of the service. First of all there were the carriages. These were 45ft. 6in. long, and had gates at the ends. They seated 48 passengers on upholstered seats with separate arm rests. At each end of the cars the seats were arranged longitudinally while in the middle there were four rows of cross seats. They were very attractively styled both inside and out, and it is significant that

79

from the very outset an ample array of hanging straps was provided for the comfort of standing passengers. Taken all round these Central London cars were quite luxurious to a degree, in the most striking contrast to the 'padded cells' of the City and South London. A six-car train had seats for 288 passengers, and in peak hours, with many standing, the train often conveyed 400 or more. Conductors travelled on each platform and shouted the names of the stations as each was approached. The signal to the driver to start was relayed from the rearmost platform on the train forward, as each was cleared of entering and leaving passengers. Externally, the carriages were finished in a two-tone colour scheme, with bodies to match the purple-brown of the locomotives, and upper panels and roof white. The ensemble looked very similar, in colour, to the style of the London and North Western Railway.

An extensive surface establishment was built at Shepherds Bush, including electricity generating station, car and locomotive running sheds; car repair and washing plants, and a machine shop. This was reached by a steeply graded line leading down into the tube tunnel. It so happened that Shepherds Bush station was the least deep of all those on the line, due to the steep falling away of the contours from Notting Hill westward. For shunting in the depot, and for hauling maintenance trains in the tube when current was switched off the Central London purchased two very powerful little 0-6-0 steam tank engines, with condensing gear, from the Hunslet Engine Co. of Leeds. Although very squat, to fit into the restricted loading gauge of the tube tunnels they were not unattractive little engines. They were interesting in being provided with duplex buffing gear—ordinary buffers and couplings for working standard railway stock, and centre couplers at a much lower level for use when they were hauling tube passenger stock, or electric locomotives 'dead'.

Reference to the connection to the surface depot at Shepherds Bush leads on to the track layouts adopted at various places on the line. It was considered necessary to have means of crossing trains from one tube to another at stations other than the terminals. At three stations, Queens Road Bayswater, Marble Arch, and British Museum, sidings were laid in between the two running lines, which permitted the removal of a defective train, or locomotive, and there was always a spare electric locomotive standing in the siding at Marble Arch. At Shepherds Bush there were scissors crossings between the two running lines at both ends of the station to provide the most complete flexibility in working. Either platform could be used as the terminating point of trains arriving from the east though it seems to have been the normal practice only to use one platform for arrivals and the other for departures, shunting the train across by means of one 'scissors', and using the one at the east end to allow the locomotive to 'run round' its train and get on to the leading end for the eastbound journey.

Another important feature of the equipment of the Central London Railway was the use of electricity for lifts. It had originally been proposed to adopt hydraulic operation; but an electrical engineer whose name will always be famous in connection with the rapid-transit urban railways, Dr. F. J. Sprague, secured a contract to supply no less than 49 electric lifts to the Central London. It is not however in connection with lifts that Sprague's special distinction rests, but in the invention of the multiple unit system of traction control. This was not adopted at first on the Central London, because as previously described the trains were all hauled by individual locomotives. It was first introduced in Great Britain on the Waterloo and City Railway, a short 'tube' line, sponsored powerfully by the London and South Western Railway, and opened in

Central London Railway: an artist's impression of the 'Twopenny Tube', as first opened.

August 1898. The multiple-unit system of traction is referred to in some detail later in this chapter, when difficulties in operating the original Central London trains are described.

The last point to be mentioned before coming to the ceremonial opening of the line and the inauguration of the public service is that of fares. When the line was originally projected, and Parliamentary powers were obtained it was intended to have two classes. So much comment and criticism had been levelled at the spartan character of the accommodation on the City and South London that the management of the Central London was at first inclined to go the other way. Their statutory powers permitted the charging of 2d. a mile first class, and 1d. a mile third, with 2d. as the minimum except on 'workmens' trains. It is interesting to note that the classes originally provided for under the Act were 'first' and 'third', without any 'second'. Nevertheless the simplicity in working from a universal fare held such attractions from an administrative viewpoint that the idea of charging by mileage was abandoned in favour of a uniform fare of 3d. first class, and 2d. second, by the year 1895. This was the situation when Sir Henry Oakley became Chairman, in 1898, and one can probably detect the influence of Granville Cuningham in making the subsequent decision to have only one class, and a universal fare of 2d. So the Central London became 'The Twopenny Tube'.

The opening ceremony took place on the afternoon of Wednesday June 27, 1900, when the Prince of Wales—within a year to become King Edward VII—drove to the Bank station, and was received by Sir Henry Oakley. A train carrying a gathering of railway representatives and of prominent City men had already left for Shepherds

Bush and a special carrying the Prince himself left at 3.36 p.m. and ran non-stop to Shepherds Bush, taking 18 minutes for the journey. In a ceremony notably brief, and entirely free from the banqueting often associated with the openings of new railways the Prince of Wales made the only speech of the day. It lasted precisely 35 seconds! He said:

'My Lords and Gentlemen, I have great pleasure in declaring the Central London Railway open. It has given me much pleasure to take part in today's proceedings. I wish to drink "Success to the undertaking", and I congratulate Sir Benjamin Baker, the eminent engineer, who has constructed this great railway. I have but little doubt that it will be an immense boon to London, and I am sure you will all join me in wishing success to the company.'

Sir Henry Oakley in a few words of simple thanks to the Prince for his attendance said that His Royal Highness had expressed a wish that the proceedings should not be further prolonged. The guests returned to the City by special train, and that was that! The line was however not immediately opened to the public, as Sir Henry and his staff wished to eliminate every possible chance of difficulty in working an enterprise that bade fair to be extremely popular. Accordingly the full train service was operated for three weeks, but with no passengers, and it was not until Monday July 30, that the line began business. The first trains left Shepherds Bush and the Bank at 5.15 and 5.20 a.m. respectively. The names of the intermediate stations, as actually brought into service were Holland Park, Notting Hill Gate, Queens Road, Lancaster Gate, Marble Arch, Bond Street, Oxford Circus, Tottenham Court Road, British Museum, Chancery Lane and Post Office. The greatest indecision over names seems to have existed over 'Post' Office'; earlier suggestions were 'Newgate Street' and 'General Post Office', though no one ever seems to have thought of St. Martins-le-Grand. One detects also the hopes of tourist traffic in having 'British Museum' as an intermediate station, instead of locating it a little farther eastwards—as now—at the important road junction of Kingsway and High Holborn.

The public flocked to travel on the new line. The news of its success quickly crossed the Atlantic and one organ of the New York press was moved to comment: 'All London seems to be as pleased with its latest novelty as a child would be with a toy.' New toy maybe, but within five years New York had an 'underground' of its own! The 'Twopenny Tube' got a most enthusiastic reception in the English press, which has never in its history been very favourably disposed towards railways of any kind. It was not only Londoners who rushed to travel on their own new railway. In the holiday months of August and September, London, as always, was crowded with overseas visitors, and one newspaper comment told how: 'Nearly every civilised nation under the sun was represented among the humanity struggling to experience London's latest sensation.' 'Under the sun' had a more direct ring about it in 1900; for in the holiday months Southern England was sweltering in a most exceptional heat wave. The London streets, at ninety in the shade were insufferable, and the people revelled in the cool air of the tube, maintained at about 55 degrees. On the very first day 84,000 passengers travelled; this total rose quite early to around 90,000, and by the end of 1902 the daily average was 130,000 to 140,000. In those early years the record was made on October 29, 1900, when the City Imperial Volunteers making a triumphal return from the South African War were accorded the honour of making a State Entry to the City. On that day the Central London Railway carried 229,000 passengers!

82

The triumph of the Twopenny Tube, for such it undoubtedly was, became tempered before the year 1900 was out by complaints of disturbance to buildings, by vibration, and these were serious enough for the Board of Trade to appoint a Committee to examine the whole question. The company itself had quickly become aware of the unwelcome characteristics of its electric locomotives, due to the heavy unsprung weight on the axles, and three of them were changed experimentally to geared drive. But the answer lay not in modifications to the locomotives themselves, but in the adoption instead of the principle of multiple unit trains. It is sometimes thought that the Central London was the pioneer in this respect. This is not so, for the Waterloo and City opened with trains of this kind in 1898, and in 1900 some fine new coaches of very modern appearance were put into service. Each of these coaches had its own motor, and could be run as a single unit, or coupled in multiple-unit with others on the principle devised by F. J. Sprague. This arrangement not only distributed the power units, and thus resulted in higher axle-loading, but it provided power in proportion to the length and loading of the trains. This was a feature found necessary in the very short length of the Waterloo and City Railway, which was heavily used in the morning and evening peak periods, but almost deserted at midday. With the multiple unit principle it was possible to run four-coach, three-, two-, and even one-coach trains if desired. The controls permitted the operation of any number of units with only one driver.

The Central London began the immediate consideration of multiple-unit operation, even though it was realised that its adoption would make redundant 30 almost new electric locomotives. In connection with this work the British Thompson-Houston Company, through which firm the Schenectady electric locomotives had been obtained, took such a serious view of the situation that they appointed a young engineer of 23, one J. P. Thomas, as London Resident Engineer, and it was as a result of the close liaison thus set up that the Central London decided to build two experimental 6-car trains, consisting of two motor coaches and four trailers. These proved so successful that the decision was taken to purchase no less than 64 new motor coaches. These were built in England by the Ashbury Carriage and Wagon Co., but fitted with American built motors. The locomotive hauled service, with a minimum headway of $2\frac{1}{2}$ minutes was operating until April 1903. After that the working was gradually changed to multiple-unit trains, and by June of that year the locomotives had been completely superseded. Not only was vibration virtually eliminated, but it was possible to speed up the service to a minimum of 2 minutes headway. J. P. Thomas spent the rest of his working life, and some of his retirement too with London Transport. He rose to become General Manager of London Transport Railways from 1933 to 1938, and when war came he was recalled from his retirement to organise arrangements for the night sheltering in the tube stations during the period of severe air raiding on London.

In view of the highly modern nature of most of its equipment it is a little surprising that the Central London was originally equipped with mechanical signalling, and the form of Spagnoletti 'lock and block' used on the City and South London Railway. This was not for want of trying on the part of those who had more advanced views. W. R. Sykes, who had installed his own form of 'lock and block' on lengthy stretches of heavily worked line south of the Thames, and who was one of the most advanced exponents of modern signalling in Great Britain submitted a scheme for automatic signalling from end to end of the Central London Railway. It was a most novel proposal, in that no signalling cables were required along the line, except for lighting the signal lamps.

Accumulators were to be carried at the front and rear of every train and on the locomotives, and the lineside signals were to be operated by power from these accumulators
making contact through wiping brushes at appropriate points along the line. But the
management of the Central London thought it was too novel, and chose instead the
well-tried Spagnoletti system. It will be told in a later chapter how this was superseded,
in 1913, by automatic signalling operated by track circuits. It is a remarkable tribute
to the skill of the signalmen, that with the original equipment of 1900, with semaphore
signals, and full-sized mechanical levers, they were able to work a conventional block-
system with such speed as to permit of a 2-minute service of trains in the peak periods.
It is of further interest to recall that this mechanical equipment for the Central London
Railway was supplied by Evans O'Donnell & Co. the founders of the Railway Signal
Works at Chippenham, Wiltshire. It is at these works, under the later ownership of
the Westinghouse Brake and Signal Company, that all the modern, highly sophisticated signalling apparatus for London Transport has been built. The only mishap that
occurred on the Central London Railway in its mechanical signalling days took place
in September 1913, unluckily just before the changeover to full automatic signalling
with track circuits. But the circumstances were very much of the transition period,
when co-acting train stops had been fitted at each of the signals. The introduction of
train stops takes us well ahead of the present period of this chapter, and so the accident
is referred to in Chapter Ten of this book.

From the summer of 1905 my home was in Reading. My father was a bank manager,
and at fairly regular intervals he had to pay routine visits to Head Office, which was
in the City. As his business was usually concluded quite briefly he frequently took me
with him, so that some 'educational' sight-seeing might follow in the afternoon. We
used to walk from Paddington to Lancaster Gate, and there take the 'Twopenny Tube'
to the Bank. That ride was a never-ending source of interest, and the station names like
'Post Office', where we got out to see St. Pauls, 'Chancery Lane', for Gamages toy shop
where they sold all kinds of model trains, and 'British Museum' became as familiar to
me as our local stations around Reading. My recollection of the tube was that it was
all very bright and pleasant; but we never travelled on it when my mother was with us!
To the very end of her long life she only once—and then by accident!—ever travelled
on the London tube railways.

The seal on the popularity of the Central London was set by friendly references to it
on the stage, and in cartoons. In 1881 the height of respectability in London travel had
been epitomised in the Gilbert and Sullivan opera 'Patience' as 'the threepenny bus
young man'. When this delightful piece was revived in the early 1900s it was easy to
amend the line to show how 'the other poet', Archibald Grosvenor—'Archibald the
all right'—had become 'with it', in contrast to Bunthorne's sham-aesthetic:
'Greenery yallery
'Grosvenor gallery
'Foot in the grave young man.'
Archibald Grosvenor was henceforth:
'a very delectable
'highly respectable
'Twopenny tube young man.'
And with the catchy rhythm of Sullivan's music in this gay duet ringing like the
wheel beats of a train at speed we can leave the Central London Railway for the present.

Electrified tracks: Aldgate station looking towards Liverpool Street.

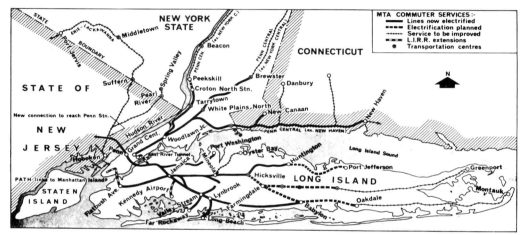

New York: a modern map showing commuter lines in relation to location of original subway on Manhattan Island.

CHAPTER EIGHT

New York: 'Elevated' to 'Subway'

The City of New York was early in the field of 'rapid Transit' railways for urban transport. Nevertheless the physical conditions and social inclinations differed considerably from those of London. Much of New York is built in a confined area on solid rock, and in the prevailing knowledge of railway construction it would have been difficult— or so it was thought—to build an underground railway in the style of the London Metropolitan. It is true that the long wide streets might have been thought ideal for 'cut and cover' methods of construction; but there was in addition a natural reluctance among the New Yorkers of the 'sixties' and 'seventies' of last century to travel underground. So instead was born the idea of the 'Elevated'. Again, the long straight thoroughfares favoured this type of railway construction. The city, built on a rectangular plan, with few if any buildings of historical or architectural importance in the central area, had no qualms about the aspect that would be presented by the overhead galleries carrying the railway, and so plans for the 'Elevated', as it became known went rapidly ahead. The first section was opened in 1872. It was extended rapidly, until there were no less than 36 miles of track in operation within the next 25 years.

Although it is slightly off the subject of 'underground' railways the early build-up of the New York Elevated, and its mode of operation is important from the way its problem influenced the subsequent construction of the very celebrated 'subway' in 1902–5. By comparison with the Metropolitan and District Railways in London, which in the first 30-odd years of their respective existences had built up studs of 66 and 54 steam 4-4-0 condensing tank engines for tunnel working in the inner area, and running the longer suburban lines of the District, the New York Elevated had, by the year 1897 no less than 326 locomotives and 1116 bogie cars. The locomotives were highly picturesque 0-4-4 tank engines, with outside cylinders in the prevailing American fashion, and the main running shed at 155th Street looked like a miniature edition of 'Crewe North', except that the whole area, being above street level was boarded over, and the rail-tops flush with the level of the boarding. The 'Elevated' cannot have been a source of satisfaction to George Westinghouse, because above all things it used the vacuum and not the air brake.

The method of operation was likewise somewhat primitive, in that no signals were used, except on a few very sharp curves where they functioned as speed restriction indicators rather than signals in the generally accepted sense. On the high elevated galleries trains followed each other at sight, at about one minute intervals, and as an English visitor once remarked: 'How fortunate it is that New York does not suffer from fogs!' The running was nevertheless extremely smart. Over one 'Elevated' route that had 25 intermediate stations in 9 miles the running time from end to end was 35 minutes. This showed an average speed of about 15 m.p.h., which was better than was achieved in 1900 with the electrically worked Central London tube railway. With a train every minute this was certainly 'some going'. It is evident that the passengers fully entered into the hustling business. The maximum allowed for any station stop was 15 seconds, and the more generally observed time was 10 seconds.

In Chapter Ten I quote some observations from A. R. Hope-Moncrieff and E. L. Ahrons upon minor traffic jams occurring with Londoners trying to get in and out of the electrified Inner Circle trains. No such confusion prevailed at any time on the New York Elevated. Porters rode on the open platforms of adjacent cars, and shouted the station names as the trains were preparing to stop; but although the cars had end doors only passengers were disciplined into a streamlined flow system, entering the car at one end and leaving by the other. The passengers from all accounts, fully entered into the spirit of the race against time, and poured in and poured out with such vigour that 10 second stops were easily practicable. The trains themselves were mostly made up to four cars, though some carried five in the peak periods. The fare was a completely uniform one of 5 cents, then equal to $2\frac{1}{2}$ pence, for any distance. The tickets could be purchased in blocks of a dozen at a time, or more, and used as required. This minimised the time taken in buying tickets for an individual journey. The British restriction that a ticket was not transferable did not apply.

Nevertheless, while the 'Elevated' was widely acclaimed on its first introduction, and always heavily patronised, its presence, and accoustic effects were not appreciated by those who lived or worked in houses along the various routes. The noise of the passing trains on the high galleries was practically continuous all day long, and to this was added the staccato exhaust beats of hard worked steam locomotives, driven 'all out' from each station stop to maintain the sharp times scheduled. To the incessant noise was added the dirt from the exhausts of the locomotives, of steam and smoke beating down; and while these side effects could be eliminated by a change to electric traction the noise would remain. For the most part the trains had a straight run. The sharp curves where signals were installed occurred where the tracks made a right-angled turn at a street corner. All-in-all, while the populace had, in 1871, demanded an 'Elevated' in preference to an underground, the general feeling by the end of the century was that things had gone far enough, and that any further extension of railway facilities within the city area should be carried underground.

This was easier said than done. But what London and Glasgow had done, and what Paris was then doing would not deter New York, and so a new Rapid Transit Subway was projected having a length of some 15 miles. Most of this was in tunnel, but about one fifth of the total was in the open. It was treated as a grand prestige job and on March 24, 1901, Mayor Van Wych, of New York, dug the first spadeful of earth. A time limit of $4\frac{1}{2}$ years was set for the construction, and work was commenced with such vigour along the route, and continued so far into the night that complaints began to pour in, once again, of the noise created. Such was the public feeling indeed that arrangements had to be made to stop all work at 11 p.m. The subway had been conceived on the most ambitious scale. There was no question of opening short sections and gradually extending. The whole job was carried through in one gigantic operation, and the remarkable thing was that there was so little dislocation of road traffic while

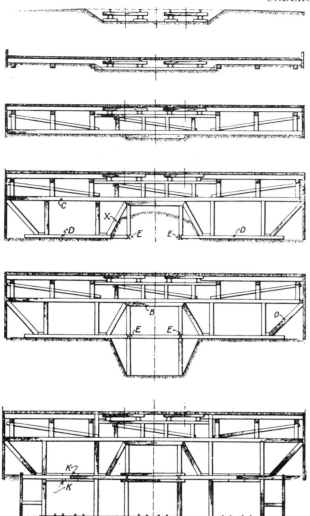

New York: Progressive stages of excavation beneath streets.

the subway was under construction. In general there were three types of tunnel used, described roughly by their cross-sectional shape. These were the rectangular, the 'barrel vault', and the circular; but the methods of construction were complicated by the extremely comprehensive nature of the track layouts used.

From the experience gained in traffic handling on the 'Elevated', and from studies of working on the London underground and tube lines the management of the New York subway decided that they must run 'express' as well as local trains, and from the very outset of the scheme it was considered essential to have quadruple tracks throughout the busiest section. One can see the ideas of the District Railway being applied here, in the proposal to have a deep level line from Earls Court to Mansion House, when the double-track route of the Inner Circle became congested. In New York it was obviously

89

G

thought desirable to grasp the nettle once and for all; having embarked upon the upheaval of digging up the streets to make the tunnels wide enough for four tracks. In any case with the rock formation below the city a deep level line under the existing one would have been an almost prohibitive task. Fortunately the streets under which the subway was to be carried were wide enough for tunnels to be built taking four tracks abreast. There was no need to indulge in the double-tiering of the tracks involved in certain places on both the City and South London, and on the Central London.

.From the very beginning the civil engineers had a tremendous task in diverting the sewers. They had been most efficiently engineered, but because of the rock formations so close beneath the surface of the ground the majority of them were quite shallow, and the task of diversion was carried out almost entirely by open excavation. There were some very complicated underground junctions of sewers that lay right in the path of the new railway. There was no chance of avoiding these difficulties by making diversions of the railway. The tunnels had to be carried directly under the main highways, and it was the sewers that had to be moved. In one instance there was a five-way junction of sewers that lay right in the path. Some extremely intricate and fascinating civil engineering work had to be carried out, in many stages, to maintain vital facilities before it was possible to begin preparations for the railway. The task was further complicated in that the construction of the sewers themselves, installed at various times, was not of uniform design; and many incidental problems were faced by the engineers when it came to opening them up, and diverting their courses.

In construction the railway tunnels immediately below busy streets, the simple 'cut and cover' method used in building much of the Metropolitan and of the District Railways in London would not have been practicable, the road traffic was too dense, and the dislocation would have been intolerable. Instead the method used on certain stretches was to dig two narrow trenches, one on each side of the main flow of road traffic. These were carried down to the full depth of the finished tunnel, and then headings were driven horizontally to link up these trenches. Little by little heavy timbering was introduced, massively strutted from below, so that the full weight of passing traffic could be taken on what amounted to a temporary timber bridge. Once this timbering and strutting was in position excavation could proceed safely, with the tunnel work extended, stage by stage, as the 'hole' below was enlarged. A remarkable feature of the work, noted with considerable surprise by the technical press of the world at the time, was that practically nothing in the way of mechanical aid to excavation was used, either when working in clay, or in going through solid rock. The tunnels were hacked out by hand digging, or hand removal of rock displaced by relatively small charges of dynamite.

On certain stretches the surface traffic was such that only one trench could be permitted. Then of course the insertion of the timber work was a more difficult operation, especially in localities where the nearness of house property involved the under-pinning of buildings. The frequency with which rock was encountered was a considerable embarrassment in the majority of locations. The proximity of tall buildings made it essential to use no more than the smallest charges of dynamite in blasting, to avoid any risk of disturbance to foundations. While the inception of the scheme was greeted with enthusiasm by the citizens the numerous inconveniences caused during its construction gave rise to frequent complaints and allegations of inefficiency. There were many evidences of work under the eyes of the people, and somewhat naturally many that they could not readily understand. New York was to experience in full measure the phenomenon of the mysterious ''ole in the road', that perennial butt of Cockney humourists. Contractors would descend upon a certain New York highway, dig a deep trench along one side—or perhaps on both sides—and then depart, leaving the trench open with nothing apparently happening. To the hustling, efficient, twentieth century American mind such a thing was quite inexplicable. It would probably never have occurred to the 'man in the street' that having started on a particular length the incidence of a major problem elsewhere had demanded the temporary switching of all available labour. Our Transatlantic friends have coined a telling phrase to describe those loungers who watch for half-hours at a time any work that is in the public gaze, always purporting to know better than the contractors themselves what is going on, and how each succeeding stage will be tackled. They call them the 'Side-walk Superintendents'. There were evidently plenty about when the New York subway was being built!

The task of excavating the tunnels beneath the busy streets was not completely solved when the side trenches were cut and the cross-timbering and strutting inserted. The spoil had to be removed. Again it was essential to cause the minimum of interference with road and pedestrian traffic, and in the majority of streets where the open trench method of construction was being used the width of those trenches was the only permissible area of access for men, tools, and tunnel lining equipment. To remove the excavated earth and rock a simple, but ingenious method was devised. Along the line of the trenches aerial ropeways were erected at intervals. These were inclined upwards from the depths of the workings to lofty sheer-legs, erected where there was space on the ground to bring in carts whereby the spoil could be taken away. These ropeways represented one of the very few instances of the use of electricity in the construction of the subway, as the buckets or nets containing the rubbish were hauled up to the sheer-legs by electric winches. By sheer weight of numbers in the labour force employed the great work of constructing the subway went forward according to schedule—despite the misgivings and criticisms of the side-walk superintendents!

On more technical grounds there was some discussion, and indeed of criticism by experienced engineers of the methods used in excavating the sections of tunnel that were too deep to be constructed by the 'cut and cover' method. Of two different

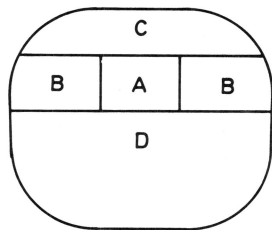

Cross section of tunnel showing
sequence of excavations.

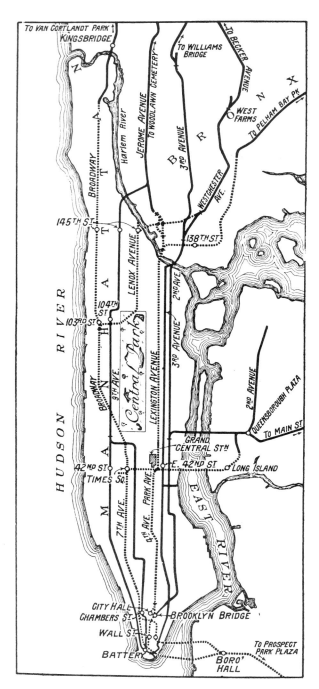

New York: 'elevated' lines in full, subway in dotted lines.

methods employed one can be illustrated by the numbered diagram on page 91 which illustrates what was termed the 'top heading' method. With this a heading of the shape by the area marked 'A' was first driven into the rock. Next this was enlarged on both sides simultaneously, by excavating the areas marked 'BB', and next the rough shape of the upper part of the tunnel was completed by excavating area 'C'. Having a wide heading extending to the full width of the tunnel the bore was then deepened to the maximum cross-sectional area required by excavating the area 'D'. There were a number of alternative methods, of which one was known as the 'drift'. The subdivision of the tunnel was similar to that shown but the sequence of excavation varied. The choice of method appears in some cases to have been that of the individual contractor—of which of course there were many on the entire subway construction— and elsewhere by the nature of the ground.

Before leaving the civil engineering work, of which I have necessarily indicated little more than the broad principles adopted, mention must be made of the finishing of the tunnels. Those of rectangular cross-section had a massive and elaborate, steel frame-work, with numerous additional vertical supports between the two central running lines on the quadruple-tracked sections. As in the case of the London tube railways a thick layer of concrete grouting was inserted between the tunnel lining and the native earth surrounding it. On the deeper level sections, where circular or barrel-vault tunnels were used, there was again a substantial concrete surround. An interesting piece of construction was that where the railway passed under the Harlem River. One would not expect to find such a section built by the 'cut and cover' methods, yet such was actually the case. Coffer dams were built along the route of the crossing, and section by section the water was excluded while the tunnel was being excavated. This was a length of circular tunnel, and when completed the top of the 'tube' was roughly on a level with the bed of the river.

If the construction of the subway was a tremendous task the scheme of its operation, traffic control and signalling necessarily involved some entirely original thinking. The whole conception centred around the original decision to run 'express' as well as local trains. Nothing of the kind had been attempted in London or on the Paris Metro; and although the Boston 'Elevated' had what was then considered a highly sophisticated system of signalling it was not adaptable to the New York Subway. In the scheme finally evolved three parties made important contributions. These were George Gibbs, consulting engineer for rolling stock and signalling; J. M. Waldron, signal engineer of the Subway, and the Union Switch and Signal Co. This latter was the signalling firm in the Westinghouse group, and which became associated for a time with signalling developments in London, through the Westinghouse Brake Company. When the conditions of the Subway came to be examined it was realised that practically nothing in the way of standard apparatus could be used. Everything had to be designed separately.

Before coming to consider the many novel features of equipment that were introduced it is important to look at the general track layout and the timetable requirements of this remarkable underground railway. The diagram on page 94 shows the track layout on the critical section of line between South Ferry, Brooklyn Bridge and 28th Street, and from the merest glance it will be appreciated that this was something infinitely more complicated than anything existing on the underground railways of London or Paris. The configuration in the area of Fulton Street, City Hall and Brooklyn Bridge savours more of Clapham Junction rather than of Mansion House or Farringdon Street! It

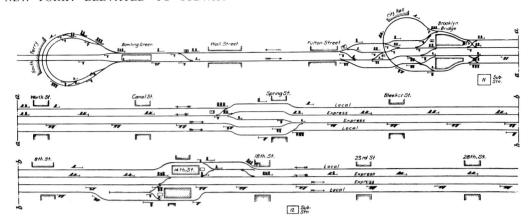

Schematic diagram of signals: South Ferry to 28th Street: New York subway.

will be seen also that at Spring Street the four tracks expand into five, and at 14th Street, if sidings are taken into consideration there are six tracks. Shades of Victoria (Underground) and Charing Cross! But even with all this proliferation beneath the streets of New York the traditions of the 'Elevated' persisted to an extraordinary degree. Only the 'express' lines were fully signalled; the local lines were operated on the 'follow my leader' basis, except as in the right-angled street turnings on the 'Elevated', where there was an imperfect view of the line ahead. The schematic diagram previously referred to, above, shows clearly the paucity of signals on the local lines, compared to those on the 'express' lines.

The signal indications were given entirely by coloured lights. There were no semaphore arms on the underground sections. The lights themselves were interesting in that unlike contemporary British practice distinction was made between the 'on' indications of home and distant signals. Here the indications were uniformly green and red, and it was left to the route knowledge of the driver to distinguish whether the signal he was approaching was a home or a distant. On the New York Subway the 'on' indication for a distant signal was yellow. But these signals on the New York Subway were not colour lights in the modern sense. The drawing reproduced on page 95 shows the front view of a stop and distant signal and it will be seen that there is only one lens for each. Inside the case there are vertical slides for each 'signal' accommodating red and green glasses in the case of the 'home' and yellow and green for the distant. These slides are moved up and down as required by pneumatic cylinders, and interpose the appropriate coloured glass between the electric lamp and the front lens. Compared to the very simple colour-light signals of the present day it was a very large and cumbersome affair, but all innovations must have their beginnings, and the signals on the New York Subway certainly 'started something'. The cross-sectional drawing reproduced on page 95 will give some idea of the extensive internals of these signals. As if this were not enough, miniature arm indicators were also provided in case the lights failed. These indicators were at 'a²' in the drawing.

An important safety provision was that the automatic train stop, which applied the brakes if a train should pass a signal at danger. The arm of the device projected above

94

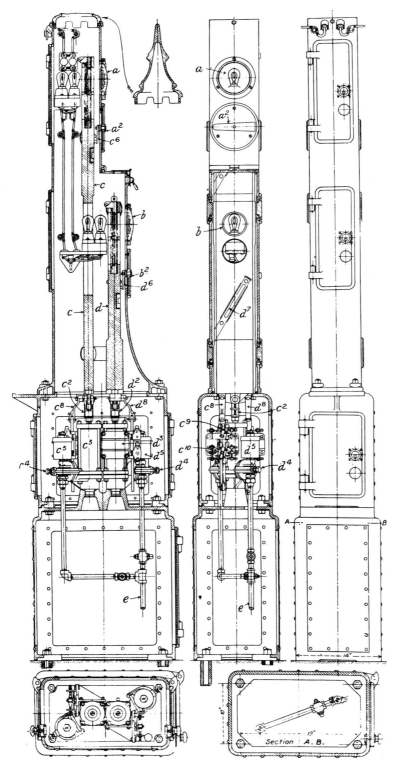

Cross-sectional drawing of signal—'Stop and Distant'—New York subway.

the rail abreast of the signal. These train stops, anticipating the system that has until recently been universally applied on the London Underground railways, co-acted with the signals in that the train stop arm was lowered when the signal was operated to the clear position. In its raised position it would engage a pendant lever on the train, which when struck thus applied the brakes and stopped the train clear of any obstruction. The signals as shown on the diagram of the tracks appear as though they were semaphores; but this was merely a conventional way of showing the difference between home and distant signals. The signals were normally in the line-clear position, and worked automatically through the agency of track circuits. Although these latter are now of almost universal application, and are familiar in their various forms to railway engineers a brief mention of the fundamental principle involved must be made at this stage for the benefit of non-technical readers. With semaphore signals and purely mechanical working a block section extends from one signal box to the next, and ordinary block working requires that no two trains may be in a block section at the same time. The first train must be seen to be clear of the section before a second train may be permitted to enter. The signalman had to observe this personally.

If one looks at the diagram of the New York Subway it can be seen that between 14th Street and Spring Street, to take a single example, there are no fewer than six block sections on the express lines, all working automatically, and with no signalmen at all. The extent of these automatic block sections is marked on the track by the insertion of insulated joints in the rails. Current for signalling purposes is applied to the rails at one end of the insulated section, while at the farther end is an electrical device called a relay. Current flows down one rail, through the relay, and back through the other rail thus constituting a track circuit. In these circumstances the relay at the far end is energised, by electro-magnetic action, and certain switch contacts are made. When a train comes on to the track however the current finds an easier return path through the wheels and axles; the relay is short-circuited, and the switch contacts are opened. This feature provides the basic safety requirement for signalling with track circuits. The train itself, by entering the track circuit puts to danger the signals in its rear, by opening the switch contacts of the appropriate relay, through short-circuiting that device. Conversely the signal at the entrance to a track circuit cannot be cleared unless the relay is energised, and that cannot take place if there is a train in section. It will be seen from the diagram that the signals on the New York Subway were mostly double. The clearing of these was controlled by *two* track circuits. If only one section was clear the signal would display one green and one yellow light, signifying 'caution' for an express train. If two sections were clear, the signal would display two green lights.

The pneumatic operation of the signals has already been mentioned. In the U.S.A. the Westinghouse company had developed the use of compressed air for operation of signals and points, and some years before it was introduced on the London underground railways it had been used at certain places on English main lines, notably at Spital-fields, on the Great Eastern, and at Bolton on the Lancashire and Yorkshire. On the New York Subway the standard electro-pneumatic switch operating mechanism of the Union Switch and Signal Company could not be used, owing to the restricted space in the tunnels, and a specially compact form had to be designed. The form of electric traction used on the Subway provided for return current through the running rails. In the ordinary way one could not have return traction current, and track circuit current flowing simultaneously in the rails; because the heavy traction currents would not only

96

swamp the small track circuit currents, but would burn out the delicate signal relays. Accordingly, alternating current was used for the track circuits. This could be super-imposed upon the direct current traction return, and the latter would not affect the signalling apparatus, which would respond only to alternating current.

At the same time a further problem was introduced. The continuity of the running rails, electrically, had to be interrupted at intervals by the insulations for the track circuits; and yet continuity in some form was essential for the traction return. To provide for this, what is termed an 'impedance bond' was connected across the rails. The coil of this provided a high inductive resistance to the passage of alternating current, but allowed the direct current to pass freely. The use of impedance bonds, which are now installed throughout the electrified system of the Southern Region of British Railways, was first made on a local railway running on the North Shore of San Francisco. It was not an underground railway but the principle there evolved, in 1903, was readily adapted to the New York Subway, and was later applied to the Central London Railway, when that line was equipped with automatic signalling. Impedance bonds were however not necessary, when the Metropolitan and the District Railways were electrified, because they used a separate conductor rail for the traction return current.

In its conception, in its construction and in the provision made for speedy and efficient operation the New York Subway was certainly a landmark in the develop-ment of underground railways. Considering its extent however, and the lavish provision for express and local trains the patronage of the line was a little modest, compared to some of the intensely worked lines in Great Britain. One can sense that so far as travel-lers were concerned, as distinct from those who lived and worked along the route, there was still a preference for the 'Elevated'. In its first full year of operation the Sub-way carried about 300,000 passengers, on roughly 15 miles of route, compared to 120,000 a day on the $5\frac{3}{4}$ miles and two tracks only of the Central London.

CHAPTER NINE

Inner Circle Electrification

The *coup-d'etat*, by which control of the Metropolitan District Railway passed, overnight at it were, from the 'Master of Bunkum', James Staats Forbes to the 'hell-bent' financier Charles Tyson Yerkes has been briefly mentioned in Chapter Three. It did no good to the District, either in its immediate effects, or in longer-term eventualities. From the very outset the whole affair got a thoroughly bad press. For one thing Yerkes himself was not the kind of man to endear himself to his newly-found British railway colleagues. That he was of humble birth and very little education is beside the point. In his early teens he worked in a flour mill in Philadelphia, but his astonishing financial acumen was shown early in life when, at the age of 22, he set up in business on his own as a stockbroker. This was in 1859, from which time onwards he followed a phaeton career, rising to heights of enterprise, crashing in bankruptcy and imprisonment, and then rising again pheonix-like to negotiate a great consolidation of urban transport in Chicago. His was the kind of career that made as many enemies as friends, and British sentiments regarded as quite repugnant the rather flagrant lobbying and electioneering methods by which he had advanced his interests in developing the North Chicago Street Railway Company. His sudden arrival in London, and his dramatic seizure of control of the District Railway was therefore regarded with the deepest misgivings.

The factor above all others however that kept him outside the comity of British railway management was that his interest in railways, *as railways*, was absolutely nil. He neither knew nor cared about the day-to-day methods of operation, safety considerations, and such like; his sole, and only concern was with the accounts. It can also be inferred that he had little time or respect for traditional British methods, and by sheer weight of dollars strove to Americanise the railway as quickly as possible. If his fellow railway managers in England were cool the railway press of the day treated his activities with disdain, when they were not being scathing. J. S. Forbes may have been a thinly-disguised old rogue, but he was a *railwayman*; and though he projected many a scheme when there was nothing in the till to pay for them they were for the most part soundly-conceived projects of railway development. The Southern Region of British Railway today has much in its network for which Forbes can be thanked. Nevertheless one cannot lay all the blame for the District Railway upheaval on Yerkes himself. There have always been Englishmen grown impatient with the apparent sloth of traditional methods, and ready to call in 'experts' from overseas; and in the case of the District Railway one such was Robert W. Perks, a London solicitor, and a considerable shareholder. Dissatisfied with the Forbes administration, he helped Yerkes to wade in!

In a very short time London was to behold the spectacle of Yerkes in action. He launched a new company, the Metropolitan District Electric Traction Co. Ltd., to carry out the electrification of the line and to build the necessary power station. He purchased the projected Brompton and Piccadilly Circus tube, to which the power station of the M.D.E.T. Co. would also supply current. It should be mentioned in passing also that following the success of the City and South London a number of deep level lines had been projected, all by independent companies, and all had languished for lack of public support, as had, of course, the Central London until other interests intervened. Yerkes and his American friends saw an opportunity to do 'big' business out of the London traffic problem, and sought to secure control of all these 'tube' projects, and in April 1902 a new company was formed, the Underground Electric Railway Company of London Ltd. to take over the M.D.E.T. and control the others as well. The principal parties to this new venture showed clearly where the influence and the investment was coming from, namely:

Speyer Brothers, of London
Speyer & Co., of New York
Old Colony Trust Co., of Boston
Teixeira de Mattos Bros., of Amsterdam.

The control of the combine was of course vested in Yerkes himself, but the participation of the Old Colony Trust Company of Boston had an extremely interesting technical sequel, as it introduced to British railway operation that most dynamic personality, Harold Gilbert Brown, at that time signal engineer of the Boston Elevated Railway.

Confidence of British railway interests in the ultimate success and profitability of Yerkes's projects was not increased by a statement he made to the shareholders of the Underground Railways company in April 1903, thus: 'In acquiring all these lines, it has been our desire to form a perfect system of intra mural transportation, and to have them all feed into the District Railway, and be fed by the same line.' This looked like out-bunkuming the bunkum of Mr. Forbes! The District was heavily worked enough without having a group of new lines feeding into it. How, and where they were going to feed in was not made clear; but one supposes that such practical considerations did not worry Charles Tyson Yerkes! When the dispute with the Metropolitan arose over the system of electric traction for the Inner Circle Yerkes was ready to sweep aside all opposition and buy the Metropolitan outright, with the guarantee of a fixed and perpetual dividend of $3\frac{1}{2}$ per cent on the ordinary shares. But although this was refused Yerkes had the satisfaction of seeing the Metropolitan brought to heel, as it were, by the findings of the tribunal in favour of the direct current system of electrification. As early as March 1902 indeed the great Yerkes company had initiated work on the power station at Lots Road, on the north bank of the Thames at Chelsea, the four great chimneys of which were destined to become one of the landmarks of London.

In the meantime the Yerkes influence was showing itself in other ways in the working of the District Railway. Some traffic had been lost to the Central London Railway, since July 1900, and also to what Mr. Alfred Powell had called asinine competition between rival bus routes in cutting fares to the borders of penury. The District had, to quote the inimitable E. L. Ahrons, been 'a real railway' in the nineteenth century in its orthodox working with steam traction. It was also orthodox in its fares' structure. Under J. S. Forbes the third class fare was the usual penny-a-mile charged by the main line railways, and in comparison with the Central London and with the City and South

London these fares were very dear. Yerkes authorised a drastic reduction, in order to compete with the tubes and the buses; but although he secured a considerable increase in the number of passengers with the total conveyed rising from 42,268,000 in 1901, to 51,168,000 in 1904, the last full year of steam operation, this increase was not anything like large enough to off-set the loss in revenue due to cheaper rates. As the company was not earning enough to pay any dividend on the ordinary shares, even before Yerkes came upon the scene, his measures made things manifestly worse. The answer of the management to all criticism was that all would be well once steam traction was eliminated—an attitude that was to have a precise echo in recent times, when British Railways in the early years of nationalisation attributed all their troubles, and their insolvency to steam traction. Another change that caused considerable offence in many influential quarters was the abandonment of the church interval on Sunday mornings. Hitherto the District, like the Metropolitan had run no trains in the inner area between 11 a.m. and 1 p.m. to avoid any subterannean rumblings being heard in the many churches, on the route of the Inner Circle particularly, during Divine service.

Taken all round, Mr. Yerkes, in a very short time had succeeded in 'rubbing quite a lot of people up the wrong way' as the saying goes. In the eyes of the press, both technical and otherwise, the District Railway could not do a thing right. For this reason the engineering features of the transition, on both the Metropolitan and the District Railways received far less attention than they deserved. *The Locomotive Magazine*, for example, which gave remarkably comprehensive coverage to all developments on the British railways, and to many overseas railways as well, virtually ignored the new equipment, yet devoted considerable space to a learned historical treatise on the steam locomotives of the District Railways which were then being scrapped as fast as the breakers' yard could cope with them. In *The Railway Magazine*, editorial opinion was vehemently expressed in a series of highly critical utterances in the 'Pertinent Paragraphs' feature that appeared every month:—but never a word about the new equipment—except when it went wrong! The fact that electrification of the District was carried out under the direction of an American engineer, J. R. Chapman, did not increase the good will towards it. After the lapse of time however it can be seen that a great job was done by all concerned, especially in view of all the difficulties inherent in the installation of an entirely new system along the tracks of the old one, while the old system is not only carrying its normal traffic, but a heavier one, due to the many extra passengers attracted by the substantial reduction in fares.

The system of electrification differed from that of the City and South London, and of the Central London in having a separate rail for the traction return current, instead of returning it through the running rails. This followed the practice adopted on certain American urban transport systems, and notably the Boston Elevated. The positive current rail was outside the track, and the negative, or return was in the middle of the four-foot. This latter feature immediately aroused criticism from the traditionalists of British railway practice, with whom the four-foot—or space between the running rails was sacrosanct, except for the installation of facing point locks. Not so many years earlier the vital importance of the facing point lock had been emphasised by accidents on main line railways caused by imperfections in the point layouts; and the facing point lock, mounted in the centre of the track had become regarded as one of the greatest safeguards in operating over junctions. The use of a centre rail for the traction meant that the facing point lock had to be fixed in a cramped position to one side or the other—

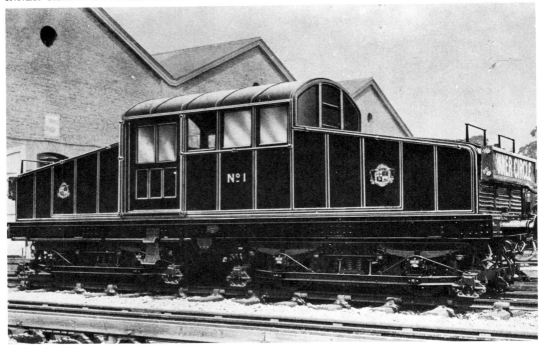

Metropolitan Railway: Electric Locomotive No. 1, as equipped for working on the Inner Circle.

a most disagreeable circumstance in the eyes of the majority of British railway engineers. Nevertheless, the insulation of the traction return current freed the running rails, and enabled them to be used for the track circuiting which was considered essential for the automatic signalling included in the general scheme of electrification. The signalling of the newly electrified Underground lines included so many features of interest and fundamental importance that an entire chapter is devoted to its earlier development.

In view of the success of multiple-unit train working on the Central London, and even more so in the U.S.A. it was natural that the same system should have been adopted from the outset for the Inner Circle. There were, however, certain services which, to quote Yerkes's phrase 'fed in', to both the District and the Metropolitan parts of the Inner Circle. Some of these had however been seriously affected by the latest railway developments in London. The 'Middle Circle' service, worked by the Great Western had never catered for truly circular traffic, but provided for through travel from West London suburbs, like North and West Kensington, to Victoria and the City. Its usefulness had virtually ended with the opening of the Central London, providing a fast and very cheap service from stations like Holland Park and Shepherds Bush to the Bank. Against this the Great Western, at parliamentary fares of a penny a mile could do nothing better than a steam all-stations service from Addison Road, or Uxbridge Road to Mansion House, via Victoria. The Great Western did not wait for the electrification of the District, and in February 1905 they cut off the Addison Road–Mansion House part of the 'Middle Circle', running only between Moorgate and

Addison Road. No problems arose therefore of working Great Western stock over the electrified lines of the District Railway. There was an overwhelming desire on the part of Yerkes and his group to be done with steam entirely, though this attitude did not prevail equally on the Metropolitan.

It was the aversion to steam traction that raised a problem for the District Railway when it came to working the 'Outer Circle'. The London and North Western Railway showed no signs of following the Great Western example and abandoning their service to Mansion House when the District was electrified. The flank of the 'Outer Circle' had not yet been turned, and as they no longer wished to have L.N.W.R. steam locomotives working through the tunnels from Gloucester Road to Mansion House some provision for electric haulage had to be made. The North Western trains on this service consisted of nine four-wheeled coaches, close-coupled, with five compartments in each of the third class carriages and four in the two first class. The tare weight was 140 tons, and as the total seating accommodation was about 370 a completely full train could scale something like 160 or 165 tons. To work these trains the District Railway built ten curious little double-bogie electric locomotives that would have been unrelievedly dull in appearance save for high clerestory roofs. They were used in pairs, and had a total motor horsepower of 800. This was considerably higher than the power capacity of any L.N.W.R. steam locomotives previously used on the Outer Circle service. They were painted crimson lake, and added quite an air to the L.N.W.R. trains, which on that service were finished in plain varnished teak. The change from steam to electric traction on the Outer Circle service took place at Earls Court. The service did not last long after the electrification of the District Line, and from New Years Day 1909 the trains from Broad Street via the North London line terminated at Earls Court.

The District Railway section of the Inner Circle electrification formed part of the general electrification of the whole line. This was inaugurated from Ealing to Whitechapel in July 1905, and the branches to the London and South Western lines at

District Railway: Electric locomotives used for hauling L.N.W.R. trains of the Outer Circle service between Earls Court and Mansion House. They were used later on the through trains between Ealing and Southend via the L.T.&S.R.

Metropolitan Railway: Multiple-unit Inner Circle train at South Kensington. Stock of this kind dated from the first electrification, in 1904, but the majority of the coaches in service up to 1951 dated from 1914 or 1920.

District Railway: a 1904 'wood-stock' trailer car, first class, including a smoking section.

Wimbledon and Richmond followed in August. Electric trains were running through the underground section from Gloucester Road to Whitechapel some weeks before electric working began on the Inner Circle. The multiple-unit trains used from the introduction of these District Line electric services were known as the 'B' stock, and while it was by that time felt inevitable that the design would be basically American much dissatisfaction was expressed when it was learned that of the 420 cars specified for the entire District service only 140 were to be built in England, and contracts for no less than 280 had been placed in France. Of these 420 cars, 192 had motor equipment, and 228 were trailers. They were designed to be worked on the multiple unit principle and the most usual formation was a 6-coach train, with 3 motor coaches and 3 trailers. They were spacious, fine looking vehicles with an appearance that suggested steel side panelling, though actually they were wooden bodied. Their high clerestoried roofs gave a particularly airy and elegant appearance inside.

In the meantime the Metropolitan Railway was going its own way so far as the provision of electric stock was concerned. Its multiple unit coaches, finished in varnished teak, with deep panelling and the company's coat of arms on the sides had a solid English look about it, and the contracts both for the cars and the electrical equipment were placed wholly with British firms. They differed in the important respect of the motor coach traction arrangements. The District cars, had only one motor bogie, each with two motors, and one trailer bogie. The Metropolitan specified its motor coaches to have both bogies powered, with a total of four motors on the coach. A standard 6-coach train consisted of 2 motor, and 4 trailer cars, though on the Inner Circle this was afterwards reduced to 4 cars, with one motor coach, two trailers, and one driving trailer. When conditions were ready for changing the Inner Circle service over to electric traction the same apportioning of the stock as in steam days was originally arranged, namely that the Metropolitan would provide all the trains on the outer rail, or clockwise direction, and some on the inner rail, because of the difference in owned route mileage. The service was planned to start on July 1, 1905, but it did not last one day, due to several most unfortunate incidents. One can detect a sense of unholy joy in a 'Pertinent Paragraph' that appeared in *The Railway Magazine* for August 1905. It began thus:

'The partial inauguration of electric working on the Inner Circle and the Metropolitan District Railway on July 1st cannot be considered a success either from an engineering viewpoint or as evidence of the business capabilities of the American financiers who now "run" the Metropolitan District Railway. The Metropolitan, under English auspices, has been electrified and ready for electric working for some months, but even now the Americans are not prepared for the all-electric working of the District Railway, and its share of the "Inner Circle" traffic.'

The events of July 1, 1905, which *The Railway Magazine* went on to describe can however hardly be laid on the doorstep of American business methods. The 'Pertinent Paragraph' continued:

'The chapter of accidents and disappointments began early on Saturday morning, July 1st, at South Acton, when, just before five o'clock, an empty electric train from Mill Hill Park fouled the points when entering the station, and jumped the line, effectually blocking the station for some hours.

'Shortly afterwards, as the first cars made their way Citywards the rain began to descend in torrents. Leaving at 5.42 from Ealing the train was delayed by signal five

St. James' Park station, showing platform train indicators.

minutes at the Mansion House, and by the time Whitechapel was reached ten minutes had been lost. The return journey was commenced at 7.33, but when Mark Lane was reached a delay of over half an hour ensued, and with stops at every station the cars eventually reached Earl's Court at 9.10 a.m. an hour late.

'Here further progress was impossible, the train service both steam and electric, coming to an entire standstill.

'The cause of the delay was the flooding of the line at Hammersmith station, and at the junction between West Kensington and Earls Court by most torrential rain. The water, owing to the absence of sufficient drainage, accumulated in such quantities as to entirely flood the rails. An earth connection was thus formed, and the whole of the electric current was diverted.

'As may readily be imagined, the utmost confusion followed upon this unlooked-for stoppage. On some portions of the line out West steam trains found themselves sandwiched between the stationary electric trains. It was impossible to move them also and the consequence was that between nine and ten o'clock the booking offices at the stations were closed, and passengers were informed that the issue of tickets was temporarily discontinued. This stoppage of traffic on a route which at that hour of the day brings thousands of business people to the City was a source of great inconvenience. The alternative vehicle to the train is the omnibus, but in face of this sudden demand the resources of the buses quickly gave out.'

One rather feels that *The Railway Magazine* had lost its sense of values in reporting this very unfortunate mischance; because however much one disliked Yerkes and his methods he could hardly be blamed for a cloudburst!

What made things infinitely worse on this inaugural day was an extraordinary incident between Sloane Square and St. James's Park. Despite the difficulties with flooding west of Earls Court it would ordinarily have been possible to keep the Inner Circle running. But early in the day there was a complete breakdown of electric current supply due to damage to the positive rail. The reason for this was an evident lack of liaison between the engineers of the Metropolitan and of the District Railways. The Metropolitan motor coaches had the pick-up shoe gear mounted outside the frames, and was designed to allow the positive pick-up to adjust itself according to the rails on curves. The mounting of the conductor rails had been arranged to work with this device on the Metropolitan but not so on the District, and an Inner Circle train of Metropolitan stock got its positive shoe out of correspondence with the live rail, dropped out of contact, and pushed it sideways smashing the porcelain insulators and completely overturning the rail for some distance. Thus, traffic on the Inner Circle was also brought to a stand. All Metropolitan trains were quickly withdrawn and steam re-instated. As the accident happened on the District line the District got the blame; but it was the Metropolitan stock that was at fault. The District coaches had the collector shoe mounted on a beam suspended between the axle-boxes, and the Metropolitan coaches were altered to this arrangement before re-instatement.

It was more than two months before electric trains were once again put on to the Inner Circle service. The introduction was gradual, as follows:

September 13: Metropolitan 2 trains
September 14: Metropolitan 1 train
September 17: District 2 trains
September 19: District 2 trains
September 20: District 1 train

It will be seen that in spite of the difference in mileage the District was quicker off the mark than the Metropolitan and on Monday September 22 the last steam trains worked on the Inner Circle. A slightly reduced service of electric trains ran on the following day, but the full electric service, as originally planned, ran from September 24, 1905.

Before the year was out the situation on the underground railways of London was thrown once again into uncertainty by the death of Mr. Yerkes, in New York, on December 29, at the relatively early age of 68. His whirlwind descent upon London had wrought a complete metamorphosis of the District Railway, and had in many respects swept the Metropolitan along with it. In a long obituary notice *The Railway Magazine* fired this parting shot over his memory:

On the Metropolitan near Harrow, with an electrically hauled train from the underground section running abreast of a Great Central train.

'Amongst British railway officers Mr. Yerkes was (and rightly so) looked upon as merely one of the usual type of American railway "financiers" whose interest in a railway *qua* railway was simply *nil*, hence the enormous sums that have been spent in electrifying the Metropolitan District Railway were not expected to produce much advantage to the patrons of the line. The conduct of the traffic since the electrification has strengthened the general opinion as to the indifferent results that have accrued from the Americanisation of the railway.'

The immediate sequel to the death of Mr. Yerkes was rather astonishing. It would seem that the American financial syndicate controlling the somewhat mysterious corporation known as the Underground Electric Railways of London Ltd., had realised the hostility to their activities that had been aroused in England, and so instead of bringing in another American as chairman they invited Sir George Gibb to take over. As General Manager of the North Eastern Railway Gibb was one of the most prominent of British railwaymen, but one nevertheless who was an outspoken admirer of American railway methods. Not long previously he had taken a party of senior North Eastern Railway officers on an extensive tour of American railways. But the mere fact that he was persuaded to relinquish his great appointment at York to take over the management of a few miles of an electric railway with a shaky reputation is enough to show the kind of money the Americans were prepared to pay in order to get the London Underground railways fairly on their feet.

The change in the chairmanship did not lessen the weight of criticism levelled at the District Railway in general, and in November 1906 *The Railway Magazine* had a 'Pertinent Paragraph' under the heading: 'Reaping the Whirlwind'. While we can nowadays discount the 'I told you so' motif that runs through this editorial comment it is worth quoting in full, as fairly summarising contemporary opinion on this most thorny question.

'The history of the Metropolitan District Railway, day by day, is exactly fulfilling the predictions that have appeared at various times in *THE RAILWAY MAGAZINE*. From the day when the electrification of the line was first suggested, we have foretold, in fairly clear language, what must inevitably result from the innovations.

'It will be seen, from the statement reproduced below that Sir George Gibb, the present chairman of the American syndicate controlling the Metropolitan District Railway, agrees with the views we have expressed on the subject:

'"In the first place, steam power is not so costly as electric. Then again, you must remember that we only carry passengers. The other railways, even if they lose on their season tickets—and many of them do—make up that loss by their goods traffic. We cannot do that, and I feel sure that not even the Board of Trade can expect a private company to carry on its work at a loss. If we were the London County Council, perhaps we might do such a thing."'

Before passing on to the final comments of *The Railway Magazine* one can well understand Sir George Gibb's feeling remarks about freight traffic, having come away from York with many a vivid recollection of the princely revenue earned by the North Eastern in short-haul coal traffic. One is also amused by his 'side-swipe' at the L.C.C.!

The Railway Magazine concluded:

'With regard to the changes in the fares, the manager explained that although the fares had been raised, they were now actually lower than when the line was first opened. When electricity took the place of steam the authorities, thinking that expenses would be much lower, reduced the fares, very considerably. Instead of the expenses being less, they were found to be heavier.

'Although attempts are being made to reduce the cost of working the line, no definite solution has thus far been arrived at, but any reform will most likely take the form of a reduction of attendents.'

Despite the continuing hostility of George Augustus Nokes, who for editorial purposes in *The Railway Magazine* turned his surname inside out and signed himself SEKON, the coming upon the Underground scene of Sir George Gibb was generally welcomed in London, and he became known as 'the straphangers friend'. It was the Rev. W. J. Scott, a lifelong railway enthusiast and an admirer and personal friend of Gibb in his North Eastern days who symbolised the gradually changing attitude in London by an amusing piece of doggerel:

'In 1900 we'd enough
'Of smoky trains that went puff-puff.
'Now we have perfection found;
'The bright Electric Underground.'

It was Scott himself who created railway journalistic history by describing for the first time in the 'British Locomotive Practice and Performance' feature of *The Railway Magazine* a run logged from the cab of one of the District Railway electric trains, from Earl's Court to Mansion House. In June 1909 he wrote:

'The signals, which on their low posts might be taken for overgrown ground discs, are then seen to be exactly at the right level to catch the driver's—I beg pardon, the motorman's—eye; the yellow distants, being really only warning or anticipatory signals, are fearlessly passed, though the driving handle is shifted to half-speed until the home signal is reached. If that be at danger, a dead stop, of course, follows.' With this reference to the signalling I am to some extent anticipating a later chapter of this book.

One of the original Metropolitan Railway electric locomotives as later modernised, and working in recent years in London Transport livery.

CHAPTER TEN

Travellers Tales

In the earlier years of the present century my present kindly publishers enriched the libraries with a series of sumptuously illustrated *Colour Books* mostly topographical in their pictures yet containing a wealth of contemporary comment. One of the most prolific authors in this series was A. R. Hope-Moncrieff, a Highland Scot, but who, by the time this series of books was under way had come to live in London. He followed his natural 'Bonnie Scotland' with delectable volumes on Surrey, Essex and the Isle of Wight, and then in 1910 he tackled London itself in a wittily written and gorgeously illustrated volume. And in this Hope-Moncrieff brought the eye of the scholar, and much-travelled man to the psychology and humanity of travel on the Underground railways. He is writing of Charing Cross, and then continues:

'Were Dickens alive today, he might tell us how the Tourist and Exchange Offices about this international rendezvous were humbly prefigured by a starting-point of coaches at the "Golden Cross", as, indeed, we know from the adventures of Mr. Pickwick. But not yet has the counsel of perfection taken form by which Charing Cross was to be a great central railway station, knotting together all the lines that come into London. Even Paris, that loves system and centralisation as we do not, was fain to scatter her terminuses far apart in the suburbs. Surely it is time to banish the pedantry of *Termini*, as to grant full right of naturalisation to the vernacular *bus*, that reached us through France, as did cab, *cabriolet*, long ago shorn of its outlandish trappings. Did we not take from Italy an idea for the catacomb lines that now act as motor nerves to this ganglion of London communications? The name of the Underground Railways, at least, came from over the Atlantic as one of those jocular metaphors our cousins are so quick to coin. In very early days of railroad enterprise sprang up a philanthropic secret society for helping runaway slaves, and Levi Coffin got the nickname of its "President", when some baffled slave-hunter is said to have declared that there must be an underground railroad to Canada from that sly Quaker's house, as his pursuers could never hit on further trace of any fugitive who gained it.

'How did Londoners get on without their "Underground", which began to break out through the streets as London became familiar to me? This convenience is supplied by two companies, the Metropolitan and the Metropolitan District, the one, as some of us know too well, paying but a small dividend, while the other, I understand, has returned to its shareholders only the consciousness of being public benefactors, execrated if ever they try to raise the fares on some vain excuse of carrying passengers at a loss. Roughly speaking, the Metropolitan takes the north side of the system, the District's domain being on the south, both of them with long feelers into northern, western, and eastern suburbs. Their rails are linked at Kensington and at Aldgate to form the Inner Circle, a joint main line, on which frequent trains run round and round in either direction. The fact of two companies being concerned should make one wary which way one turns, as each may be more concerned to carry the traveller on its own metals than on the shortest segment of the circle. I have known country cousins who, living at Brompton and desiring to reach Kensington, innocently took an almost complete round under London to reach a point not a mile off. One hard winter, how a tramp spent his last penny on a short-stage ticket, then passed the rest of the day in that snug round-about. But only very cold and impecunious travellers welcomed the Stygian atmosphere of the Underground in its days of steam traction, when the northern stretch, from Edgware Road to Kings Cross, had a specially foul reputation, and one drew a breath of relief on coming into the open air reaches, where also, the trains are gloomily walled out from all brighter aspects than a show of mendacious advertisements. In one such gap near Gloucester Road Station, a moving scene was once enacted, when marriages still had to be performed before noon. A block in the line had held up a train containing a bridegroom in gallant array. As twelve o'clock drew near anxiety made him bold. Amid the cheers of his fellow-passengers, and the secret sympathy of protesting officials he and his friends stormed the *glacis* to rush, begrimed and bleeding, to the altar at which a distressed bride awaited him.

'The use of electricity has now purged the Underground caverns; and the suburban branches run mainly in the open air. Within the last few years the Circle has been ramified and transected by deeper tunnels popularly called Tubes, which at many points are brought into touch with it by means of lifts and subways, sometimes so long that in all weathers one can here get a considerable amount of exercise under cover, and in atmosphere kept bright and clean by electrical apparatus, when fog or rain oppresses the upper world. New York, jealous of our "rapid transit" tried to go one better by its spidery Elevated Railway; but then took to burrowing underground after the mole model of London. Our first Tube was from Clapham to the City, which for some time remained alone in its fulginous glory. Then came the more renowned "Twopenny Tube", straight through the centre of London, so called because at first it was found possible to simplify the ticket system: one had the new experience of paying twopence for any distance, passing through a turnstile, descending by a lift, to be bustled into a long car, whisked through a longer hole and again lifted up into the open air. Now, several of these Tubes, the longest of them stretching from Hammersmith to Finsbury Park, are connected at several points; and through bookings between them have brought back the old ticket encumbrance. One can thus travel comfortably from almost any part of London to another for a few pence.

'All these fresh aids to locomotion seem to call forth as well as to supply a want, for at certain times of the day they will be found inconveniently crowded. On the District Railway, of a foggy evening, one must expect to travel in a mass of human beings literally packed like sardines; and we old fogies at all times may think ourselves lucky to get a seat, where the young and lively press in before us as to a pool of Bethesda. One has seen a Judge on his way to court standing buttressed by fellow-swayers, while the bailed criminal he was to try might be sitting comfortably, for the nonce, in the same car. From America has been imported the art of strap-hanging, not to be done grace-fully by all amateurs; and a point of manners arises which is said to have become rather honoured in the breach across the Atlantic. Courteous youth will take pleasure in giving up his seat to a lady; but one has also known a strapping damsel make place for a tottering greybeard. Some little time ago, I saw a scene in the Underground that was quite *fin de siecle*. A lady with a child pushed her way into a crowded carriage, to whom a tired-looking City gentleman, since so it must be, gave up his seat. She thanked him, made the child sit down, and stood waiting till someone else rose up for herself, as did not I. Young John Bull used to be taught more modest manners, but from Brother Jonathan he can learn how youth is the age of honour as well as hope, after which hoary old age must expect at the best to take a back seat. Another symptom of Americanisation is the hustle and flurry of these impatient trains that have gone to cut short the lives of many weak-hearted citizens, in danger of being knocked off their legs by dashing youngsters. Hindoos who spread their bedding on the station platform below the unheeded time-table; Andean Indians who may have to wait a week for the next train; Spaniards, whose favourite time for setting out is *manana*, might all be the better of this smartening discipline, but we should seem already quite enough versed in the text "Time is money". Sharp Yankee critics, however, find fault that at every stop one or two seconds are wasted by Mr. Bull's inveterate want of spryness, the blame rather to be laid on Mrs. Bull's headlong eagerness to get into a carriage before other people have got out of it.'

E. L. Ahrons, in his dual capacity as railway enthusiast, and insatiable humorist began an essay on the Underground lines in this wise: 'In the latter part of the nineteenth century both the Metropolitan and the District were really railways; now alas! they appear to be glorified overcrowded electric tramways. This, of course is a pure matter of personal opinion.

'The former steam railways', he went on '—at least the Inner Circle portion—had one advantage which disappeared with the steam locomotive. In the old days they provided a sort of health resort for people who suffered from asthma, for which the sulphurous and other fumes were supposed to be beneficial, and there were several regular asthmatical customers who daily took one or two turns round the circle to enjoy the—to them—invigorating atmosphere. But today the sulphur has all gone, except in the speech of a few irritable travellers, and has been replaced by an indescribable atmosphere of squashed microbes, and the sounds emitted by a hustler with a trumpet. Having unburdened my soul of the above, I may as well proceed to return to the nineteenth century.'

One cannot leave the human side of the Inner Circle without referring to the occasion when it figured prominently in one of the Adventures of Sherlock Holmes, and when with his usual powers of analysis and deduction Holmes established the connection between the theft of most of the plans for a new secret submarine from an Admiralty drawing office, and the finding of a body of a young engineer from that office on the track of the Inner Circle near Aldgate. Only the most pedantic commentator could find fault with the liberties Conan Doyle took with the railway geography of Gloucester Road, where the body of the murdered man was put on to the roof of an Inner Circle train; but save in the most trifling *minutiae* the details of railway working are entirely authentic and convincing.

For a final memory of steam days on the Inner Circle it is fascinating to read once again an article published in *The English Illustrated Magazine* nearly 80 years ago, written by an artist correspondent who was given a footplate pass and rode round the

113

'Circle' anti-clockwise on a District Railway train. Boarding the engine at St. James's Park he wrote:

'I was accommodated with a position near the left-hand tank, whence I could get an uninterrupted view ahead; but it has its drawbacks as the water in that tank was hot. No time is wasted at stations on the Underground, and a minute later the train was off—off into a black wall ahead with the shrieking of ten thousand demons rising above the thunder of the wheels. The sensation altogether was much like the inhalation of gas preparatory to having a tooth drawn. I would have given a good deal to have waited just a minute or so longer. Visions of accidents, collisions, and crumbling tunnels floated through my mind; a fierce wind took away my breath, and innumerable blacks filled my eyes. I crouched low and held on like grim death to a little rail near me. Driver, stoker, inspector, and engine—all had vanished. Before and behind and on either side was blackness, heavy, dense, and inpenetrable.

'Westminster Bridge, Charing Cross, and the Temple were passed before I could do or think of anything beyond holding on to that rolling rushing engine; then finding that I was still alive and sound, I began to look about me. Inspector Exall put his head to my ear and shouted something at the top of his voice, but I could only catch the word "Blackfriars". I looked ahead. Far off in the distance was a small square-shaped hole, seemingly high up in the air, and from it came four silver threads palpitating like gossamers in the morning breeze. Larger and larger grew the hole, the threads became rails, and the hole a station; Blackfriars, with rays of golden sunlight piercing through the gloom.

'Off again, a fierce light now trailing out behind us from the open furnace door, lighting up the fireman as he shovelled more coal on to the furnace, throwing great shadows into the air, and revealing overhead a low creamy roof with black lines upon it that seemed to chase and follow us. Ever and anon the guard's face could be dimly seen at his window, more like a ghost than man; while in the glass of the look-out holes were reflected the forms of engine-men, like spirits of the tunnel mocking us from the black pit into which we were plunging. Then again we would seem to stop, and to fall down, down, down, with always the wild shrieking surge and ceaseless clatter of the iron wheels.

'Soon ahead of us gleamed pillars of crimson stars, the signal lights of the Mansion House. Between this station and Mark Lane there is nothing particularly noticeable, saving the approach to the latter; where ghostly-looking figures paced a hidden platform across which fell great golden beams that looked like impassable barriers. Yet, ere one could take a second glance, the beams were riven assunder, and a black engine blotted them out with clouds of writhing steam. Next to Mark Lane, and almost close to it is the old Tower Station, now disused. We sped past its deserted platforms and limp signal posts, and a few minutes later steamed into the central station, Aldgate. The fireman at once jumped off the engine and made the necessary arrangements for filling our water tanks. So quickly was this done that probably none of the passengers noticed any difference in the length of the stoppage, and in a very short while we were off again into the tunnels, two minutes sufficing to bring us round a sharp curve into Bishopsgate.

'Aldersgate, the next station, was opened in 1865, and for many years was comparatively deserted by passengers. The opening of the markets hard by has altered all this, and it is now one of the principal stations on the line. All about this section we encountered other lines which sometimes dived under us, at other times merely diverged in various directions. Outside Aldersgate the line is ventilated by a series of arches, which give a fine effect of light and shade, making the tunnel look like an old-time dungeon.

'From Farringdon Street to Kings Cross is the longest stretch without a station, and the driver here gave us an exhibition of full speed, and No. 18 came into Kings Cross at the rate of some 40 m.p.h. The average speed of trains between one station and another is from 20 to 25 m.p.h.

'The road now began to be uphill, and at the same time the air grew more foul. From Kings Cross to Edgware Road the ventilation is defective, and the atmosphere on a par with the "tween decks, forrud" of a modern ironclad in bad weather, and that is saying a good deal. By the time we reached Gower Street I was coughing and spluttering like a boy with his first cigar. "It is a little unpleasant when you ain't used to it," said the driver with the composure born of long usage, "but you ought to come on a hot summer day to get the real thing!" Fog on the underground appears to cause less inconvenience than do the sultry days of July; then the atmosphere is killing. With the exception of this one section (between Kings Cross and Edgware Road) I found the air far purer than I had expected, and the bad air so much complained of by the "sewer rats"—as those who habitually use this circle are called in "the City"—is due in a great measure to their almost universal habit of keeping all the windows and ventilators closed.

'The finest bit of scenery on the underground is the Baker Street Junction, where a second tunnel leading to the St. John's Wood line branches out of the main one. It is no longer used for through trains, however, owing to a fearful accident that occurred here some time ago, and Baker Street is now the terminus of that line. On the left through the main tunnel lies the station, a medley in crimson and gold; on the right the daylight creeps in, and the picture is a harmony in blue and silver. It is a novel and unexpected sight to see the ordinary black coat of respectability look crimson, as it does when seen after the intense blackness of the tunnel. But like all other scenes, this was brief and momentary; then a dream of the past. There is a similar and much-used junction before Praed Street, but it is provided with a big signal box where the tunnels meet.

'The ventilating holes in the tunnel roof all about this part give a beautiful effect of light striking into darkness; especially one before Edgware Road is reached, where the silver column of light fell on a green signal lamp, set low on the permanent way. Just before Praed Street we got into daylight again—the line passing through a sort of valley formed by high houses on each side.

'Hitherto, though we had passed many, I had scarcely noticed the trains that we met; but about here I changed over to the right side of the engine in order to get a better view of the coming train. I had not long to wait. Far away in the distance was an ever-increasing speck of light—the headlight of an approaching train. A moment later, it had come and gone—a silent flash of light, so silent that it might have been a phantom; our own engine made too much noise for any other sound to be audible. Curiously enough, an approaching train is totally unlike what one would imagine it ought to look like. A strong light bursts from the furnace if it chances to be open, and illuminates the tunnel overhead, the carriage windows and brass work make lines of light that run off and die in the blackness through which it is rushing.

'At High Street, Kensington, engines are changed so we jumped off—at least my guide did—my attempt to follow his example being calculated to cause an impression that I had taken the platform to be a seat—but all this is by the way. Engine No. 18 went off into a shed to rest awhile, and No. 7, a precisely similar one, backed on to the train in her place. This resting of engines is rendered a frequent necessity from the strain caused by the numerous stoppages; incessant running in one direction has also been found bad for them as it wears away the wheels on one side sooner than on the other. To remedy this, the engines half their time run "backwards forwards" as they say in the West of England.

'Off again; and this time downhill. We dashed rapidly through the grass embankments outside Gloucester Road, past some men posting bills on the advertisement hoardings that border the line below South Kensington, now deep in a tunnel, now traversing a cutting open to the sky; until we shot once more into St. James's Park 70 minutes after leaving it. We had covered some 13 miles in our trip round London; seemingly no great distance for the time occupied; till one recollects that it entailed no less than 27 stoppages, with a watering and change of engines into the bargain. It is these stoppages that make the journey as long as it is; if a train went round at its usual rate it would be back at the starting point in less than 40 minutes, while if it went full speed some 20 minutes would suffice.

'However, the 70-minute trip is quite rapid enough for all practical purposes, and is only rendered possible by the excellence of the brake arrangements, and the perfection to which the block-system of signalling has now been brought. The length of the stoppages could not well be reduced; indeed, they are already too short if we are to believe the tale now current of a wandering Jew sort of passenger—a lady of advanced years who can only alight from a train backwards. Every time she begins to get out a porter rushes up crying, "Hurry up, ma'am; train's going!"—and pushes her in again!

' "This finishes our journey," said the inspector, as, taught by previous experience, I cautiously crawled off the engine—"unless you'd like to go round again." I declined.'

CHAPTER ELEVEN

London Underground Signalling

The electrification of the Inner Circle saw the beginning of a complete change in signalling methods on the underground railways of London; and as these changes came to form the basis of an even greater metamorphosis in the signalling of the British main line railways the techniques and the men responsible for them require much more than a mere passing reference. Up to the time of electrification of the District Railway four men were principally involved, two American and two English. It was my privilege to know all four of them, and at various times to work under them. In the U.S.A., George Westinghouse was actively developing the signalling side of his business in the early 1890s. His thinking was far in advance, not only of the traditional British manual block system, or yet of the systems of 'lock and block' that were being propounded by Sykes, Spagnoletti, and others. In the development of the London underground railways he saw an opportunity for an extension of the activities of the London branch of his empire, the Westinghouse Brake Company. At the same time, wise from his personal experiences in England he felt that it was no use trying the direct marketing of American practice and apparatus. One recalls the classic instance of the British railway manager who was once asked why he did not adopt the Westinghouse brake: he replied: 'Sir, I am an Englishman!' And that precisely was that!!

There must be no such stumbling blocks over the introduction of Westinghouse signalling. The systems must be engineered to suit British practice, in England, and the apparatus manufactured there. There must be skilled engineers who could discuss and work out plans with British railway officers. There must be no need to refer problems to the U.S.A. But before there could be any discussion of schemes there must be apparatus, if not actually on the shelf, as it were, but designed, tooled up and ready for production in England. At the start this would necessarily be of American type, for Westinghouse had made considerable progress in this direction by the mid-1890s; but the American designs had to be adapted to British manufacturing methods, and the first step was to find a man who could do this. In 1889 a young designer of 26, who had been trained under W. R. Sykes, and was thus well-versed in the most forward-thinking British signalling methods, had joined the Westinghouse Brake Company in London. This was Walter Allan Pearce, and it was he who was selected to specialise in signalling. He was sent to America, and for two years, from 1893 to 1895 worked in the signalling company of the Westinghouse group, the Union Switch and Signal Company of Swissvale, near Pittsburgh. On his return to England he began systematically to prepare a complete range of designs that could be manufactured in the London works of Westinghouse, at Kings Cross. Many years later, when I myself became Chief Draughtsman, I had these beautiful drawings in my care—works of art, every one of them, and symbolical of a more leisured age, despite their having been made under the auspices of a hustling American organisation.

Drawings and production facilities were only one side of the problem, and in the later 'nineties' business in underground railways was quiescent in England. But the arrival of Yerkes changed all that. Westinghouse then had in London a very able manager in John Wills Cloud, an American of forthright, but charming personality. He was an expert in all matters connected with the air brake, but although he then had Pearce as designer, neither he nor Pearce were sufficiently versed in the latest electrical techniques to 'sell' the system in England. A specialist was needed, and in 1902 Cloud was sent to the U.S.A. to find one. By that time it was evident which way the wind was blowing in London, and it was perhaps no more than natural that Cloud went to one of the most spectacular of the Yerkes railways, the Boston Elevated. The signal engineer there was Harold Gilbert Brown, then no more than 27 years of age, but already having displayed a remarkable flair for electrical invention. He had perfected a system of track circuiting on electric railways, and as the Metropolitan District was almost certain to be equipped for electric traction in the same way as the Boston Elevated 'H.G.B.', as we always knew him later, seemed the ideal man for the job. At less than a fortnight's notice he packed up home and family and sailed for England. With Cloud at the head of affairs, and two such men as Pearce and H. G. Brown, the Westinghouse Brake Company in England was well prepared to take on electric signalling.

The influence in those early days was however not entirely American. In 1903 a young Cornishman of 17, Bernard Hartley Peter by name, joined the staff of the Metropolitan District Railway. In earlier days that railway had of course, been mechanically

Metropolitan District Railway: the original Signal Engineers office at Earls Court, with early semaphore signals.

118

signalled, with a form of Sykes 'lock and block', and Peter, young as he was, became entrusted with preparations for the new signalling necessary with electrification. With the contract awarded to Westinghouse he necessarily became closely associated with Pearce and H. G. Brown—an association that was to last for the rest of their lives. Peter was of course very much the 'baby' of the trio. In 1904 when preparations reached their greatest intensity, he was only 18, whereas 'H.G.B.' was 29 and Pearce 31. And although Peter represented the customer, contractors in those days sometimes had a rather high-handed way of doing things. Pearce in particular—as I came to know only too well!—had a fiery disposition, that concealed a warmhearted nature; he had also a high-pitched voice, that got higher and more squeaky as his temper shortened, and put one in mind of Cecil Rhodes, who was once admonished and told to 'stop squealing like a damned rabbit!' Many years later when making a presentation to him on his retirement from Westinghouse, Peter admitted that in the early days he was unashamedly frightened of Pearce! Nevertheless, his tact and powers of persuasion must have been considerable, for that irrascible designer, clever engineer though he was, did not take readily to innovations; and yet for the District Railway electrification he was induced to provide two novelties, both of which were 'world-firsts' in railway signalling practice. Before describing these however the general layout of signalling on the District section of the Inner Circle must be made clear.

In steam days there were no fewer than 13 signal boxes between South Kensington, where the Metropolitan and District lines converged, and Minories Junction, where the Inner Circle turning sharply to the left diverged from the Whitechapel and Bow line. It was at this junction that the 'body' in Sherlock Holmes's 'Adventure of the Bruce Partington Plans', fell off the roof of the train. The new scheme was for the whole of the line to work automatically between Minories Junction and South Kensington except at Mansion House, where a number of trains terminated. These included those of the 'Outer Circle' hitherto operated by the L.N.W.R. With automatic signalling the ordinary method of describing trains forward from station to station could not be applied. On the Inner Circle the last man, other than platform staff, to see eastbound trains would be the signalman to South Kensington. There would be many trains on the line between there and Mansion House, where some would need to be switched into the terminal platform and others to the through line, proceeding eastwards to Minories Junction. It would have been quite impracticable to have sent advice of the order in which trains were travelling, for example, first Whitechapel, second Inner Circle, third Barking, fourth Mansion House, and so on. There would be so many 'in the pipeline' so to speak, that the Mansion House man would be apt to lose count, and sooner or later one of them would be switched on to the wrong line. So with close collaboration between B. H. Peter and the Westinghouse company a system of *automatic* train description was worked out.

The system was initiated by the signalman at the commencing point of the stretch of line concerned, after which it worked automatically. One can take the particular case of South Kensington: as eastbound trains were passed forward the signalman turned the pointer of his 'transmitter' to the route of each train concerned, and then pressed the plunger. At each of the intermediate stations there was a receiver on which the indications transmitted from South Kensington were 'stored'. The question of route setting did not arise until a train was approaching Mansion House, but a very important feature of the system was the train indicating at the various stations. The arrangement

The ingenious electro-mechanical apparatus for operating the train description system installed on the Metropolitan District Railway in 1906.

Acton Town signal box: the first-ever illuminated track diagram installed in 1905 when the station was known as Mill Hill Park.

121

of 'storing' the indications enabled the illuminated indicators to be operated showing the destination of first, second and third trains. After the passage of a train the indications would automatically be stepped one forward, the 'second' becoming the 'first' and so on. The receivers were so designed that no fewer than 32 trains could be 'stored', and in the morning and evening rush hours there could easily be more than 20 on the line between South Kensington and Mansion House. The various appliances were electro-pneumatic in their actuation and although at first glance the electrical circuits were rather terrifying they were, in their essentials very simple. In later years I took a hand in the adaptation of this system to train description between Buenos Aires and Temperley, in the intensively-used suburban area at the Buenos Aires Great Southern Railway, and did not acquire any grey hairs in the process! The train indicators were a much appreciated feature of the District line electrification in London.

The second great innovation in the resignalling of the District Line was the use of illuminated cabin diagrams at the junction signal boxes. The first of these was actually not underground, but similar ones were brought into use shortly afterwards at Earls Court, South Kensington and at Minories Junction. The pioneer of them all was at the station then known as Mill Hill Park, now Acton Town. From the earliest days of signal boxes a plan of the tracks on a large scale was usually hung, like a framed picture, over the interlocking lever frame. This track plan showed all the signals in their correct geographical positions and everything was numbered to correspond with the numbering of the levers themselves. It was however purely a plan, and quite inanimate. The signal box had to be so positioned and so provided with large windows that the man could personally observe the passage of the trains, and judge the correct moment to operate and restore signals to danger after the trains had passed by. If there did have to be any signals that were out of sight of the box, small electrical repeaters were mounted on the instrument, just above the lever handles, and below the track diagram. Generally speaking the area of control of a signal box was limited to what the man could see. It was realised however that if full advantage was to be taken of modern techniques—techniques, that is, that were modern in 1904—means would have to be found for controlling larger areas, extending beyond what the man could see. Where the underground was concerned there was little then he *could* see.

B. H. Peter, in consultation with the engineers of the Westinghouse Brake Company, conceived the idea of making the cabin track diagram *live*. The installation of track circuiting throughout provided a ready means of doing it. The tracks on the cabin

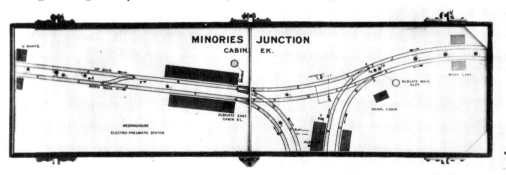

Close-up of a typical illuminated diagram of the original 'strip-light' type, installed at Minories Junction, at the eastern extremity of the Inner Circle.

Rear-view of a 'strip-light' diagram, showing how the lamps were partitioned off into groups to light the various 'strips'.

diagram could be sectioned off in correspondence with the track circuits; the narrow band representing the rails could be made of translucent material and lamps placed behind. When the track was clear the lamps would be lighted, and where there was a train on the line its presence would be shown to the signalman by a dark length, due to the lamps being extinguished. Like all great inventions it was extremely simple in conception, but a good deal of trouble was experienced in the early days, with various quite incidental details. For instance, the lamps were lighted for much longer periods than they were extinguished, and the front plate of the diagram with the translucent stripe in the tracks got dangerously hot. The manufacturing techniques with electric lamps were in a fairly primitive stage at that time, and really suitable miniature lamps were not available. The quantities at first required were so small that there could be no question of getting anything made specially. Last, but not least, signalmen used to pulling full-sized levers and looking out of windows to see each train, were really scared of this new-fangled instrument, with a locking frame composed of miniature levers that could be operated with little more than a flick of the wrist, and this vivid constantly-changing array of lights on the track diagram above. Many years after the event Peter told me that he spent most of the first week that Mill Hill Park was in service, operating the frame himself while the signalmen looked on.

Although illuminated track diagrams have been greatly improved in detail the principle is universally applied today in all modern signalling plants. In many large installations the signalmen do not see any trains during their days' work. They operate, with every confidence and success, busy junctions 20 and 30 miles from the signal box. Mill Hill Park, and the plants that followed soon after it on the underground sections of the District Railway, did more than create signalling history; they marked the beginning of an entirely new epoch in railway signalling and traffic operation. Only one point of principle, and that a secondary one, has been changed in later years. It is

123

Electro-pneumatic semaphore
signals at Earls Court East.

one of the fundamentals of railway signalling that any failure, either of apparatus or system should be on the side of safety: if the wire pulling a semaphore signal should break the arm should go to danger; if a wire in any electrical circuit should break the signal should go to red—and so on. It was natural that the same principle should be applied to the first illuminated diagrams. If a lamp should burn out the track would appear dark, and give the impression that there was a train on the line. But the over-heating of the diagram cases was a serious matter. Various modified forms of illuminated indication were tried, in some cases using a single spot light for each track circuit, instead of the original strip lighting. Many years later however it was felt that the safeguards in operation were so many that there was no need to apply the 'fail-safe' principle to the lighting of illuminated diagrams, and the generally accepted modern method is to light the track to show the presence of a train rather than its absence. This means that lamps are not lighted for such long periods. But with this secondary change in principle, the illuminated diagram, as first installed by B. H. Peter at Mill Hill Park, is absolutely standard practice on railways all over the world.

124

The first track circuits on the London underground railways were designed by H. G. Brown, and were generally the same as those he had installed on the Boston Elevated Railway. The interesting feature is that he used direct current for the track circuits. Although there was a separate current rail for the traction return there was always the liability of the relays to be energised by extraneous currents, and so give a false clear indication. In the chapter of this book dealing with the New York Subway I described how this difficulty had been overcome by the use of alternating current track circuits, the relays of which would not respond to stray direct currents. At the time of the electrification of the District and Metropolitan Railways however the development of alternating current relays was not in a very advanced stage, and H. G. Brown's patent enabled direct current to be used with complete success. He used two relays for each track, but they were so connected up electrically and so interlocked in their control, that although it was possible to energise either one or both of them by stray currents while a train was actually on the line it was impossible for them both to be energised in the *normal* direction, and so permit the controlled signal to clear. The special feature was that they were *polarised*; that is, their coils were direction-sensitive to the current flowing. In correct track-circuit operation both relays were energised in the normal direction; but for every conceivable condition of stray currents in the rails one or other of the relays were energised in the reverse direction, and in such conditions the signal circuit was maintained broken and the signal at danger. Many of the track circuits on the London underground railways with Brown's polarised relays remained in service for upwards of thirty years.

On the District Railway all the signals were operated electro-pneumatically. Where these were in the open, as at South Kensington, or at the head of station platforms that

Pneumatically operated tunnel signal: a ¾-side view showing mounting in tube tunnel.

Pneumatically operated tunnel signal: the driver view. Note also the automatic train stop mounted at track level.

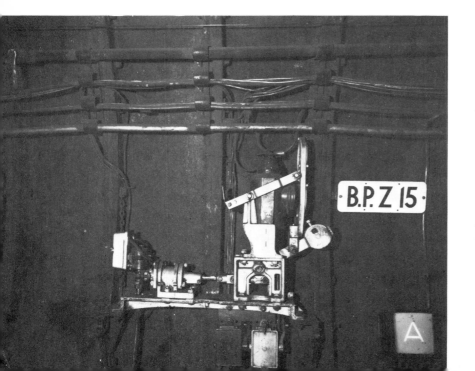

Pneumatically operated tunnel signal: a side view showing the mechanical linkage whereby the air-cylinder operates the spectacle plate in front of the lamp.

had some daylight full-sized semaphore arms were used, clearing to an angle of 60 degrees to the horizontal. In the tunnels light signals were used, but of a vastly more compact design than that of the New York subway. A spectacle casting containing coloured glasses was moved in front of the lamp unit; but instead of the familiar movement of the spectacle on an ordinary semaphore signal, in a plane athwart the track, the tunnel signals had a horizontal pivot, at right angles to the track and moved in a vertical arc around that pivot. They were extremely neat little units, and a characteristic example of Pearce's elegant designing. The train stops were adjacent to the signals and had trip arms similar to those on the New York subway. Normally there were no distant signals at all—signals showing just red and green for 'stop' and 'proceed'. In a few instances where motormen got a restricted view 'distant' signals were added, and these provided the very first instance in Great Britain of the yellow light being shown for 'caution' and of the signal arms themselves being painted yellow.

Taking matters apart from details of engineering equipment the system *in toto* was unquestionably the most advanced piece of railway operating technique so far seen in Great Britain, and probably in the whole world. American techniques in track circuiting and automatic signalling had been skilfully enhanced by the addition of illuminated diagrams in the signal boxes at the junctions, and by the train description and illuminated platform indicators. But in *The Railway Magazine*, G. A. Sekon in continuing his campaign against the 'District' was ready enough to find fault, while giving no description of the basic principles of the system, nor the slightest credit to

Miniature electro-pneumatic semaphore signal, used for shunting purposes.

127

those who had carried it out. With its management thus prejudiced this important organ of railway news completely failed to record one of the most important railway events of the Edwardian era in England. Instead there was published in April 1906 an ill-humoured 'Pertinent Paragraph' under the heading: 'Railway Accidents and Automatic Signals', thus:

'The automatic signals on the Metropolitan District Railway have not proved remarkably successful; already two collisions have occurred that the signals should have prevented. These automatic signals have a trigger, which, when the signal is at danger, should engage with the trip cock on the vehicles of the train, and by opening the cock apply the Westinghouse break and so stop a train that over-runs the danger signal. Splendid in theory, but, unfortunately, theory and practice with regard to automatic signals (as well as many other things) do not always agree.

'In the first collision the trip cock was not actuated sufficiently to fully apply the break, and in the second, the distance between the "automatic" stop signal and the point of collision was not sufficiently long to enable the break to bring a train of the weight of the one in question and travelling at a high speed, to a stop, with the result that a collision occurred.

'In the second place the driver of the train deliberately over-ran the signal to allow his train to be automatically stopped by the signal apparatus.

'The absence of signalmen at automatic stop signals is, undoubtedly, a predisposing cause towards slackness on the part of the motor men; with a signalman watching them, and the knowledge that they would be reported if they over-ran a stop signal, the drivers would take a care to stop. On the other hand, the knowledge that no one is watching them and the belief that they will be automatically stopped by the danger signal is likely to engender slackness in working, and its natural results—accidents.'

Passing over the perhaps-unintentional and unkind reference, three times, to the Westinghouse brake as a 'break', I should add that both accidents were of a relatively minor character; and that despite the dire forebodings of Mr. Sekon the District went on to establish a magnificent record of safety in operation. In 1907 the close association between the Westinghouse Brake Company and the District Railway was further strengthened when C. E. Strange the Signal Engineer was appointed Business Manager of the brake company. B. H. Peter thereupon became Signal Engineer of the District Railway, at the age of 21. In the meantime events were moving in other parts of London, and on March 10, 1906, the first of the tube railways financed by the Yerkes group was opened—that between Baker Street and Waterloo. This soon earned the nickname of the Baker-loo, and so it has remained ever since, when its extremities now lie far beyond the two original termini. The first intermediate stations were named Regents Park, Oxford Circus, Piccadilly Circus, Trafalgar Square, and Thames Embankment. The last named was soon re-christened Charing Cross in view of its interchange facilities with the District station of the same name on the Inner Circle.

As on the Central London there was a uniform fare of 2d. and throughout from 7.30 a.m. to 11.30 p.m. there was a 3-minute service. The total journey time from Baker Street to Waterloo was about 15 minutes. The system of electrification was that of the District rather than that of the Central London, with a fourth rail for traction return. This same system was used on the two additional Yerkes tubes: the Great Northern, Piccadilly and Brompton, opened on December 15, 1906, and the Charing Cross, Euston and Hampstead on June 22, 1907. The three new tube railways were grouped together under the title of London Electric Railways, and in 1908 Peter was appointed Signal Engineer, in addition to retaining his post as Signal Engineer of the District Railway. The signalling arrangements on all three lines of the L.E.R. were similar to those of the District, except that special arrangements had to be devised for accommodating both signals and point operating mechanisms in the confined space between the outer profile of the tube trains and the tunnel walls. Space was saved by building the units so that they were parly recessed into the segments of the tube sections, and it was certainly a novel arrangement to have the electro-pneumatic point operating gear half-way up the side of the tunnel, working the points through rods curved to suit the shape of the tube.

Here I must break for a moment from purely signalling matters to explain certain changes in organisation that eventually led to new signalling requirements. I have mentioned in an earlier chapter how following the death of Mr. Yerkes at the end of 1905 the direction of District Railway affairs, and of those concerned with the tube railway then under construction were taken over by Sir George Gibb, the former General Manager of the North Eastern Railway. Gibb did not stay long and in 1907 he was succeeded by Mr. A. H. Stanley (afterwards Lord Ashfield). It was he who began to complete co-ordination of the London underground railways, and the first steps towards this were seen in 1913, when the Central London and City and South London Railways were absorbed into the L.E.R. Consideration had already been given to the modernisation of traffic working methods on the Central London, by elimination of the original mechanical signalling and lock-and-block working; but so far as the other underground lines there remained the difference in the traction system, which on the Central London involved the return traction current passing through the running rails. It would have been possible to make a straight adaptation of H. G. Brown's system from the Boston Elevated Railway, but in the years since the electrification of the District the science of alternating current track circuiting had advanced considerably, and these more modern developments claimed attention.

In the meantime the signalling profession as a whole received an unexpected and important fillip from activities on the District and London Electric Railways. B. H. Peter, young as he was, had a major problem of administration on his hands in that the systems and apparatus in use had virtually no counterparts anywhere else on the railways of Great Britain at that time. He had to recruit and train all his men, and while he did a great deal to imbue them with his own interest and enthusiasm something more was needed. Accordingly he inaugurated what was known as The Signal Engineering Society. News of this reached the main line railways, and at first it was regarded with some suspicion. At that time the only professional associations of men concerned with railway work were certain very exclusive 'clubs' to which only the most senior men belonged, and only then by invitation. Peter himself, as Signal Engineer of the District Railway, was a member of the Association of Railway Companies Signal Superintendents and Signal Engineers, but in seniority he was a mere boy compared to his colleagues on the main line railways. In 1908, the president of the senior engineers' association, W. C. Acfield of the Midland Railway, wrote to Peter and asked him just what was going on at Earls Court. He replied as follows:

Dear Sir,   THE SIGNAL ENGINEERING SOCIETY

This society was started by some of the men on the District and 'Tube' railways staff during the last winter.

There are about 150 men concerned on these lines with the signalling work, and many of them wished to join some society for getting in touch with outside work.

They found however that there was no society for which they were eligible, so started their own, to which anyone employed in the design, construction or maintenance can belong. The Society is in no way in opposition to your association, and is merely to encourage the men to take an interest in signalling work. Papers are read on various subjects, visits are arranged to works, etc., and small concerts held.

Yours very truly

(Sgd.) B. H. Peter.

The news of this activity on the District and Tube railways spread to other administrations, and it was studied very carefully. The wheels of innovation are apt to move slowly at times, but in the early spring of 1910 eight signal engineers met together in London to consider the formation of an association of railway signal engineers, not only for the 'top brass' but for those engaged in signalling work using the expression in its most comprehensive sense. It is indeed significant of the esteem in which Peter was held that he was invited to join the select gathering. The other seven were the signal engineers or telegraph superintendents of the London and North Western, Midland,

A typical electro-pneumatic type of interlocking frame of the 1905–1915 era; Earls Court East signal box.

130

North Eastern, Lancashire and Yorkshire and Great Central Railways, and two of the most senior assistants from the Great Western. From this beginning, sparked off by the enterprising activity of the District Railway, was born the Institution of Railway Signal Engineers, which in 1972 celebrated the Diamond Jubilee of its incorporation. In their signalling the underground railways of London made history in more senses than one, and later chapters of this book will show that the system has continued to be a veritable pace-maker right down to the present day.

The M(onroe) D(octrine) Railway.

BROTHER JONATHAN to METROPOLITAN RAILWAY: "Well, whatever your Company may do, I reckon I mean to keep *this bit* for myself.

Flashback to 1901: a cartoon from 'The Railway Magazine' concerning proposals for electrifying the Metropolitan District Railway.

CHAPTER TWELVE

Continental Developments: the Madrid Metro

In the early years of the twentieth century Spain would not generally have been regarded as a country to be found in the forefront of railway development. Its trunk routes were roundabout, planned to serve the maximum number of towns between the major centres of population, while international communications were dogged by the great inconvenience of a break of gauge at all railway exchange points on the French frontier. Trains were slow in themselves, and railway business was conducted at the leisurely tempo of life generally prevailing in Spain at that period. But the beautiful capital city was even then experiencing the traffic congestion in its central districts typical of all great cities, and with the examples of successful underground railways in London, Paris and New York, proposals for a similar metropolitan system were formulated in Madrid. The practice in other countries was carefully studied, and in May 1914 definite proposals were submitted to the Government of the day. Then came World War I, and although Spain was relatively unaffected by the cataclysm of restrictions, rationing, and other direct consequences, the involvement of the countries on which reliance would have to be placed for equipment and rolling stock for the new line naturally retarded developments. Nevertheless the project went ahead, and in January 1917 the concession was granted for the construction of four underground lines.

It was evident from the outset that the new railway was based very much upon the French model. As had been the case in Paris the system was planned as a whole, so that Madrid would eventually have a closely integrated and comprehensive underground network. Not only was the French system of traction employed but, astonishing also, the gauge of 4ft. 8½in.! Whether the municipality of Madrid had the same ideas about excluding the main line railways one cannot say; but it seems extraordinary that in a country with a standard rail gauge of 5ft. the British and French 4ft. 8½in. should have been chosen for the Metro. The first section of the underground system, from Puerta del Sol to Cuatro Caminos was ceremonially opened by King Alphonso XIII in October 1919, but to one whose acquaintance with Madrid is purely that of a visitor it seems a rather curious section for an inauguration of so important a development in the life of the capital city. It was rather like having a terminus at Piccadilly Circus, and running out to Islington or Hackney. Furthermore the line did not, as in Paris, traverse the major tourist routes, or the principal boulevards; it was obviously designed for the convenience of the citizens of Madrid, in getting to and from their work and not as a facility for visitors.

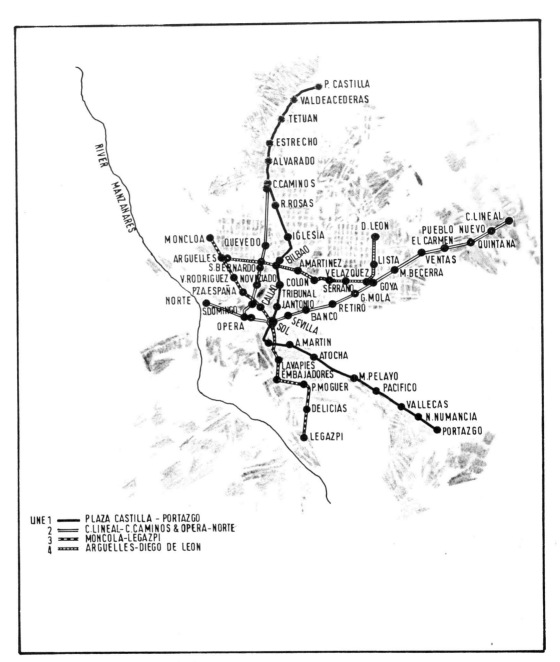

The Madrid Metro: original plan.

Again, in contrast to London, and to a lesser extent to Paris the first section of the Madrid Metro provided no connection whatever to any of the main line stations. The accompanying sketch map shows the first underground in relation to the Norte, Charmartin, Delicias and Atocha stations. It must be appreciated that at the time the Metro was built there was practically nothing in the way of commuter traffic on the Spanish main line railways, and there would be no incoming business to be collected daily from outlying districts. There was no cause for the Metro to be anything but a purely self-contained metropolitan entity. On the accompanying map the original station names are quoted, though some of these, as with a number of the London underground stations have been changed in the course of time. It was certainly appropriate to make Puerta del Sol the starting point, for this is the very hub of Madrid's teeming life—far more so than any of the *plazas* in the chain of grand boulevards that extends northward from the Atocha railway terminus. 'The Gate of the Sun': a traveller from England once said that if you lost yourself in the tangle of streets between the Prado and the Royal Palace you always seem to arrive in the Puerta del Sol, which was a good thing. You could once more take your bearings and start again! And so, what better starting point for the new Metro, for both the *Madrilenos* and such foreign visitors who ventured down its staircases. The first intermediate station, with an entrance like a glorified newspaper kiosk in the middle of the road, used to be called Gran Via; but in the reconstruction after the end of the Civil War it was renamed 'José Antonio', after the son of General Primo de Rivera, who was shot by the Communists during the war.

One's first impression upon entering any of the stations on the original line is of the faithful copy Madrid made of the Paris Metro. Construction-wise the route followed the main streets and there was no excavation under any existing buildings. The cross-section of the double-line tunnels at the stations has the same elegant elliptical shape as in Paris, and the walls and roofs are lined with white and coloured tiles. A major point of difference however is that current collection is from overhead wire, with a tramway type of 'trolley pole' on the motor coaches instead of the more sophisticated 'pantograph' on main line electric trains. On the newer lines of the Madrid Metro, opened subsequently a more modern form of pick-up has been adopted, though the tramway type of contact wire still prevails. On this system, as if to emphasise the difference and 'splendid isolation' from the Spanish main line railways, they use left hand running, as in England. The Madrid Metro is double-tracked throughout, with double-line tunnels constructed on that form of 'cut-and-cover' used for most of the underground lines in Paris. The original trains in 1919 were mostly two-car, consisting of one motor coach of the type shown in the accompanying drawing, and one trailer. Some extensive provision was made for future development of traffic, because all the stations were made long enough to accommodate trains made up to five of these 2-car units. The normal maximum complement of the original cars was 76 passengers, 24 seated and 52 standing. It would seem that the patronage of the Metro came rather slowly, for in 1920 the total rolling stock owned by the line amounted to no more than 11 motor coaches and 10 trailers.

The original line between Puerta del Sol and Cuatro Caminos was no more than $2\frac{1}{2}$ miles long, and some of the intermediate stations in their abbreviation of the names of the districts they served could be misleading to strangers. One of them, for example, is Bilbao, and far from suggesting that the Metro stretched as far as the Biscay coast, it merely indicated the Glorieta de Bilbao, or Bilbao circus. One of the most unusual names on this first line is 'Iglesia', at the Pintor Sorolla road intersection. As *Iglesia* simply means a church the designation seems rather vague, though no doubt the *Madrilenos* had no difficulty from the outset. The original northern terminus at Cuatro Caminos, in the Garcia road, lay just beyond the extensive basins of the Isabel II canal. As in Paris, and originally on our own 'tube' railways in London, there was a uniform fare. What is more remarkable is that this principle still prevails today in Madrid; although the system has greatly extended. In 1919 and for some little time afterwards the fare was 15 centimes. At the contemporary rate of exchange this was approximately three halfpence! The gradients apparently made a considerable difference to the running of the trains, and the northbound journey, against the grade was evidently much the harder of the two. In those days not all the trains stopped at all stations, and in making the downhill run from Cuatro Caminos to Puerta del Sol, and calling at only three of the six intermediate stations the time for the $2\frac{1}{2}$-mile run was only 8 minutes— a very smart average of nearly 19 m.p.h. In similar circumstances against the gradient the time, northbound, was 10 minutes.

During the 1920s the system was extended considerably. The original section, now known as Line 1, was continued to Atocha, and the first sections of Line 2 were built. The map reproduced on page 134 shows the present extent of the four lines envisaged in the original concession of January 1917, though lines 3 and 4 were not built until a much later time. The civil war, which broke out in 1936, had a devastating effect upon all railways in and around Madrid, and although Line 3 had been planned by 1935, to be constructed in two sections, the first from Puerto del Sol to Embajadores, and the second northwards to Arguelles neither was completed until some years after the end of the war. Although this is to some extent anticipating, the damage to the railways of Madrid during the civil war was not merely that by aerial attack, as in London. The northern suburbs of the city were virtually front-line territory; there was incessant shelling, much street fighting, and normal railway operation, on this side of the city at any rate was at a standstill for months on end. The Metro experienced, in a much less organised form, the human problems that were to arise in London when the Nazi 'blitz' came in 1940. Terrified civilians of all ages flocked to the Madrid Metro stations for shelter from air-raids. With the overhead contact wire there was no danger from the running rails, and when trains were not running, as was very frequently the case in that chaotic period the refugees sought even greater protection by going into the tunnels, and dossing down on the permanent way. Such was the situation of near-panic that frequently prevailed that the railway officials often had the greatest difficulty in getting these shelterers to leave the tunnels, even after an air raid had ended.

Somewhat naturally very little maintenance work was done on the Metro during the period of the civil war, and when it ended, in 1938, the entire plant was in a state of great dilapidation. In due course it was nationalised, and in the period of notable recovery that subsequently took place, while the rest of Europe was involved in the second world war, several new lines were opened. The long projected Line 3 from Puerta del Sol to Arguelles was opened in 1942, by which time work had also commenced on Line 4 from Arguelles to Goya. Only then were the lines envisaged in the original concession in prospect of realisation. In 1942 the system had 14 route miles in operation, and it was carrying 220 million passengers a year. Visitors have remarked upon the fact that the Metro always seems to be full, no matter what the time of day

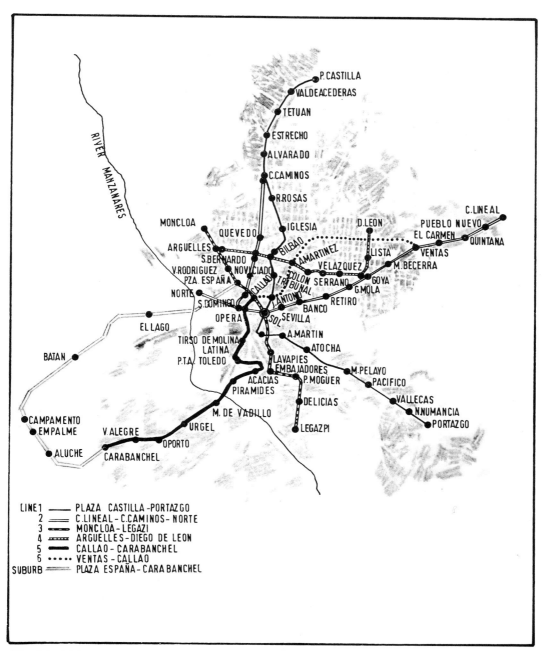

The Madrid Metro: as developing today.

K

happens to be, and the packed cars of the original design, which were in general use until the opening of Line 5, in 1968, had a very simple and effective form of ventilation. Unlike the London and Paris 'underground' trains, their Madrid counterparts do not come to the surface at all. The cars have clerestory roofs, but the window spaces in these roofs are devoid of any glass and provide some ventilation for the pack of humanity wedged below!

One is accustomed to the somewhat flamboyant interiors of some Continental rolling stock, plastered as they are with advertisements of all kinds; but on the Madrid Metro, the proliferation of 'don'ts' reaches record proportions! One is not allowed to smoke, to indulge in street, or rather train vending, to hold the doors open—against the pneumatic door engines—, nor to attempt to enter or leave the train after the whistle has started to blow. But our Continental cousins seem to love blowing whistles, and as they start the very instant a train has come to rest at a platform nobody takes any notice of this particular command. Only the time-honoured English injunction, not to spit, seems to be missing, and one loses the opportunity of turning two carriage notices of the Midland Railway into a rhyming couplet by which my housemaster once convulsed an audience at an English public school:

'Do not spit, to stop the train
In case of emergency pull the chain!'

But this is straying far from the Madrid Metro, and its bewildering geography for a stranger. At Puerta del Sol, which for all the extensions still remains the very heart of the system, one can buy a very good map; but, unfortunately it omitted to include the number of the lines, and so where the subterranean passages at the exchange stations are signposted: 'This way to Line Two', or words to that effect, the stranger can be completely baffled. This omission was happily rectified in the admirable brochure issued when Line 5 was inaugurated in 1968. Whether this brochure would provide any assurance against the pitfall of getting into a train on Line 1, 2 or any other of the lines that is going the wrong way is another matter. One can do this easily enough on the most familiar ground. At the very time of writing this chapter I dashed down a staircase into a train on one of the surface lines of London Transport, and was momentarily flabbergasted when the doors closed, and the train set off in the 'wrong' direction —wrong for me that was!

But I must return to the more technical features of the original Madrid metropolitan line, and particularly to the methods of operation. The practice of the Paris Metro was followed closely in the original signalling. No track circuits were used, which was unusual by that time in the working of rapid-transit urban railways. The Hall signal company of America had however achieved a notable degree of success with its very simple automatic system, using treadles, and the authorities of the Madrid Metro were no doubt attracted not only by the relative cheapness of the system, but also because the apparatus was easy to maintain and adjust. Even upon the most sophisticated railway systems of the world at that time the science of track circuiting was in no more than an evolutionary stage, and there would have been no experience at all of it on the main line railways of Spain. An underground railway planned to carry a great number of people is hardly the place for technicians to learn what to them would have been a new art! The signals themselves were colour-light, and all alike in having only two aspects: red for 'stop' and white for 'proceed'. The aspects were controlled entirely by the treadles, operated by the wheels of the trains. In later years as Line 1 was extended

138

it was necessary to instal crossovers and sidings at certain intermediate stations, and these of course required the use of interlocking between points and signals and track circuiting. At the same time the signal aspects have been changed to the familiar red, yellow and green. Nevertheless the white light has been retained, for use not as the normal clear, but in a particular circumstance as follows: if the approach to a station is being made under clear signals, and the track circuit immediately ahead of the station platform is also clear, white is used as a clear aspect preceding the green, as an additional indication to motormen of the state of the line ahead.

The controls of the signalling are now all-electric, the original Hall system having been dispensed with. On Line 1 the points and signals at intermediate stations are electrically controlled, but the turn-round at the terminal points is automatically controlled by track circuit. On Lines 2 and 4 however, which are not so extensive there are no more than a few all-electric interlockings. A number of intermediate crossovers are included, but these are not used in the ordinary course of the daily service. Arrangements are available for these to be worked by hand in emergency, subject of course to the taking of various special safety precautions. Some of the most interesting signalling on the Madrid Metro is to be seen on Lines 3 and 5, both of which are operated solely from centralised traffic control machines installed at Puerta del Sol. But before coming to consider the signalling I must make much more than a passing reference to Line 5. This represents the very latest development of the Madrid Metro and was not brought into service until 1968. It incorporates a number of features new to the system and serves parts of the city that have not hitherto enjoyed the facility of rapid travel to the centre. At the time of writing only the southern half of the line is in commission, as shown on the accompanying sketch map. The north-eastern continuation from Callao to Ventas, which will be known as Line 6, is to have a still more modern form of control, with completely automatic operation of the trains.

Reverting to Line 5 however, it will be seen from the map that it originates below Line 3 at Callao and passes beneath Line 2 at Opera. There is no physical junction between the lines, and the new line was tunnelled at a considerably lower level. It is, in fact, a deep-level line in every respect, and reaches its maximum depth at Latina station, which is no less than 90ft. below ground level. The general depths however vary mostly between 35 and 55ft. This characteristic has of course necessitated the use of escalators, and these are of a most pleasing and spacious type, far removed from giving an impression of descending into the bowels of the earth. The railway itself is unusual, among deep level tunnelling projects in urban areas in being double tracked throughout, and it was no surprise to learn that the difficulties in construction had been numerous and serious. These, of course, arose from the nature of the ground through which the tunnels had to be bored. The line was carried beneath some of the older parts of the city, and while the well established principle of routeing the line beneath streets was generally followed, the narrowness of many of the streets, and the precarious nature of the foundations of many old buildings rendered the task of tunnelling a highly delicate one. In this connection the use of double line tunnel did not help, for it precluded use of the expedient frequently adopted with the London tubes of bringing one single-line tunnel vertically above its fellow, when running below a narrow street.

There were many places along the route where water bearing strata was encountered, some complicated by carrying a strong dose of magnesium sulphate in solution. Special difficulties with water were experienced between the Plaza de Isabel II and the Commandante Las Morenas, neither of which have stations on the new lines. But underground deep beneath this area there was such an abundance of water that chemical injection was applied to consolidate the ground prior to the excavation proper being commenced. Another difficult section was where the line was carried beneath the Manzanares river, between the stations Piramides and M. de Vadillo. This was the first instance of any Madrid underground line being carried under the river, and a system of reinforced concrete protecting aprons was used to safeguard the workings. Generally a high degree of mechanisation was used in all the tunnel excavations, and to provide the necessary safeguards against water, pumping machinery was installed, as in the case of the Severn Tunnel, in Great Britain; this was considered necessary in Madrid because of the numerous instances of water bearing strata through which the tunnels of Line 5 pass, and also due to the proximity of the River Manzanares.

The *décor* of the new line, while following generally upon the construction methods adopted from the outset in Madrid, is attractively modern. There is a lot to be said for a double line station, when the wide platforms are kept so clean and so brilliantly lighted as those on Line 5. There is a scheme of diffused lighting from the walls, and a profusion of strip lighting above each platform edge. Imitation can be the most sincere form of flattery, and the adoption of a 'totem' device like that of the London Underground, but with the station names encompassed with a red diamond instead of the London 'ring', makes a distinctive and easily recognisable *motif* for the Metro as a whole. The new trains are attractively styled, but at the same time clearly designed to provide for a maximum of standing accommodation in the rush hours.

Line 3, which as previously mentioned was brought into service during the period of reconstruction following the end of the civil war, was equipped with a system of signalling control that was then novel so far as underground railways were concerned. It is a form of Centralised Traffic Control developed by the Swedish firm of L. M. Ericsson, and now used extensively on the State Railway of Sweden. One normally associates the term Centralised Traffic Control—or C.T.C.—with sections of single line railway extending far into mountainous or sparsely populated territory, where trains are few. And Ericssons have certainly developed it to full advantage for service in Sweden. But the system is also readily applicable to one man control of a single underground railway, such as Lines 3 and 5 in Madrid. On these lines some trains run from end to end, while others serve only the busy central area, and are turned round at one or another of the intermediate stations. The general principle of control has some points of similarity to that of programme machine working on London Transport. In both cases the operation is largely automatic until it is necessary for the operator at line headquarters to take direct control. The working of the system can perhaps be best appreciated by taking a look at the control centre of one of these lines at Puerta de Sol. The point that immediately strikes one on entering the room is the positively minimal amount of equipment. There is a single desk, with a few telephones that might be those of a senior business executive of the most modern type, a small push-button console, and a recessed portion in the centre. Standing some little distance in front of the desk is a much-miniaturised illuminated track diagram, on which the movement of trains throughout the line are constantly indicated.

Ericssons have developed their particular form of illuminated diagram to suit very extensive areas of railway operation, often covering up to a hundred miles of route; and so that the indications of train movement on a large diagram can be readily seen

140

from the operator without his moving from his chair the diagram itself is curved to make the front face roughly radial from the operators' chair. This may seem a logical enough feature of design; but even with modern manufacturing techniques it is not the easiest thing to produce a radially shaped case into which numerous miniature electrical appliances have to be fitted. But the immediate impression created by these diagrams at Puerto del Sol is of the beauty of their finish. While the illuminated diagram shows the immediate on-line position at any moment, and provides the tool of control needed by the operator of any departure from timetable, or emergency movements have to be quickly organised, further apparatus is provided to furnish a complete and permanent record of the day's working on the line. I mentioned earlier that in the middle of the operating desk there was a recessed portion; this has a glass cover, that shields an apparatus for automatically recording train movements.

Railway operating managers are constantly concerned with the day-to-day variations of train working from that carefully planned and set out in the timetable. After occasions of delay, or fluctuations in movement the subsequent 'inquest' is frequently faced with the question: 'What did *really* happen?', or how did such-and-such a situation really build up. Those who had to deal with things at close quarters were probably too much engrossed in their immediate problems to be aware of the situation as a whole, and when the 'inquest' is concluded the operating manager has most likely gained no more than an imperfect idea of the entire happening. When the principle of C.T.C. was developed for lengthy stretches of single line in the Middle-West and Western states of the U.S.A. the automatic train graph recorder was considered an essential part of the equipment. The movement of trains through the various track circuits is automatically registered on the graph by electrically operated pens, which make marks on a continuous roll of graph paper, moving forward in synchronisation with the time of day. Thus the time of a particular train passing through a certain track circuit is marked at the appropriate time of day on the graph. In the earliest American examples of this form of apparatus the automatic recording merely took the form of making marks at certain strategic points, and to complete the record of train movement the operator had to join up the marks by ruling a pencil line from point to point. There was no great difficulty in this, with only a few trains on, maybe, 100 miles of railway. But on a rapid-transit system like the Madrid Metro, and like some of the Swedish lines signalled by Ericssons, it would be an impossible task, and the progress of the trains is therefore recorded at many intermediate points. The operator has no work to do on the graphic record. The compiling of the register is entirely automatic.

So far I have said nothing about the control of the various junctions, crossovers, and sidings that are included in the track layouts of lines 3 and 5. Everything is done from a small push-button desk unit, as and when it is necessary to institute individual remote control. Otherwise the line is entirely automatic. If it should be necessary to change the routeing of a train, which can be done at the stations where there are points and crossings, the operator at the Puerta del Sol control office presses the button appropriate to that particular station; that connects him, as it were, to the local 'exchange', and he can then move the points and clear the signals by electronic remote control apparatus. On Line 5, for the first time in Spain, automatic train control has been added to the signalling. This is achieved by what are termed 'coded' track circuits. In the ordinary form of track circuits the current flows continuously, and the controls governed by the track circuit current are either 'on' or 'off'. In coded track circuits the current is pulsating, being interrupted so many times a second according to the state of the line ahead. The trains are fitted with apparatus for interpreting the codes flowing in the rails, and this apparatus, and the codes picked up, regulate the speed of the train. On the Madrid Metro the controlled speed, according to the state of the line ahead are 43, 31 and 22 m.p.h.

At the present time two further lines are under construction, to be numbered 6 and 7, and on these it is intended that fully automatic train operation shall be installed. It is perhaps anticipating the strict chronological order of this book to mention this remarkable feature, because its introduction has already preceded by some little time by fully operative installations of A.T.O. in London and Rotterdam. But the Madrid Metro in its steady expansion, and sophisticated equipment is well to the fore in the development of urban rapid transit practice.

CHAPTER THIRTEEN

The Post Office Tube

In the first years of the present century congestion on the streets of London had reached an unparalleled extent. The success of the deep level tube railways, and of the electrification of the Inner Circle—whatever its financial results—had taken a good deal of passenger business from the streets; but horse-drawn omnibuses continued to operate in large numbers and the electric underground railways had done practically nothing to relieve the pressure of goods traffic. Some of the main line railways, notably the London and North Western, Midland and Great Northern had established goods depots of their own in the City, in addition to their major goods termini adjacent to their principal passenger stations; but there were large areas not served directly by rail between Camden and Haydon Square, for example. The main line railways therefore owned large fleets of horse-drawn delivery wagons and vans. Doré's famous drawing of Ludgate Hill, showing the entire roadway one solid, well-nigh immovable jam of vehicles was no doubt an exaggeration; but it was nevertheless symbolical of the general tempo of traffic on the London streets.

At this time the Post Office, with a standard letter rate of one penny, was providing a remarkably comprehensive service of mail collection and delivery throughout the day. Mail trains equipped with travelling post offices ran in the mornings as well as at night, and the congestion on the streets of London was a serious hindrance to rapid conveyance of traffic between the major postal centres in London itself, and the main line railway stations from which the more important mail trains were operated. In addition to the special and exclusively postal trains that ran from Euston to the north, and from Paddington to the West of England there were regular Continental mails via Cannon Street and Dover, while in those years prior to air travel the regular Indian, South African, Australian and American mails were of great importance. It was in these circumstances, of great difficulty and delay in the transport of mail within and across London that the idea of a tube railway exclusively for Post Office use was conceived. The original idea was to link up all the main line termini dealing with important mail traffic, and thus include Euston, Paddington, Kings Cross, Liverpool Street, Cannon Street and Waterloo with the major sorting depots at Mount Pleasant and St. Martins-le-Grand; but like the passenger tube railway network the project was authorised in stages.

The first plan was to eliminate the tremendous congestion on the principal east–west route of mail traffic, and the route authorised, as shown on the map on page 144, ran from the Eastern District main post office in the Whitechapel Road, via Liverpool

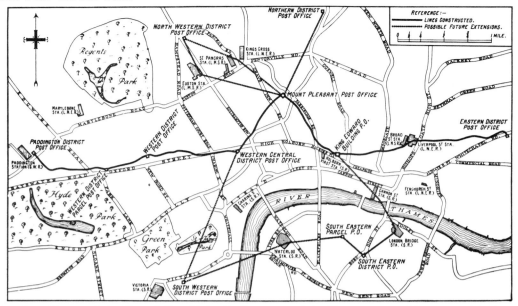

London: Route of the Post Office Tube Railway as originally constructed in 1927 with lines then considered for future extensions, but which have not been built.

Street, Great Eastern station, the G.P.O. at St. Martins-le-Grand, Mount Pleasant sorting office, the Western Central, and Western district main post offices, to Paddington. It was evidently considered more important at first to connect the Western Central main post office in High Holborn than to extend the circuit further to the north to take in Euston. It was after all in the central areas that the greatest congestion occurred, and connection with the principal mail departures from Euston from 8.30 p.m. onwards, was made at a time when traffic on the streets would have eased somewhat. As the map shows however some considerable extensions to the original line were envisaged in the early 1930s. The line was planned as a deep level tube running between 70 and 80ft. below the surface. Work was commenced in 1914, but after the outbreak of war operations were suspended, and they were not resumed until the mid-1920s, by which time prices had fallen to a level that enabled contracts for equipment and rolling stock to be placed at figures not too widely divergent from the original estimates. The period of industrial disturbance following the General Strike of 1926 was a cause of further delay in completion. However, as finally brought into service the railway was an immediate success. Something like a quarter of the mail vans hitherto working on the streets of London were withdrawn, and the savings in operating costs of the postal service were very substantial.

On a railway designed purely and exclusively for the conveyance of parcels and mails the scheme of operation could be quite different from one involved with large numbers of passengers. The safety provisions in connection with train movements concerned solely the efficient handling of traffic. A collision would be an operating nuisance rather than a hazard to human life, and so from the outset it was agreed that the trains should be driverless, and their movements regulated by the application of traction current to the rails instead of by signals of the orthodox kind. Then, as there would be no regular

144

operators riding on the trains, the size of the tube tunnels could be made no larger than required to accommodate rolling stock designed expressly for postal traffic. To mini-mise the cost of construction only one tube was run between stations. The rail gauge is 2ft., and both tracks could be accommodated in a tube 9ft. in diameter. This at the same time gives ample space for two trains abreast, and is convenient for men to enter to perform essential maintenance. The original rolling stock consisted entirely of steel motor wagons with an overall length of 13ft. 5in., a width of 2ft. 10in. and a height of 4ft. 11in. They were energised from a centre current rail. These wagons could be operated singly, or in 'trains' of two, or three. They were designed for maximum carrying capacity, and when fully loaded could take $\frac{1}{2}$ ton of postal matter. The original equipment of the line was 90 wagons, so that 45 tons of mail could be on the move simultaneously. In 1930 some 750 tons of mail were dealt with daily by the Post Office in London, so that the opening of the railway clearly made a massive contribution. The maximum speed of these wagons was 35 m.p.h., an impressive performance on 2ft. gauge!

The underground stations at the General Post Office, 'King Edward Building', and at Mount Pleasant were, from the outset, the two major centres of activity on the system. There could be no question of a simple, continuous circuit as on the Inner Circle, of a straightforward to and fro movement as on the deep-level passenger tubes. Both 'King Edward Building', and 'Mount Pleasant' were intermediate centres of traffic where trains terminated, and originated. Facilities had to be provided for ter-minating trains to be cleared and berthed till required again, or to 'run round' if needed to return immediately. Both these important stations were similar in this respect, but at Mount Pleasant there was also located the car shed and maintenance depot. There was no question on this railway of bringing cars to a surface depot for stabling, or repair; everything was done underground and the car shed at Mount Pleasant was quite a remarkable affair. The track layouts at these two intermediate stations are shown on

Post Office Tube Railway: loading one of the automatic trains with mail.

Post Office Tube: a scene at one of the major stations with the special containers being loaded.

this page, and they require some special mention. On the platforms the loading and unloading of mail is entirely uni-directional, and this dictated the provision of the run-round loops at each end. One platform deals solely with eastbound traffic, and the other with westbound; so that if a train from Paddington arrives at Mount Pleasant, and terminates there it is unloaded, and then run round to the westbound platform for the return journey. This co-ordinates with the streamlined flow of traffic handling on the platforms themselves.

Still referring to the platform working, the platform faces are approximately 200ft. long and thus capable of accommodating at a maximum about 14 of the standard wagons. But to provide for flexibility in operation it will be seen that crossover roads are laid in intermediately along the platforms, so that a train from the rear end of the platform could be dispatched while one at the head end is still loading, or another could be brought in to the head end while the rear end was occupied. It will be seen also that at the eastern end of both stations head-shunts are provided for berthing stock not immediately required, in addition to the run-round loops at both ends. To avoid any difficulty with conflicting routes in these quite complicated layouts all the crossings of one line across another are made by what the Americans term 'grade separation', or what in the open air we call 'flying' or 'burrowing' junctions. In providing the additional access to the car sheds at Mount Pleasant this principle involved some quite intricate tube tunnelling. At both stations the plans reproduced on this page suggest the existence of certain 'blind' tunnel entrances; at the eastern end at King Edward Building, and at the western end at Mount Pleasant. It was considered desirable to facilitate the possibility of further extensions by actually building tunnels of larger

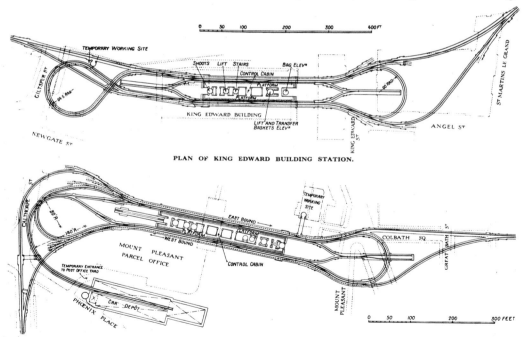

PLAN OF KING EDWARD BUILDING STATION.

MOUNT PLEASANT STATION.

The London Post Office Tube Railway.

Post Office Tube Railway: the control cabin and switchboard at Mount Pleasant in 1935.

section, with so-called 'step-plate' connections at the site of future junction points. At King Edward Building these connections were for the proposed line to London Bridge and the South Eastern District loop to Waterloo, while those at Mount Pleasant provided for two further extensions, to the Northern and North Western main district post offices, and to Euston.

On the two-track tube sections between stations the track sections are so proportioned as to provide for a headway of 2 min. between successive trains. Each main section of conductor rail is automatically made 'dead' as the train leaves it, and becomes 'live' again when the train enters the next section but one. There is thus a 'dead' section between two successive trains. Just as the track circuits on a passenger-carrying railway govern the aspects displayed by the signals, which are observed and obeyed by the train drivers, so the direct energisation of the track rails governs the movement of trains on the Post Office Tube. It is intriguing to realise also that precisely the same principle is used for the control of train running on many, highly sophisticated electric model railways of today. On the Post Office Tube the working at intermediate stations and at the major junctions is regulated by individual operators. One could not call them signalmen on a railway that has no signals, so instead they are usually referred to as 'switchmen'. The traffic position in the tunnels approaching a station, and the destination of each train is indicated to the switchman on an illuminated diagram designed on just the same principles as those introduced by B. H. Peter on the Metropolitan District Railway in 1905. To receive a train the switchman operates the appropriate points to set the route, and energises such sections of live rail as are necessary, leaving a section 'dead' at the location where it is desired to bring the train to rest.

Post Office Tube: one of the automatic trains at speed.

Post Office Tube Railway: a tunnel junction at Mount Pleasant.

The points are electrically worked, but without one of the refinements required legally where passenger trains are concerned. The Board of Trade, and more recently the Ministry of Transport required that all points run over by passenger trains in a facing direction should be equipped with facing point locks, and that the signals reading over such junctions shall not be cleared until the plunger of the facing point lock is fully home. The interlocking between levers provides the necessary safeguard of this requirement. But whereas a derailment at facing points on an ordinary railway could result in loss of life, on the Post Office Tube it would have no more than a 'nuisance value'. In consequence the point operating mechanisms have no facing point locks, and are much simpler as a result. Even so, 'nuisance' in a complex layout like those at King Edward Building and Mount Pleasant could mean considerable delay, and a very complete system of interlocking was installed between the points and energisation of the conductor rails, while the principle of track circuiting used on passenger railways, to preclude the establishment of conditions that could result in a collision is applied on the Post Office Tube to prevent energising the sections of live rail in such a way as to have a similar result.

The vertical profile of the line was arranged on the 'dipping gradient' principle, like that of the Central London, to provide for rapid acceleration from station stops, and to assist retardation when coming to rest. The stations were much further apart than on the underground passenger lines, and even with no higher maximum speeds than 35 m.p.h. it was possible to maintain end-to-end average speeds of 20 m.p.h. This was a vast improvement over the speeds of 5 to 7 m.p.h. which were about the best one could expect with road vehicles. In the state of the London streets in the early 1900s motor vehicles would have shown little superiority over horses, so great was the congestion in certain areas. But average speeds of transit on the Post Office Tube Railway were greatly superior to those on the passenger lines due to the relative infrequency of stops, and to the mechanised arrangements for loading, which will be mentioned later. During the 1930s when the line had got fully into its stride it was carrying $6\frac{1}{2}$ million letter bags per annum, and 4 million parcel bags. On weekdays the line was continuously open, with trains running to a regular schedule except between 7 a.m. and 9 a.m., when there was a two-hour break for maintenance work. By 7 a.m. all the night mails coming into London would have been dealt with, and distributed to the major district post offices along the line. The special postal trains were due into Euston and Paddington by 4 a.m., and the Irish Mail arrived at Euston just before 6 a.m. There were no trains on the Post Office Tube Railway on Sundays. During what could be termed the 'normal' periods of the year the weekly car miles run averaged about 34,000. In the autumn, which was then a traditionally busier time for the Post Office the average usually showed an increase to about 38,000, while at the height of the Christmas rush with every one of the 90 cars in continuous use the weekly average was known to rise to 68,000 car miles—a remarkable performance on a 2ft. gauge line only $6\frac{1}{2}$ miles long.

The means of access to the railway at the various stations was planned on the most comprehensive scale, full advantage being taken of the experience gained with tube railways. Lifts were provided for both mails and men, while in addition each station had necessarily its emergency staircases. These, together with the lifts, were reached from the basement levels of the various post-offices beneath which the underground stations were located. There were some significant differences between the constructional methods employed on this line and on the underground passenger railways in

150

Post Office Tube
Railway: a loaded train
emerging from tunnel.

London. In the case of the latter several instances have been mentioned in this book, of where sharp curvature and the aligning of tubes one above the other was necessary to keep the tunnels beneath the streets. With the Post Office tube the accommodation of both running lines in one tube made things simpler, while the narrow gauge tracks and relatively light-weight of the trains was likely to cause a minimum of disturbance from vibration, especially when located 70 to 80ft. below ground level. At the stations however it was another matter. These had, of necessity, to be located immediately underneath the buildings of the various post offices with lifts, conveyors and staircases connecting directly with the basements. Some very careful work was necessary in underpinning large buildings, especially at Mount Pleasant and King Edward Building, when the access ways to the tube railway were under construction.

At all stations the transfer of mail and parcels is entirely mechanised. There are spiral

151

chutes for downward mails and lifts for the corresponding upward traffic, and the mechanisation extends to the point of actually loading bags on to the trains. The arrangements at the various stations can be imagined by picturing a series of circular shafts connecting the sorting rooms above with the station platforms below. At their lower ends the shafts run the length of the platforms, in which there are openings every few yards. In these shafts beneath the platforms there are electrically driven conveyor belts, and when a train is unloaded the mail bags are dropped through the openings in the platforms on to the conveyor belt on which they travel to the elevator that takes them up to the sorting rooms in the post offices at street level. The mail bags are untouched by hand from the moment that they are dropped through the platform openings until they arrive in the sorting rooms. In the reverse direction bags for loading descend by one or another of the spiral chutes, and then at platform level they are loaded into special containers. These were designed so that they could be readily wheeled across the platforms and loaded into the trains, and proportioned to fit neatly into the spaces available on the train wagons. Wagons, containers, and station layouts were indeed designed as one comprehensive project.

The car shed at Mount Pleasant, as shown in one of the photographs reproduced on page 153 has an interesting layout. To economise space the track connections include many sharp curves, while the intricacies of the connections, and the individual operations involved place it outside the sphere of control of the switchmen. The tracks are not electrified, and once the train wagons have arrived on to the approach tracks to the shed they are propelled, marshalled, or parked as required by special electric locomotives deriving their power from batteries. The shed includes an extensive bay on one side where servicing and repair work is done. This is of course greatly simplified because all cars are alike.

The arrangements at the western terminus of the line, beneath Paddington station, were interesting, and are shown on the plan on page 154. I write of these arrangements in the past tense, because they were modified when the Great Western station was modernised so far as its platform layouts were concerned in the early 1930s. The Post Office Railway has its own terminus beneath the Paddington District Post Office, in London Street, adjacent to the arrival side of the main line station and the dotted lines on the plan show the layout of the underground tracks, with the usual 'run round' and lay-by sidings. As originally arranged the connections between the tube postal station and the Great Western platforms were of two kinds. There were shoots for arriving mail and parcels from the buffer stop ends of platforms 8, 9, and 10, at which the principal express passenger trains used to arrive. These would be carrying small amounts of mail. Along platform 11 however, at which the West of England postal special arrived there were no fewer than 8 shoots, conveying mail down to the Post Office Railway station. Outgoing mail was taken by a separate elevating conveyor to a distributional centre at one corner of the circulating area always known as 'The Lawn'. The special enclosure dealing with mails includes three conveyor bands, two bringing mail bags from the Post Office Railway, and the other, travelling laterally, to serve as a distributing band from which the mails are transferred to platform trolleys.

From its first opening, in time for the Christmas rush of 1927 the Post Office Tube Railway was a great success. By holding back the time of placing contracts for the rolling stock the total cost did not greatly exceed the pre-1914 estimates. The cost was of the order of $£1\frac{1}{2}$ million, and in the later 1930s it appeared in Post Office accounts as an

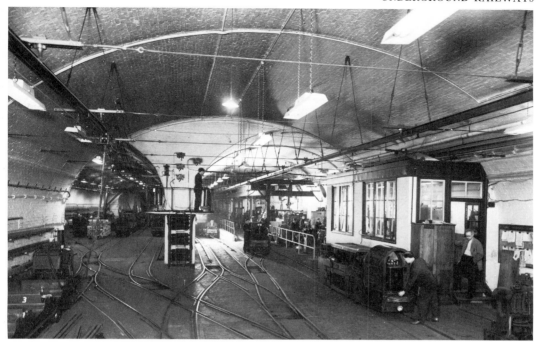

Post Office Tube Railway: the large underground repair depot and workshop.

Post Office Tube Railway: one of the latest type of traction units, with four standard containers loaded.

L

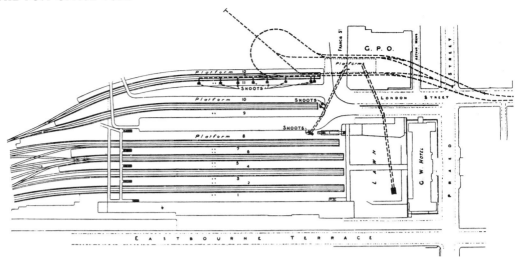

Original arrangements at Paddington Station, Great Western Railway, showing connections to Post Office Tube Railway.

asset valued at around £1,100,000. With the changing trends of postal service, and the marked lessening in importance of Cannon Street and Waterloo stations for overseas mail, due to air transport, the extensions originally envisaged and for which provision was made in the excavations for the necessary junctions, have never been constructed. As a single purpose underground railway however the Post Office Tube remains a uniquely interesting example.

Post Office Tube Railway:
the switch frame and control panel at King Edward Building, 1962.

CHAPTER FOURTEEN

Integration in London

The underground railways of London suffered the penalties of all pioneer works, and from a characteristically British way of doing things. Earlier chapters of this book have described how successive lines were the fruits of individual enterprises. There was no central direction, and both the traffic facilities and engineering details were settled to suit the judgment of the several managements. Another chapter of this book has told how the Paris 'Metro' was planned as a single entity and a later one describes the even more rationalised case of Moscow. But one could never have imagined such precise planning to have taken place in any British city, let alone London; varying interests went ahead in their several ways leaving it to later enterprises to profit by the mistakes, and errors of judgment, that were inevitable. This is not to place any form of stigma upon such courageous achievements as the first section of the Metropolitan, upon the City and South London, and above all upon the 'Twopenny Tube'; but sooner or later their vagaries and pronounced divergencies in practice would have to be resolved. So far as management was concerned the gathering of the City and South London, and of the Central London into the London Electric Railway group even before World War I, was no more than a first step; but already there was a master-mind at the head of affairs in the person of Albert H. Stanley, who in later years we came to know so well as Lord Ashfield.

It is sometimes felt that the enticement of Sir George Gibb from the general managership of the North Eastern Railway to become Managing Director of the District Railway and the three Yerkes tubes in 1906 was no more than an interim measure; but it was Gibb who secured the services of Albert Stanley, in 1907, when the latter was no more than 33 years of age. As the history of the North Eastern Railway, and subsequently of the London and North Eastern so frequently showed, Gibb had the priceless managerial quality of being able to pick his men, for promotion; and the selection of Stanley as a man of immense potential stemmed from several years earlier than Gibb's underground days, when he had led a party of North Eastern officers on a visit to the United States. Stanley himself was English to the core, having been born at Derby in 1874, but very early in life he went to the U.S.A. and joined the Detroit Street Railway Company on the traffic side. But when that concern adopted electric traction, he left his existing appointment to obtain training in mechanical and electrical engineering in the shops of the company. His enterprise, and his now varied experience was quickly appreciated by the management, and before he was 28 years of age he was appointed General Superintendent of the company. At the age of 29 he was appointed Assistant

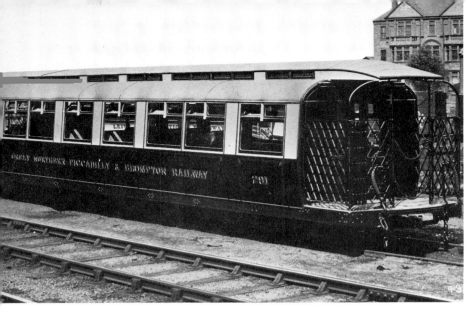

Before the integration began:
Great Northern, Piccadilly and
Brompton Railway, one of the f
all-steel cars used on a British
railway, 1905.

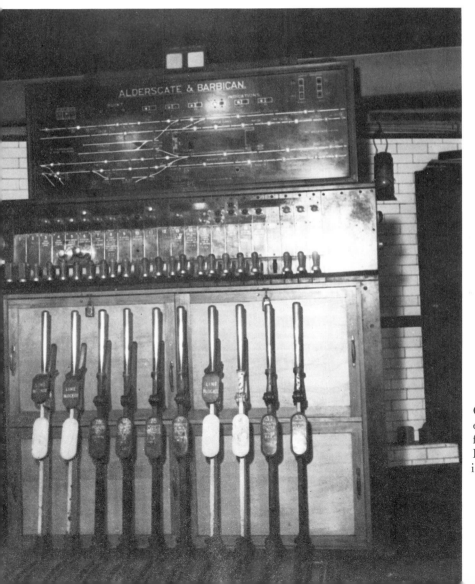

City Widened Lines: an early
electro-mechanical locking
frame at Aldersgate and
Barbican modernised with
illuminated diagram.

General Manager of the Street Railway Department of New Jersey, and in February 1904 Manager.

Gibb and the party of N.E.R. officers had made their tour of the U.S.A. in 1901, and it was then that he became aware of Stanley's talents. In response to Gibb's invitation he came to England in April 1907 to become General Manager of the Underground Electric Railways Company of London Ltd., and in 1910 he succeeded Gibb as Managing Director. His work in commencing the complete integration of the tube railways received remarkably early public recognition with the honour of a knighthood, in 1914, but a completely unprecedented distinction was bestowed upon him in December 1916. At that time Lloyd George had succeeded Asquith as Prime Minister, and was in process of forming a National Government on the broadest possible basis, to reinforce the very small War Cabinet; and as a member of this Government he chose Sir Albert Stanley as President of the Board of Trade. Stanley had then just turned 42 years of age, and was by some years the most junior member of the Government. But that he should have been chosen by Lloyd George at that most critical time in our national history was indeed a measure of the man currently in command of the Underground group. On taking up Government duties he had of course to resign his post on the Underground railways; but this resignation was naturally no more than temporary, and in August 1919 he rejoined the group as Managing Director, being also elected to the Chairmanship. In the New Year Honours of 1920 his war services were acknowledged by the award of a barony, and he became Lord Ashfield of Southwell. He was then barely 46 years of age, and for nearly 30 years subsequently his name became synonymous with all activities on the London Underground railway system.

The grouping of the main line railways of Great Britain in January 1923 left the London Underground railways unchanged, and the Metropolitan remained outside the Ashfield 'empire', for another 10 years. In the meantime however a most important facet of underground railway strategy in London began to unfold. Although the various electric tramway systems around London were also mostly under Sir Albert Stanley's managership, even before the outbreak of war in 1914, and although the most careful measures were taken to co-ordinate their working with those of the tube railways, the idea of the 'tubes' being neat little, self-contained services, shuttling to and fro deep beneath the London streets began gradually to disappear. At the outlying tube termini, such as Golders Green and Shepherds Bush there was the inconvenience of interchange between tram and train, and although the Underground organisation remained faithful to the trams for many years to come, in popular sentiment they gradually became as outmoded as the steam locomotive became on main line railways in later years. The underground policy became one of extending the 'tubes' into the dormitory suburbs of London, and the developments eventually carried out under the 'Ashfield' administration linked the central tube network with some of the largest of the main line railways running north, east and west of London.

It is fascinating to reflect upon the similarity that developed between this new policy and that so vigorously and enthusiastically pursued by James Staats Forbes when chairman of the Metropolitan District Railway. Forbes may have been something of a buccaneer: a man who pursued his ideas regardless of whether they were going to bring an adequate return to the shareholders. But he had his finger on the pulse of traffic, and could see where the flows were likely to be strongest. He pushed out the western tentacles of the District Railway to link up with the London and South Western at both

157

The Thames Tunnel at Wapping, on the East London Railway: a train of the modernised District Railway 'F' stock of 1920 emerging.

Wimbledon and Richmond, exercising running powers over their tracks for considerable mileages, while his link-up with the Great Western at Ealing Broadway was a vastly better proposition than the old steam-worked service between Southall and Victoria, operated by Great Western trains. And from 1910 onwards A. H. Stanley, as he was then, began to do exactly the same with the tubes. The three Yerkes lines, 'Charing Cross Euston and Hampstead', 'Piccadilly', and the 'Bakerloo', had all proved remarkably successful; but it was the carrying of the first named to its surface terminus at Golders Green—from its first opening in June 1907—that gave another clue to future advancement. That terminus was then literally in open country, and in a very short time a teeming suburb had grown up around the station. This demonstrated the power of the tube railways to create traffic. The Hampstead line was of course a purely 'underground' enterprise. No other organisation was involved traffic-wise, or financially interested; and gratifying though the results were, particularly in the housing developments at Golders Green, any development on similar lines was ruled out, for a time, on the grounds of capital cost.

It was then that the 'stop-at-nothing', 'go-it-alone' Yerkes technique began to give place to the more subtle tactics of J. S. Forbes, but with the solidarity of management now being so efficiently practised by A. H. Stanley. The first evidence of this was seen in the north-westward extension of the Bakerloo line. The original Yerkes scheme had envisaged an extension of the tube railway from Baker Street to Paddington, and this was undertaken and brought into operation in December 1913. This however was no more than the first stage of a much more ambitious development. The London and North Western Railway, like the Great Western, but totally unlike all the railways entering London from the south of the Thames had never been one to offer much of a commuter service. Its partner, the North London, tapped a fairly populous residential district and conveyed many season-ticket holders to and from its City terminus at

Broad Street; but Euston was essentially a 'long distance' station. The L.N.W.R. had no particular cause to try and build up traffic round London; it earned a princely revenue in the conveyance of freight, and its long-distance express passenger trains were the most punctual and best patronised of any in the country in the years 1905–10. North-west of central London the stations on the main line between Willesden were far apart, as befitted a country district, and in the $26\frac{1}{4}$ miles between the last mentioned station and Tring on the crest of the Chiltern Hills there were no more than 8 intermediate stations.

Unconsciously perhaps, the North Western was nevertheless building for the future. These stations had a service that was of a semi-main line character. Modern, smooth-riding commodious carriages were provided on all trains; the service was operated with the smartness, courtesy and punctuality characteristic of 'The Premier Line', of Great Britain, and more and more people began to live near to these 'country' stations and to commute in the greatest comfort to and from Euston. Season-ticket rates were extraordinarily cheap—not only by present standards(!), but in comparison with many of those prevailing elsewhere at the time. At no place was the housing development more pronounced than at Watford, and the management of the L.N.W.R., quick as always to sense the significance of a developing traffic, decided upon a remarkable scheme of expansion. There were never any half-measures about North Western development. It had always been the policy of the company to plough back a considerable proportion of its profits into improvements of its traffic handling facilities; and now, from 1910 onwards a plan of enormous development in the London area was set in motion. The outer suburban traffic was to be fostered for all it was worth, and since the quadruple-tracked main line from Euston was already well occupied with long distance passenger and freight trains an entirely new line was to be built alongside for the increased suburban trains. New intermediate stations were to be built, on the new lines only, and eventually the whole suburban network, including the North London Railway was to be electrified.

The Underground group saw an unrivalled opportunity of participating in this great scheme of development. While many passengers from the North Western country suburbs would undoubtedly wish to travel to Euston or Broad Street, there would no doubt be many others who would appreciate a direct connection to the West End; and so the L.E.R. negotiated an alliance with the L.N.W.R. that was eventually to prove most profitable to both. Plans were put in hand for the extension of the Bakerloo tube from Paddington to come to the surface at Queens Park, $3\frac{1}{2}$ miles out of Euston, and feed into the Watford 'new line' of the L.N.W.R. When the latter was electrified the tube trains would be able to run through from the Elephant and Castle to Watford. To facilitate this working the North Western agreed to adopt the same system of electrification as the District and the three 'Yerkes' tube lines, namely 600 volts direct current, with a fourth rail for traction return. This was an arrangement entirely in the style of J. S. Forbes, as he had engineered to get the District trains to Wimbledon, and Richmond over L.S.W.R. tracks. The North Western entered whole-heartedly into the Watford alliance and for the through service to the Elephant and Castle the tube trains were jointly owned, and painted in the historic 'sepia and white' colour scheme of the L.N.W.R. carriages. At the time of the nationalisation of British Railways, when the harassed and newly-formed Railway Executive was trying to decide on colour schemes for the unified stock, a two-tone livery reminiscent of the L.N.W.R. was officially

159

Lord Ashfield of Southwell. From 1907, as Mr. Albert Stanley,
General Manager and later Managing Director of the Underground
Railways of London, Ltd., and Chairman from 1919. Chairman of
London Transport from 1933 to 1947. He was Knighted in 1914 and
raised to the Peerage in 1920.

described as 'plum and spilt milk'. This may have been appropriate to a pre-grouping
North Western coach in dingy, or travel-stained condition, but was no more than a
shabby echo of the *real* North Western. The 'tube' trains that ran through to Watford
certainly looked very fine in their pristine condition, though very odd in their greatly
dwarfed profile when they came alongside standard North Western stock on the surface
part of the line.

Work was going rapidly ahead with this great scheme of expansion when war broke
out in August 1914. At first work was continued. The new lines of the L.N.W.R.
between Willesden and Watford had been opened in February 1913, with steam traction, and despite the war work was pushed ahead to complete the link up between the
Bakerloo tube and the 'new line'. The North Western constructed two new tunnels to
carry the new line under Kensal Green Cemetery, while the Underground extended
the tube westwards from Paddington. By May 1915 it was possible to inaugurate a
Bakerloo service to Willesden Junction, and despite the war a high priority was given

160

to the completion of the North Western part of the electrification. By April 1917 the Bakerloo trains were running through to Watford. The complete North Western scheme, with electrification into Euston was not completed until 1922 however, and then the normal pattern of service on the 'new line' between Queens Park and Watford, was that one train in three was through to the Elephant and Castle; the other two were 'full-sized' North Westerns, for Euston and Broad Street respectively. On the Bakerloo line itself only a proportion of the trains ran through to Watford. The greater number terminated at Queens Park, and provided a Watford service by connection with the North Western trains.

The second 'Underground' probing into the country was in close association with the Great Western Railway, and although not brought into service until August 1920 was the consummation of a scheme projected as long previously as 1905. This was the Ealing and Shepherds Bush Railway, linking up the Central London with the Great Western main line at Ealing Broadway. The immediate post war years were a time of much discussion on the future of transport ownership and policy, and not long after his resumption of executive duties as chairman and managing director of the Underground group Lord Ashfield, as he had then become, expressed the opinion that future railway development would largely involve the connection of tube and underground lines with surface railways in order to facilitate the distribution of passengers from the various suburban areas throughout the business and industrial areas of great cities, as distinct from the concentration necessarily associated with the large main line terminal stations. The Ealing and Shepherds Bush Railway was designed to connect the Central London tube with the Great Western main line, but whether any extension of the electrified area to Southall, or even to Slough was contemplated at the time of its original projection it is not possible now to say. After all, Slough is only one mile further from Paddington than Watford Junction is from Euston, and longer-distance commuter travel on the Great Western bore a very strong resemblance to that of the North Western prior to 1914.

In any case this second 'country' project, on which the Underground group cashed in, was very similar, in that the 'new line' was built and owned by the main line company. For the Great Western however there was more to it than a link-up with a busy and profitable tube railway; and although it is somewhat outside the Underground story the Ealing and Shepherds Bush Railway provided connections between the main, and the Wycombe lines of the Great Western Railway, and the West London Railway at Wood Lane. It was this facility with the valuable relief route that it provided in war time that enabled the fairly heavy civil engineering to be continued during the first world war. In Chapter Seven of this book reference is made to the car sheds and maintenance depot of the Central London Line Railway, which was on the surface, beyond the western end of the line at Shepherds Bush. The establishment of the famous White City Exhibition grounds at Wood Lane, adjacent to the C.L.R. depot, was accompanied by the building of an additional line from Shepherds Bush tube station to a new station just below ground level at Wood Lane situated on what became a run-round loop for Central London trains, while serving the White City. This line provided an almost ready-made connection to the new Ealing and Shepherds Bush Railway, and required only two short lengths of cutting and tunnelling to bring the Central London fully to the surface. The new station and loop at Wood Lane was brought into service in May 1908, on the opening day of the Franco-British Exhibition at the White City.

Metropolitan Railway: the signal
cabin at Edgware Road 1927. This
railway prior to the formation of the
L.P.T.B. used the all-electric system of
interlocking as distinct from the electro-
pneumatic of the District and the tubes.

Central London Railway: control
cabin for extension to the Ealing and
Shepherds Bush line.

So far as the Ealing and Shepherds Bush Railway was concerned the Great Western was able to use it for goods traffic from April 1917, but the electrification was not carried out until after the war. The through tube train service from the Central London line to Ealing Broadway began in August 1920.

The scene now moves to the City and South London, which in 1920 was still operating with its original electric locomotives, and in much the same gloomy conditions that had led to its carriages being known as the 'padded cells', and the whole outfit to be nicknamed 'The Drain'. It had been extended to Euston, but the reduced diameter of the tunnels, 10ft. 6in., precluded the use of standard tube stock, as running on the three 'Yerkes' lines. The merest glance at the tube railway map of London would be enough to suggest what advantages might be derived by a southward extension of the Hampstead line to link up with the City and South London at Kennington, and a further connection between the two lines near Euston. The obstacle to all this was the size of the City and South London tunnels, and the drastic decision was taken therefore to reconstruct the whole line to standard dimensions. When major railway civil engineering works are in progress on surface lines, with the exercise of much ingenuity means are devised of keeping a train service going; but it is another matter underground, and virtually impossible in two single line tube tunnels. There was nothing for it but to close the line completely during the enlargement. To lessen the inconvenience the closure was applied in three stages:

The London Rush-Hour: Piccadilly Circus station.

163

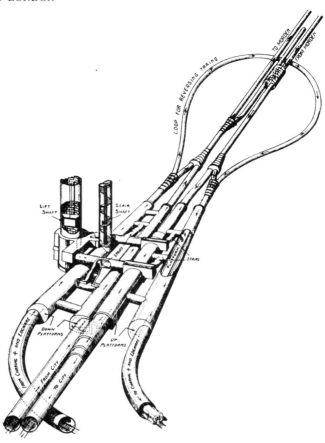

Perspective view of Kennington connections, at junction of Northern and City Lines.

August 1922 to November 1923: Euston–Moorgate.
November 1923 to April 1924: The entire line, from Euston to Clapham Common.
April 1924 to December 1924: Moorgate–Clapham Common.
A special bus service was operated over the closed sections during the enlargement.

The connections to the Charing Cross, Euston and Hampstead line—now known as the Northern Line—involved some highly interesting work at both junction points. At Kennington provision had to be made for trains from both Hampstead and City line trains either to terminate or to continue to Clapham Common. The accompanying perspective drawing shows how it was done, deep underground, without having any conflicting routes. It was a masterly piece of underground surveying. Its counterpart, to the north of Euston, was even more elaborate. There Camden Town was made the exchange point, and trains travelling from the Charing Cross line, or from the City line could be routed northward either to the Golders Green or Highgate lines. Again there were no conflicting crossings, and the burrowing of the tubes beneath each other involved some highly intricate construction work. The accompanying illustration, page 165, explains more than whole chapters the nature of the work involved.

At the same time Lord Ashfield's policy of extending farther into the country suburbs was exemplified by carrying the City and South London outwards to Morden, mostly in tube tunnel, serving Balham, Tooting and South Wimbledon, and coming to the surface only just before the terminus. At roughly the same time the Hampstead line was extended entirely above ground from Golders Green to Edgware. I have vivid recollections of the engineering work involved in this latter project. As a university student it was part of my training to visit works in progress, and a party of us went to Golders Green one fine winter's day, but one which followed a period of heavy rain. We clambered up half finished viaducts and embankments in footwear highly unsuitable to the conditions of mud that prevailed. I learned to my cost the extraordinarily adhesive properties of the London clay, applied when soggy wet and drying afterwards on one's shoes! By the autumn of 1926 therefore tube trains passing through central London were penetrating variously, as far out as Ealing Broadway, Watford, Morden, and Edgware. It was a very notable achievement in railway development, but the

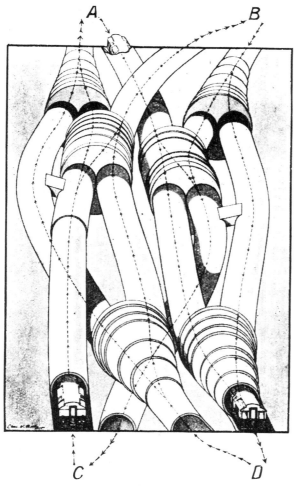

Reproduction of part of poster, showing arrangement of tubes at Camden Town at junction of Northern and City Lines.

increased traffic was bringing heavy pressure to bear upon the carrying capacity of the tube lines in the central area, certain sections of which were, from this time onward, being worked virtually at their limit.

The extensions from both ends of the Piccadilly line, from Finsbury Park to Cockfosters in the north and from Hammersmith westwards to permit of through running by tube trains to Hounslow and South Harrow, were a natural development of the same policy. These were completed by 1932; but on July 1, 1933, the London Passenger Transport Board came into existence, and this change brought to an end the independent existence of the old Metropolitan Railway. It is of interest to recall that when the L.P.T.B. was set up there were five distinct railways still operating underground lines in London. Although there had been close co-ordination, under Lord Ashfield since 1913, as *companies* the Metropolitan District, the City and South London, the Central London, and the London Electric (three Yerkes tubes) had continued to exist; and these four, together with the Metropolitan were now fully amalgamated in the railway system of the L.P.T.B. Lord Ashfield was appointed chairman, and his policies continued without intermission. The big shake-up took place on the Metropolitan, on which details of operation, rolling stock, and fixed equipment differed in many respects from the former 'Ashfield' railways. The most striking evidences of the new regime were to be seen on the surface lines beyond Finchley Road, with which I am not primarily concerned in this book; but some further development of the Ashfield policy was to be seen in the construction of a new 'arm' of the Bakerloo tube, springing from a junction at Baker Street. It was carried northwards beneath the 'country' line of the Metropolitan to surface at Finchley Road, and then form part of a quadruple tracked line to Harrow-on-the-Hill. Bakerloo trains could henceforth run either to Queens Park and Watford over the former L.N.W.R., or take the new line to join the Metropolitan at Finchley Road. Through trains were run to Stanmore, using the new Metropolitan branch from Wembley Park. Needless to say this brought additional pressure on to the central section of the Bakerloo, from Baker Street to the Elephant and Castle, and the means developed for coping with this pressure are described later in Chapter Sixteen.

By the mid-1930s it was only the Central London among the original tube railways that had not 'sprouted' at both ends; but its turn was now coming, and the L.P.T.B. entered into an alliance with the Southern Area of the L.N.E.R. in prompting an extension eastwards from Liverpool Street. It was to prove very much of a combined operation, for the L.N.E.R. had in prospect the electrification of the suburban lines of the former Great Eastern Railway, and the two schemes were planned so as to avoid any proliferation of service. The L.N.E.R. project was to electrify the East Anglian main line as far as Shenfield, and to extend this over the Southend branch; the L.P.T.B. was to extend the Central London tube to make surface connection with the Woodford and Hainault group of Great Eastern suburban lines, as the Bakerloo had done with the L.N.W.R. at Watford. The joint planning of the two administrations agreed that Stratford was a natural and vital exchange point. If the tube line was brought to the surface there interchange could be easy and rapid, just across platforms. Passengers from the Shenfield line could change into tube trains to reach the West End direct, instead of having the far less convenient change at Liverpool Street. Interchange could also be made with steam trains from other parts of the L.N.E.R. suburban area. Beyond Stratford however it was desirable for the Central London line to descend once more into tunnel, for a few miles at least; and this conception led to some of the most interest-

Piccadilly Circus, on the escalators in the evening rush hour.

London Rush Hour: the driver's view when entering Charing Cross station, Northern Line.

167

ing tunnelling work in the history of the London tubes, so far. In the winter of 1938–9 I was privileged to see some of this work at first hand, and although the job of tunnelling with shields was nothing new at that time the nature of the ground provided the engineers with some pretty little problems.

Between Bow and Stratford the course of the Central London extension crosses the delta of the River Lea; the Hackney and Leyton marshes are near at hand, and the river itself is flowing in five separate channels. A deep level tube line would have been a fairly straightforward proposition, but just where this difficult ground was encountered the line was rising to the surface to reach the exchange platforms with the L.N.E.R. at Stratford. It was here that I had an opportunity of seeing the work in progress. In the River Lea area, where the railway was rising to the surface the new line was carried immediately beneath the embankment of the L.N.E.R. main line, and the tubes were carried through some very difficult ground. In a typical location there was ordinary gravel for a few feet, and then after a shallow layer of mottled clay there came a section of silt, stuff that is little removed from wet mud. Not until some depth below the line of the new railway was the hard blue London clay reached.

I was taken into the tunnels down a working shaft adjacent to Pudding Mill river. At this point the line was so near to the surface that a minute's descent on a vertical ladder brought us to the workings. Where the tunnels are driven through water-bearing ground the construction has to be carried on under compressed air and the first business was to go through an air lock, from the open air to the sealed chamber within. Owing to the presence of the L.N.E.R. embankment the working shaft was situated to one side of the line of the new tube railway, and the passageway containing the air lock was at right angles to the tunnels. The passage through the air lock is a strange experience. The chamber itself has a distinctly forbidding look; it is sealed off from the open air, and from the portion of the tunnel already driven, by massive steel doors only about five feet high. Once inside the air pressure is allowed to build up gradually, and the increase is quickly felt by a slight pain in one's eardrums. My guide suggested swallowing repeatedly; this I found a very successful remedy, so that by the time we were up to the working pressure and the inner door came swinging open I had grown more or less accustomed to the unusual conditions. The pressure being used on this particular section was $8\frac{1}{2}$ lb. per sq. in. above atmosphere; this is comparatively low, for on stretches where the actual working face was in 'the water', as they usually termed the silt, an air pressure of 25 lb. per sq. in. above atmosphere was found necessary.

The interior of a tube is a fairly familiar sight nowadays, though when one comes to examine it 'in the raw' so to speak, there are many interesting and perhaps unexpected features in its design. The tunnel walls consist of a series of cast iron rings, each 20in. long, and each complete ring is made in seven sections. These rings have deep flanges on each side through which the adjacent rings are bolted together. The flanges are finished off with a smooth surface so that when adjacent sections are bolted together they make a good joint; the inner edge of the joint is caulked with lead, so that should any water manage to creep through the joint of the flanges none could possibly percolate through into the tunnels. During constructional work the compressed air keeps back all the water, but one cannot retain compressed air when the line is open. The amount of metal used in tube construction is perhaps not generally realised. A single ring weighs roughly 1.2/3 tons, and this is only 20in. long; a mile of single line tunnel weighs over 5000 tons.

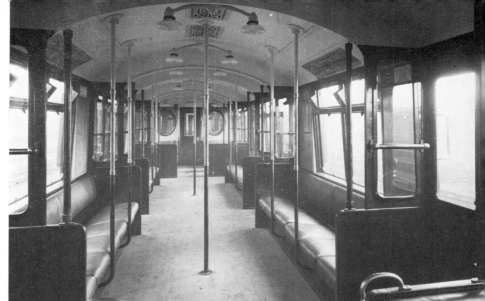

ing Stock Evolution: Interior
20 District Line third class

Interior of 1949 Tube
Stock.

ing Stock Evolution: Interior
60 Metropolitan line stock.

M

The Standard London Transport miniature lever interlocking frame, and colour light signals for electro-pneumatic operation of points, at Cromwell Curve, Gloucester Road.

We now set off towards the working face. Along the completed line of tunnel a light railway was laid, and on this the material excavated was brought to the shafts for conveyance to the surface. One quickly notices too, a slight fogginess in the atmosphere; this is characteristic of tunnels under air pressure. My guide told me that in the sections under high pressure 25 lb. per sq. in. or so, this slight mist develops into a real 'fog'. After about 10 minutes walking on longitudinal planks resting on the cross sleepers of the railway we came to the shield itself. One's first impression is that of the comparatively few men at work. It took a gang of only six men to drive the tunnel for this tube railway.

The shields being used for the construction of this part of the line may be likened to a short length of tubular tunnel, with the addition that the forward end was provided with a hood extending round the upper half of the circle of the tunnel. Before the shield can advance a narrow trench has to be dug in the working face; this trench is semicircular and accommodates the hood of the shield when the latter is pushed forward. The hood also supports the roof. Across the middle of the shield, at right angles to its axis, is a bulkhead that can if necessary be made watertight.

The 'knife', as the hood is sometimes called, is driven forward in steps equal to the length of one tunnel ring. Around the inside of the tubular shield are fixed 20 compressed-air rams, so arranged that their pistons push in a line parallel to the direction

170

of the tunnel. These pistons push against the flange of the last tunnel ring fixed in position. After the shield has advanced, that portion of earth inside the hood has to be excavated. On the particular section I visited all this excavation was being done by hand, and the gravel was shovelled through one of the bulkhead doors into the wagons waiting just outside. While this was being done the pistons of the rams are withdrawn, and a further 20in. long section of tunnel lining can be fitted into position. How much force is necessary to drive the shield takes some realising; the rams work at 3000 lb. per sq. in., and the maximum combined thrust of the dozen of them is just over 600 tons. The rate of progress naturally varied according to the nature of the ground, but when matters were going fairly smoothly an advance of 40in. or two section lengths, during an eight-hour shift represented an average rate. This is equal to about 55ft. per week.

Owing to the nature of the ground it is not always possible to go straight ahead with the full-sized tunnel, which is 12ft. in diameter. An interesting case occurred where the line of tunnel passed very close underneath that channel of the Lea, which is known as Waterworks River. The ground just beneath the river bed was so very 'lively' that it was necessary to inject chemical consolidating matter in order to make it sufficiently solid to drive a tunnel through it, even in compressed air. A fair proportion of this consolidation was applied from above, from a boat, but this was not possible in mid-stream where there is a pier of the bridge carrying the L.N.E.R. Accordingly from the

Camden Junction: Signal box controlling the intersection of the City and South London and Northern Line. The signalman sees none of the trains—only their indications on the illuminated diagram.

171

Central London Line: the north-eastern extension in 1937. View showing air locks leading into section of tunnel constructing under air pressure, between Liverpool Street and Stratford.

Central London Line: constructional work on the L.N.E.R. main line at Stratford where the 'tube' comes to the surface.

172

nearest point reached by the full-sized tube tunnel a pilot tunnel 7ft. in diameter was driven underneath the Waterworks River. From this the chemical consolidation was injected upwards, and the ground thus rendered sufficiently stable for the full-sized tunnel to be constructed.

One of the most complicated pieces of work was necessary just to the east of Stratford station, where the new line, after making a surface connection with the L.N.E.R., was burrowing again. In a very short distance the tracks had to pass under the four-track main line to East Anglia. Head room was not sufficient to drive a tube tunnel, and so the engineers had to resort to the cut-and-cover method. Now it is one thing to build a tunnel in this way when the ground on the surface is clear, or even below a city street as with the Metropolitan, but quite another matter when cutting under one of the busiest main lines of the country! Little by little the L.N.E.R. tracks were underpinned, and the permanent way carried on heavy cross-girders. It was a lengthy process, for to put in the cross-girders entailed complete possession of at least one of the four roads, and that could only be obtained at weekends.

Further complications at this point—if any were needed!—were caused by the bottom of the new cut-and-cover section being 'in the water'. The cross-section of that part of the tunnel was rectangular, and the vertical side walls were based on tubular sections filled with concrete. These foundations were constructed in just the same way as an ordinary tube tunnel, under compressed air. The two foundation tubes were linked together by a third tube of oval section, in which the formation to carry the permanent way was eventually built up. It was hoped that this extension of the 'tube' system would be completed and in operation early in 1940; but the outbreak of World War II postponed work indefinitely and as it turned out the first use of that part of the tunnelling that was finished was not for running trains, but as deep-level air raid shelters.

CHAPTER FIFTEEN

The Moscow Metro

If the city council had had its way Moscow might have had its first metropolitan underground railway at roughly the same time as that of Paris, and several years before the construction of the New York subway. As long ago as the year 1900 the council was discussing it; but as soon as the proposals became known any suggestion of it was immediately ruled out from two quarters that then apparently had far greater authority than the Moscow city council. These were the Russian Imperial Archaeological Society, and the Archbishop of Moscow. Both combined to issue a virtual embargo upon the scheme, upon the grounds that the tunnelling work, and the running of trains underground would gravely endanger the foundations of many churches and buildings of historic interest. Moscow of course was, and still is rich in historical buildings, but not more so than London or Paris; and in Czarist days the general layout in the city centre was far more spacious. One presumes that the outline proposals discussed by the city council provided for the underground railway to run beneath the streets, as elsewhere; but the opposition of the Archbishop and of the Archaeological Society killed the idea stone dead, and it was not until Russian affairs had become stabilised under the Communist regime that further consideration was given to the construction of such a railway.

In the meantime with the rapid growth of the city itself the passenger transport problem was becoming acute. With the number of journeys made on the existing trams and buses rising to more than 1,500,000,000 by 1930 the city council once again turned its attention to an underground railway. This time is received the immediate support of the Central Committee of the Communist Party, and in March 1931 the general scheme of the 'Metro' was sanctioned by the Council of People's Commissars. As in Paris, but totally unlike the situation that had existed for so long in London, the plan for the entire system was worked out at once. In Paris however, while the general scheme for the complete underground network was worked out as a single exercise the actual construction proceeded by stages; only one, or two lines were tackled simultaneously. In Moscow, once the scheme was settled and authorised construction was started of practically all sections at once, to provide 68 miles of underground railway. The general plan of the 'Metro' followed the historic development of the city itself, in which the main highways all radiated from the centre point of the Kremlin. The main line railways, as they were constructed, developed on much the same lines as those of Paris, with many terminal stations, serving lines radiating in almost every direction of the compass, to reach Leningrad, Archangel, Gorki, Kursk, Astrakan, Kiev, Warsaw

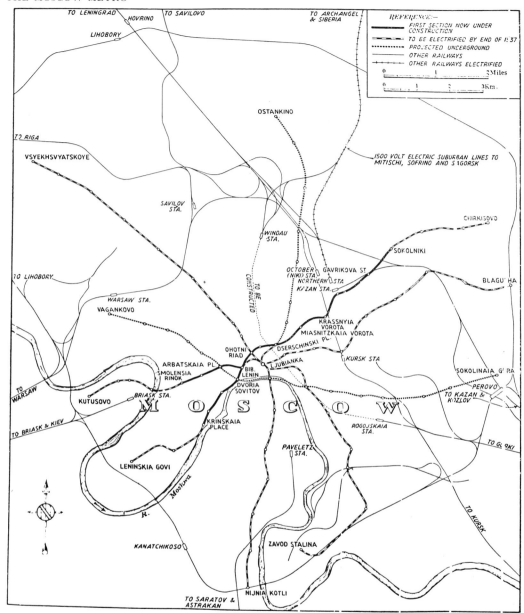

The Moscow Metro: a contemporary plan at the time of the first opening.

and Riga. They were connected on the periphery of the city area by a circular route that was in many respects a counterpart of the Grande Ceinture line around Paris.

The 'Metro' was planned to fill in additional 'spokes' in the wheel of railway communications centred near the Kremlin; but whereas none of the main line termini were situated nearer than about 2 miles from the centre the underground was planned to consist of six diametrical lines, crossing, and in most cases connecting with each other

176

Moscow Metro: Exit stairway at Sokolniki station.

near the city centre, and thus providing no fewer than 10 radiating routes into the suburbs, together with the sixth radial line which linked the Windau and Rogojskaia main line termini. In addition to this radial network, a supplement to the original scheme proposed a 'belt' railway of about $2\frac{1}{2}$ miles in diameter, skirting the city centre, and crossing all the radial lines at interchange stations. The similarity to the Ashfield conception in London will be immediately apparent, if one accepts the Oxford Circus–Piccadilly Circus–Leicester Square triangle as the 'centre'. For there one can see the 'diametrical' lines of the Central London, Piccadilly, Bakerloo and Northern lines crossing one another and inter-connecting by passenger subways, while the London 'Inner Circle' provides the exact counterpart to the Moscow 'belt' line. Actually Soviet engineers made a long and detailed study of the London network before embarking upon their own project, and the fact that the Moscow plan, conceived as a single entity, so closely resembled the complex that had been built up in London in nearly 70 years of unconnected private enterprise, many vicissitudes of fortune, and drastic changes of managerial policy is remarkable. Of course, the London underground of the 1930s had then enjoyed the guiding hand of Lord Ashfield for more than 20 years, and in that time he had succeeded in tying up a great number of the original loose ends.

The general scheme of things in Moscow, at the time the first section of the 'Metro' was under construction is shown in the map on page 176. The first line to be built was that shown in the thick black line, from Sokolniki south-westwards to the city centre, where it forked into two sections leading to temporary terminals at Smolensia Rinok, and Krinskaia Place. This was a potentially very busy route as a beginning, because

177

at the second station from Sokolniki, named Komisornel, ready connection was made with no fewer than three main line termini—the October, Northern and Kazan stations, and an assemblance not unlike the relative proximity of Euston, St. Pancras and Kings Cross, in London. The length of this first section of the Moscow Metro was $7\frac{1}{2}$ miles, of which $5\frac{3}{4}$ miles represented the 'main line' from Sokolniki to Krinskaia Place. The geological formation of the ground made it difficult to reach a decision concerning the method of constructing the tunnels. There were mixed layers of sandy loam, with strata of hard loam, while in places along the projected line of the railway a solid band of limestone existed. The Moscow city authorities conferred with Russian specialists, and with experts from London, Paris, New York and Berlin. The Russian engineers favoured a deep tunnel throughout, on the London tube model, because it would not disturb road traffic, and it would not be subject to the rigours of the Russian winter during the constructional period. Furthermore all the men, equipment, and materials required could be drawn from the Russian mining industry.

It has nevertheless been the experience of those most involved, in tunnelling of any kind that one is always venturing into the unknown, no matter how carefully and scientifically the preliminary surveys are made. Just after World War II there was the remarkable case of the new Woodhead Tunnel on the London and North Eastern Railway, at the summit of the cross-country line between Sheffield and Manchester. Here the new tunnel was bored no more than a dozen yards or so abreast of the original tunnels driven by Joseph Locke when the line was first built. The records of construction were apparently well documented, and the likely troubles well known; yet in relatively modern times and in subterranean conditions believed to be fully understood the engineers struck a wealth of dire trouble. How much more hazardous therefore was the task of boring through unknown ground likely to be! And sure enough the Russians ran into trouble even before the working shafts were sunk to the projected level of the railway. Of the first $7\frac{1}{2}$ miles roughly $3\frac{1}{8}$ miles was planned to run in deep tunnel, with another $3\frac{1}{8}$ miles on a form of 'cut and cover' referred to in contemporary technical literature as the 'Berlin system'.

For the deep level sections which extended from the station Bibliotek Lenin to Komsomolski Platz 40 shafts were sunk to depths of from 50ft. to 130ft. below ground level, and the average length of tunnel driven from each shaft was about 110 yards. Great difficulty was experienced in sinking many of the shafts. In certain cases they had to go down through quicksand, and although the workings were in the centre of wide thoroughfares, the influx of quicksand into the unfinished shafts was so enormous as to cause cavities on the ground that imperilled adjacent buildings, with risks of subsidence. In one case the pressure of this treacherous strata was so great as to cause partial failure of a pallisade of sheet metal piling. I have already referred to the use of compressed air sections when building the London and Glasgow underground railways. In Moscow, compressed air caissons had to be built, and the shafts lined with concrete before they reached fully to the projected line of the railway tunnel. In another case where water and quicksand were present a compressed air-lock was constructed as a working area for sinking the shaft, and below it compressed air was blown into the surrounding ground to lessen the friction involved in driving the lining rings downwards.

To avoid the need for passing through airlocks in ascending or descending through the working shafts, and the consequent delay in conveying men, materials and equip-

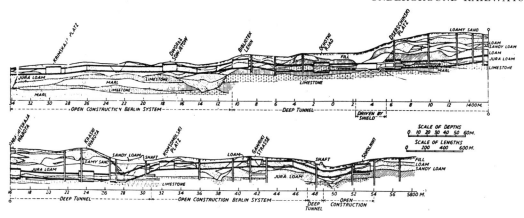

Moscow: a schematic cross-section showing the nature of ground tunnelled through.

ment a technique of freezing the ground encircling the shaft was employed in certain instances. These shafts were mostly around 20ft. in diameter, and where there were tall buildings in close proximity the danger of the shaft caving in unexpectedly was an ever-present hazard. In such cases a high degree of stabilisation during the shaft sinking work was secured by freezing the ground to form a solid wall of ice just over 3ft. thick round the shaft. Then the core of earth inside was excavated, and preparations made to insert a lining of reinforced concrete one foot thick. This brought another problem to the engineers. While the atmosphere in the shaft was at just about freezing point, 32 deg. Fah., the frozen walls of the excavation were no more than 10 to 14 deg. Fah. Now concrete sets most readily at equable summer air temperature of around 60 to 65 deg. Fah. Below 40 deg. the 'mix' then in use set slowly, and below that temperature scarcely at all. So here was a nice little problem! To get the concrete to set satisfactorily it would have to be heated, and naturally if it was then applied to the ice it would cause melting. The difficulty was overcome by first applying a layer of insulating material to the frozen earth; then the concrete was heated electrically, and thus applied it made a satisfactory lining without impairing the solidarity of the ice wall outside. Once the concrete was set it could be allowed to cool down to the air temperature in the shaft.

On this page there is reproduced a geological section of the 'main line' of this first section of the Moscow Underground, and it will be seen that only for a distance of some 400 yards near to the Dserschinski Platz station was the shield form of construction used in the deep level section. Here the line passed beneath the Neglinaja canal and the ground was particularly bad. The shield used for this section was purchased from England, and the experience with it so satisfactory that further ones of similar design were built in Russia to expedite the construction on some of the later lines in the underground network. An interesting feature of the Moscow railway is its use of double line tunnels on the deep-level sections. The stations are of the island type, and from the platform ends the tracks pass through short lengths of single line tunnel of 18ft. internal diameter; these merge into double-line tunnels between the stations. Practically all the excavation was done by hand, and in firm ground, or rock, the 'top heading' method referred to in connection with the New York Subway was used; this involved the driving of what was termed in Moscow a 'crown gallery', and then constructing the

179

THE MOSCOW METRO

arch. After that the lower portion was excavated in the form of procedure described
for New York. Nevertheless boring into the 'unknown' beneath Moscow the engineers
encountered several locations where large quantities of water burst in to cause serious
flooding, while elsewhere there occurred subsidences, in unstable ground. These were
overcome by the introduction of compressed air caissons.

Another method for preventing damage and flooding of the workings in wet and
unstable ground that was satisfactorily applied was the chemical solidification of the
earth. A series of tubes one inch in diameter were driven fanwise into the ground. These
tubes are perforated, and the chemical solutions injected are thus forced through the
perforations in the tubes into the ground. The solutions used set the ground solid in
about 20 minutes, making it completely water-tight and attaining a high mechanical
strength. A shell about 3ft. thick was, by this means, formed around the tunnel profile.
It was not a cheap process, any more than that of freezing the rings around the working
shafts. It was stated that the consumption of chemicals was about 84 gallons per cubic
yard solidified. At a rough estimate this would involve the use of about 6300 gallons of
chemicals for every yard the tunnel advanced. On the sections where this procedure
was used the rate of advance was about $6\frac{1}{2}$ ft. per day. This result must be considered
in relation to the much greater amount of excavation required in a double-line tunnel
for rolling stock much larger than that used in London, and on the Russian gauge of
5ft., against 4ft. $8\frac{1}{2}$in. On the section driven by shield the rate of advance was about

The Moscow Metro: a striking example of station architecture.

Moscow Metro: a night view of Arbatskaia Square Station.

10 to 13ft. per day, in comparatively soft ground. There the tunnels were lined with pre-cast concrete blocks.

On the sections constructed on what was termed the 'shallow tunnel', or Berlin system—another version of the familiar 'cut and cover' method—for one length of more than $1\frac{3}{4}$ miles the street beneath which the 'Underground' is carried was so wide that excavation for the double track railway was made alongside the roadway without any interference with traffic, or the need to underpin any adjoining buildings. The ground water level was between 10 and 15ft. below ground level and the strata encountered included sand, loam, mixed rock, hard rock, and solid clay. Most of the excavating, as in deep tunnels, was done by hand, with no more than a limited use of pneumatic drills.

181

Removal of the spoils was one of the greatest difficulties; most of it was conveyed in wheelbarrows, and it was difficult to co-ordinate the removal from the workings with transport arrangements to clear it away from the sites. Further difficulties arose through the necessity to continue constructional work through the depths of the Moscow winter. The open cuttings in the streets were covered with planks and insulating material, and steam heating applied liberally below ground; but the difficulties over removal of spoil were sometimes accentuated when it could not be quickly cleared after being wheeled away from the excavations. Large heaps of spoil became frozen solid, and had to be re-broken before it could be moved. All this, it will be appreciated, required a large labour force, and on this first section of the Moscow Underground, only $7\frac{1}{2}$ miles, the number of men regularly employed was 30,000.

The 'cut and cover' sections, both of the shallow tunnel (Berlin) type and of the shallow subway (Paris) type, were made 25ft. wide, with a headway of 12ft. 9in. above rail level. At the stations, of course, the width was much greater, extending in certain cases to 82ft. and there some diversion from the straight, and underpinning of buildings was necessary. There were however some sections where the ground water level was so deep that there was no risk of infiltration or flooding, and the open trench system of excavation could be used, without any protective side piling, as in the so-called 'Berlin' method. On the 'shallow subway' sections the space for the tunnel walls was first excavated by digging two trenches of the full depth. Then the walls were built, in concrete, and the roof added, after which excavation could proceed between the walls and under the roof. Taking all in all the constructional methods used on the first sections of the Moscow Underground were of much interest in the examples they provided of procedures adapted not only to the physical conditions of ground and extremes of climate, but in use of indigenous materials and machinery.

The stations have no counterparts on underground railways anywhere in the world. The main objects sought in developing the station designs were to provide friendly and convenient room for the public, and to avoid any suggestion of a 'basement', let alone a drain! There was, from the outset no attempt at standardisation, rather the reverse. Each station on the original line was built to individual designs of leading Russian architects, and the results were striking, to say the least of them. The only thing in common was the huge sign 'METRO' outside! I have not had the opportunity of visiting Moscow personally; but the accompanying photographs, reproduced on pages 177, 180 and 181 convey something of the air of extreme opulence that characterises the Moscow Metro from end to end. The walls, roof and pillars of most of the stations are covered with white and pink marble, some columns being partly covered in black marble by way of contrast, while in some stations artificial lighting is supplied through a roof of coloured glass. The interchange stations, with their spacious open staircases, wide platforms, lofty ceilings and soft diffused lighting are as far removed from the normal London conception of an interchange station—such as Leicester Square, or Holborn—as one could possibly imagine. In London one is always 'in the tube'; in Moscow it is hardly ever so. Whether such incredibly lavish stations were really necessary is another matter; but economies apart, the Moscow railway is unquestionably the most *beautiful* underground system in the world.

Coming now to its engineering features and operation, the intense involvement of the U.S.S.R. in World War II naturally retarded development, but by the year 1962 there were some 50 miles of line open, and more were under construction. The system of electrification was 750 volts direct current with traction return through the running rails, as originally provided on the Central London, and at present standard on the electrified system of British Railways, Southern Region. Later information is that the voltage has now been increased to 850. The trains used on the first section opened consisted of two-car units, with one motor and one trailer car. These could be built up on the multiple unit principle to a maximum of eight car trains. The cars themselves were 61ft. long, and provided seating for 55 passengers, on longitudinal seats. As the cars were no less than 8ft. 10in. wide there was ample space between the seats for standing, and it was expected that a maximum of 250 passengers could be accommodated in each car in the rush hours. This meant a total of something like 2000 passengers to a train. With automatic colour light signalling that was designed to permit the running of 48 trains per hour the new line was able to carry quite a lot of people in the rush hours!

The general layout of the original cars was interesting. Each had four sets of double sliding doors on each side, providing a 4ft. wide opening. Operating of these doors was entirely controlled by the driver, through small pneumatic door-engines. At first the seats were not upholstered, though handsomely finished in polished oak. The side walls were finished in mahogany, and glass shields were fitted adjacent to the door openings to protect seated passengers from being unduly disturbed by those entering and leaving. The external appearance was very smart. The cars were painted blue with a silver waistband under the windows, and a grey roof. The traction motors had a total of 820 horsepower for each 2-car set, so that a maximum length 8-car train had 3280 motor horsepower available. The motor coaches weighed about 49 tons, and the trailers $32\frac{1}{2}$ tons, and contemporary literature suggested that when fully loaded these weights would be 69 and 52 tons respectively—a remarkable increase. One normally reckons passengers at 15 to the ton, when estimating the increase over tare weight to be provided for in fully laden coaches. The suggested increase of 20 tons in each case would mean 300 passengers and even with the spacious layout of the new coaches this would be a pretty jam. Otherwise one can only assume that the average Muscovite travelling on the 'Metro' in the mid-1930s weighed about 13 stone—men, women and children alike. The maximum speed of these original trains was 32 m.p.h., providing a scheduled average speed of 16 m.p.h.

The later stock introduced in 1950, had greatly improved operating characteristics. In the Type 'G' trains the tare weight of the motor cars was reduced to 44 tons, and in the later series 'D' this was further reduced to 36 tons. These latter have a maximum speed of 47 m.p.h. and a headway of $1\frac{1}{2}$ minutes between trains is being maintained during the busiest periods. At the present time there are about 1500 cars, motor and trailer, working on the 'Metro', and they carry an average of around 3 million passengers a day. With the improved rolling stock now in service the overall speed from end to end of each line is about 25 m.p.h., though in comparison to London this is in greater measure due to the longer distances between stations than to higher maximum speed of the trains themselves.

CHAPTER SIXTEEN

London: Towards Automation

The fourth decade of this century was a time of notable advance in railway signalling practice all over the world, and on all kinds of railways. The attention of operating men was attracted to the systems of remote control being applied to lengthy stretches of line in remote territories in the Middle-West and Western states of the U.S.A., and the British associates of American manufacturing companies pioneering these developments were busy scanning their own markets for possible applications of similar apparatus. An opportunity presented itself in the projected Stanmore branch of the Metropolitan Railway. This was planned originally as a double track line running from a junction with the main line at Wembley Park. Colour light signalling was to be installed throughout; but instead of having a signal box to control terminating and reversing movements at Stanmore itself the signalling arrangements were designed on the remote control principle known commercially as 'Centralised Traffic Control', or C.T.C. It was necessarily a trial installation; an opportunity for British engineers to become familiar with a novel technique, and as such it marks an important milestone in British signalling history. The fact that it took place on a surface, and not on an underground line, and that it was in any case short lived may suggest that any reference to it is out of place in this book. But it postulated a principle that was developed to a high degree of perfection in later years on the busiest underground lines in London.

The terminus at Stanmore was operated without the attention of a signalman on the spot. The man controlling the working was at Wembley Park, $4\frac{1}{2}$ miles away. With the general introduction of illuminated track diagrams there was, by that time, nothing unusual in traffic being worked without the signalman seeing the actual trains. The faithful indication of their presence and movement on the illuminated diagrams was entirely adequate for purposes of traffic regulation. When it came to longer distances from the controlling signal boxes however economics began to enter into it, in the form of the cost of the cable. For carrying the currents necessary for point operation the cables were of no inconsiderable size, and while a layout like that of the Camden Town junctions could be readily designed for control over direct wires, with no function more than a hundred yards or so from the signal box, it was another matter when cable had to be carried for several miles. It was in this respect that the American principle of C.T.C. sparked off a new, and wholly British development in the way of remote control.

As in the days of the District line electrification, so in the exacting years from 1930 onwards the London Underground claimed some of the most outstanding personalities in the signalling world. Peter had been succeeded, as signal engineer of the Ashfield

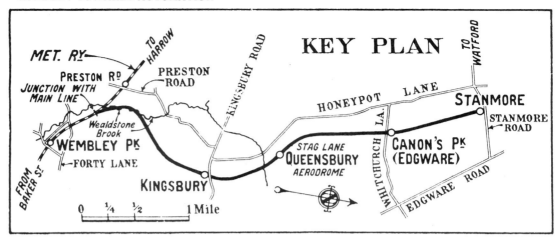

Metropolitan Railway: the Stanmore Branch.

group by Philip Whysall and in 1919 he in turn was succeeded by W. S. Every. It was the latter very able engineer who began the 'modernisation', of an already very modern system. The management of the London Underground held the philosophy that a collision was unthinkable in the confined spaces of the tube tunnels, or indeed anywhere on this very heavily worked railway; and in consequence the financial allocation to signalling each year was more generous than on the main line railways. Every and his staff certainly took full advantage of this attitude, and as the years went by every device that human ingenuity could produce to lessen still further the risk of failure was adopted. I have heard engineers from other administrations speak a trifle scornfully of what they regarded as extravagance in signalling equipment on the Underground; but one has always got to study this against that inexorable background of packed trains following each other through the tube tunnels at intervals of less than 2 minutes, and attaining speeds of about 45 m.p.h. between stations. There is another factor that is sometimes not appreciated, and that is the very limited time available for maintenance. All routine work has to be done in the middle of the night, and the fact that so much of the apparatus is housed in the sheltered climatic conditions of the tube tunnels does not provide immunity from an occasional ducking. For to assist in keeping the atmosphere fresh the tubes are hosed down every night!

At the time of the formation of the London Passenger Transport Board Major R. F. Morkill was signal engineer of the Metropolitan Railway. Prior to joining that railway, in 1925, he had wide experience of signalling in Canada, South Africa, and with the Railway Operating Division of the British Army during World War I. It was, no doubt, his broad outlook—far beyond that of London commuter problems—that influenced his decision to try the American form of C.T.C. on the Stanmore branch. When the L.P.T.B. was formed however W. S. Every was by some years senior to Morkill in office, in addition, of course, to being signal engineer of the 'group' that was henceforth to call the tune on the Board, and Every naturally secured the post of signal engineer of the L.P.T.B. From that time onwards the signalling and operating methods on the Metropolitan lines were gradually brought into line with District and 'tube' practice. An early decision was to standardise the method of point operation. From the time of

186

Night maintenance work in the tubes. Routine changing of signalling relays.

Night maintenance work: adjustments to electro-pneumatic point mechanism at Cromwell Curve.

electrification of the District Railway the Westinghouse electro-pneumatic system had been used in all the tunnel sections—even extending, as previously mentioned in Chapter Nine, to pneumatic working of the light signals in the tunnels. When the Hampstead line was extended from Golders Green to Edgware, entirely on the surface, a trial had been made of all-electric point operation, to obviate the need for carrying an air main out in the country. Furthermore, the Metropolitan Railway had standard-ised electric, rather than electro-pneumatic working of points. But the experience gained by Every and his staff on the Edgware line convinced them of the advantages to be derived from complete standardisation of the electro-pneumatic system, and this was applied, as opportunity presented itself throughout the Metropolitan lines.

In the meantime another outstanding Underground engineer was coming to the fore in the person of Robert Dell. His ingenuity in designing equipment to suit the particular conditions of the L.P.T.B. railways brought him rapidly to the position of a senior assistant to Every, and the widest possible experience both 'inside' and throughout the operating network of the London underground railways developed in him a remarkably even balance between the intricacies of mechanical and electrical design, and what was a thoroughly sound proposition for installation and maintenance. An early example of this, before even the L.P.T.B. was set up, was the introduction of relays with detach-able terminal boards. The vital function of relays in the increasingly elaborate signalling circuits was resulting in an ever-increasing number of wire connections requiring to be made to them. If a relay had to be removed for maintenance or repair much valuable time was taken up in disconnecting all these wires, and attaching them to the replace-ment unit. Furthermore, the most careful checking had to be carried out subsequently to make sure none of the wires had been inadvertently attached to the wrong terminals. This if course could have disastrous results. Dell conceived the idea of making the mechanism—the section of the instrument containing the moving parts—separate from the terminal board, and capable of being jacked in. Then, when removal was necessary no wires need be disconnected; the mechanism could be unjacked, and a new one substituted in a matter of minutes. This principle proved a great success in practice, and it was extended to many other items of equipment. The pneumatic cylinders of point mechanisms and train stops, for example, were in future designed so that they could be removed without disconnecting any air pipes.

The years from 1935 onwards witnessed the introduction of push-button control panels for main signal boxes in a few notable instances on the British main line railways, incorporating interlocking through electrical circuits instead of through the old-established mechanical mechanisms. The highest degree of safety was built into these so-called relay-, or circuit-interlockings, and the concentration of control they pro-vided, and the miniaturisation of the equipment appealed to the majority of railway operating men and signal engineers, at a time when costs were rising. The reduction in size of the control instruments had a particular attraction for Underground men, where, as Every once exclaimed at a meeting of engineers: 'God knows what it costs to dig a hole in the ground!' In apparatus however, like for like, it was considered that relay interlocking was more expensive than the older standard methods of using a miniature lever frame, and Dell himself was strongly averse to using electrical methods for the vital function of the lever interlocking. He was to prove himself one of the most advanced thinkers of the profession, yet in all the developments that followed he stuck resolutely to simple mechanical locking for maintaining the integrity of the point and

188

Robert Dell, O.B.E. F.I.E.E. Past-President, Institution of Railway
Signal Engineers.

signal operational control. At the same time he appreciated the advantages to be derived from panel operation of large areas, from the viewpoint of the actual tasks performed by the signalman, and he developed, on certain of the surface lines of the L.P.T.B. a system of remote control, that with subsequent refinements was to be widely adopted on the underground sections later. I should mention that on the retirement of W. S. Every in 1940 he became Joint Signal Engineer, with Major Morkill, and in 1942 assumed the supreme command.

In applying the principle of panel operation he had predominantly in mind the need for rapid restoration in case of any failure, and for simplicity in maintenance. The late 1930s were a time of increasing awareness of the danger of war, and it was quite clear that a single bomb could completely immobilise a panel interlocking. While not ruling out the attractive principle on that account he sought means of continuing work as quickly as possible after any untoward incident. His determination to retain mechanical interlocking between vital functions *plus* the strategic needs, largely prompted the form of the first L.P.T.B. remote control schemes. Miniature-lever power interlocking frames, with mechanical locking, would be installed in small signal boxes adjacent to the junctions concerned, but these frames would be so designed that they could be operated without human aid, by remote control, from a central panel. In the event of any severing of the remote control wiring or damage to the central instrument, a signal-man could be put into the small box, and work the frame in the normal manner. Although the incorporation of the additional mechanism for remote control into those locking frames involved some intricate, and relatively expensive design the saving of manpower in operating such a group of interlockings was important at a time when there was an increasing shortage of skilled operating staff. The accompanying plan shows how the principle was applied at Harrow-on-the-Hill, with three small remotely-controlled locking frames of 35, 47, and 35 levers normally actuated remotely from a central control panel.

In the remote control of these miniature lever frames the action of a man pulling the

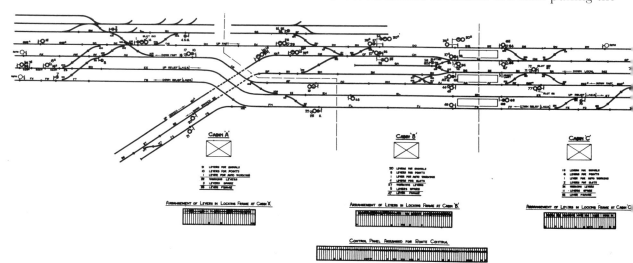

Signalling arrangements at Harrow, including power-worked, remote-controlled interlocking frames.

levers had to be simulated. I need not go into the finer points of the design work that was involved—nor of the grey hairs developed by some of us who were involved! But in basic essentials the push and pull movement was provided by small pneumatic cylinders, controlled by electrical currents transmitted from the central push-button panel. Like all Dell's innovations, once the initial headaches were surmounted it worked with complete reliability. Small though the standard miniature lever frames were they were not ideal for space economy, where one had to dig a hole underground, and the next step was to produce the so-called 'interlocking machine'. This in all essentials was exactly the same as the remotely controlled power frame except that it was arranged with everything within a very narrow vertical 'slice', so as to be accommodated in a restricted space—not flat against a wall, for there had to be room for a man to get behind it, but with no more than that. Again the interlocking between the levers was entirely mechanical, and the remote actuation by means of small air cylinders. Both with this form of interlocking machine, and with the older and more conventional form of interlocking frame, all the vital signalling equipment was close at hand; but the remote control, which merely acted as the initiator, from the push button panel, was contained in very small, and cheap telephone wiring, and the impulses transmitted by the functioning of small, cheap, Post Office type relays. Dell emphasised the difference in the equipment for the vital signalling and interlocking circuits connected with the interlocking machines, and the non-vital transmission between the central panel and the interlocking machine controls. If, in telephone parlance, the signalman or the apparatus transmitted a 'wrong number' to the interlocking machine the safety features inherent in the latter would make it incapable of responding. But more picturesquely, if the interlocking machine was asked to set up a dangerous condition it just would not play!

The gradual introduction of these remotely controlled interlocking machines was only a step on the fascinating road to complete automation. The next one was the automatic working of junctions. Train operation on the London Underground lines is probably the most precisely regulated to be found anywhere in the world. The occasions of hold-up are so rare that they create 'front-page news' when they occur. It was this regularity that led to the conception of automatic junction working. It was first tried out in a very simple and innocuous way, at trailing layouts. On some of the main line railways the practice of having 'loose' trailing points is used. The switches are unconnected by rodding to any operating mechanism, and a train 'trails' them for whatever direction it is approaching. For example, if a train is trailing in from the left hand road at a converging junction, and the points are lying for the right hand direction the leading wheels of the locomotive, or motor coach, push the 'loose' points over, or 'trail' them, as it is termed. In certain cases where the preponderance of running at such a junction is for one of the two converging lines the points are held by a spring to be normal for the busiest route. When a train from the less-busy route trails through the points are pushed over against the spring.

This method of obviating the need for any operating mechanism for trailing points could not be used very well on the tube lines, where the trains themselves are very light, in relation to the heavy standard permanent way, and the first step towards automatic working was to provide for power working of the switches by the standard electro-pneumatic mechanism controlled on a 'first come, first served' principle. As an actual example the trailing junction at Baker Street on the Bakerloo Tube may be taken.

191

There, the two 'country' lines, the one from Watford and the other from the Metropolitan Extension line converge. On these two lines 'check-in' track circuits are installed at an appropriate distance from the actual junction, and if the first train to arrive on either of these was one on the Watford line the checking-in action would set the trailing points for this train, and when they were proved electrically to have moved correctly the signal reading over the junction would clear and the train could proceed. If in the meantime a train from the Metropolitan Extension line checked-in also, electrical interlocking between the junction controls would prevent any interference with the route already set up for the Watford line train, until that train had actually passed over the junction, and cleared into the section ahead. Any risk of a collision on the junction through one train inadvertently over-running a signal at danger is eliminated by the existence of the automatic train stop. If the signal were at danger the arm of the train stop would be in the raised position, in accordance with the standard practice, and in the event of an over-run the trip arm on the brake gear would be struck. This causes a full emergency application of the brakes and the train would be brought to rest short of the point where its presence could cause a collision.

Nevertheless, the 'first come, first served' method of working trailing junctions automatically was no more than a very preliminary first step. The main objective was to work *facing* junctions automatically and thus eliminate the need for signalling at small

One of the latest type of electro-pneumatic train stops, with cover removed for routine inspection. The trip arm can be seen in the raised position.

192

One of the new type Interlocking machines replacing the conventional form of lever frame: Watford Junction, Metropolitan Extension Line.

Camden Junction: a battery of programme machines, regulating traffic automatically according to time-table.

A close-up of a programme machine showing the roll containing destinations of successive trains.

interlockings, of which the example of Baker Street, on the Bakerloo tube line is no more than one among many. One method of doing this would have been to introduce some method of link-up between the train description apparatus and the junction working. Still referring to the Bakerloo line, northbound trains originating from the Elephant and Castle are 'described' for the purpose of displaying the first and second train destinations on the illuminated platform indicators: and of course these destinations would determine the routes to be followed at the facing junction at Baker Street. Before the days of automatic junction working it was the responsibility of the signalman at the Elephant and Castle to set up the train descriptions of northbound departing trains, which would be then transmitted sequentially along the line. In the normal run of day-to-day working the sequence of trains is exactly to timetable, and Robert Dell developed the idea of pre-setting the entire day's programme, and enabling it to be run without any human intervention.

He invented an apparatus known as a 'Programme Machine', which carries, on a punched tape, full details of the train service for an entire day. There would need to be one of these programme machines for every pair of points, facing or trailing, and from the information contained on the tape it would set the routes for the trains over a junction in timetable order. Each train, on passing, would cause the tape to be advanced one step, thereby initiating any change in the setting of the points that may be required for the next succeeding train. At the same time it was of course appreciated that any such form of automation would require the most careful 'supervision'. Machines can misbehave, and with a device depending upon sequential stepping utter chaos in the way of train delays and wrong setting up of routes could ensue. There could never be any danger of collision, because however remote and automatic the controls the ultimate safety of train running over the junctions is ensured by the interlocking machines with their mechanical interlocking mechanisms. To provide the necessary surveillance and supervision of areas under Programme Machine working small supervisory control rooms were established, with illuminated track diagrams showing the whereabouts of every train.

Even in the supervision however a high degree of automation was introduced. The controller in one of these rooms could be a very busy man, often with a score of trains at once on the illuminated diagram covering an extended area. And so the programme machines had a feature included in them for automatically drawing attention to any irregularities in the working. For instance, if a train on its programme is more than a predetermined number of *seconds* late in arriving at the junction it sounds an alarm, to draw the controller's attention. Conversely, but without drawing anyone's attention, it delays the clearing of a starting signal if a train should arrive before its time. This might appear unlikely on so intensely worked a system as the London tubes; but at 'off peak' periods station times could be cut below normal, and a train proceed through the automatic sections quickly to arrive at a junction before its scheduled times. If it was working on the 'first come, first served' system, it could take the road ahead of one from the converging route that it would normally have followed, and so throw the planned sequence out of gear. The programme machine also provides a continuous check on the correct operation of the train describers and of the destinations displayed on the illuminated platform indicators.

This fascinating conception of programme machine working, so successfully applied now on many London Underground lines, is not confined to the relatively simple track

Servicing a programme machine in the relay room at Parsons Green.

The Leicester Square Control Room, where lines under programme-machine control are under constant surveillance.

layouts of the tube lines. The equipment of the programme machines enables them to deal with the case of a train originating from an intermediate point on the route, such as starting out from a siding. Then the interposing of such a train into the sequence already flowing is accompanied by appropriate changes in the destinations and descriptions displayed on the platform indicators. Then, in connection with late running, the machine can have features designed into it to enable a train that is waiting to be signalled forward, out of sequence, if the preceding train is late by a predetermined amount. The controller, having been advised by the audible alarm signal of the late running, could if necessary forestall the automatic changing of the sequence; but if he does not find it necessary to do this, the programme machine having signalled the waiting train forward, out of sequence, stores the information that this has been done in an electronic 'memory', and when the late train does arrive it is duly inserted in the first convenient part of the sequence and its destination displayed appropriately on the platform indicators.

London Transport were so confident of this epoch-marking innovation that they authorised its installation in a big way from the very outset, and it was applied to the alternative routes afforded by the Northern and City and South London lines through the very centre of London. The programme machine working extended from the celebrated quadruple junctions at Camden Town over the City and West End routes via Bank, and Charing Cross respectively, to their convergence once again at Kennington. In addition to the programme machine working at Camden Town and Kennington there was a further installation at Euston, where some of the trains running over the City line terminated. The facility for interposing trains into the programme was utilised here. The control room for this installation was sited at Leicester Square, and it was equipped with a complete illuminated diagram; a set of push buttons, to enable the routes to be set by hand if necessary; the set of 'alarms' from the programme machines, by which the controller is notified of any irregularity in the working, and finally the facility to cancel any train off the programme, in the event of stock not being available, or from any other mischance.

The extent of the Northern and City line programme machine installation, with no signalmen at all, and with only a single controller keeping an eye on the smooth working from the supervisory room at Leicester Square was no more than a start in the application of this remarkable technique. Although it is carrying the story of the development through the 1950s, and ahead of strict chronological order so far as underground railways in other countries are concerned, it has been stated that the ultimate intention is to invest control of the entire working of London Transport railways in Central London in no more than four supervisory control and regulating rooms as follows:

A. Metropolitan and Bakerloo.
B. Northern and Victoria Lines.
C. District and Piccadilly.
D. Central Line and its extensions.

At this stage it is perhaps expedient to refer only to Group C. leaving the wider conception to Chapter 19, in which I deal specifically with the Victoria Line, and its developments. At the time when I had an opportunity of seeing the works the arrangements on the District and Piccadilly Lines had reached the stage of putting the complicated western extremities of the old Metropolitan District Railway under programme

197

Interlocking machines in the 'tube'; automatically controlled signal box at Kennington.

machine operation from South Kensington through to its western connections with the Southern Region of British Railways, at Turnham Green and Putney Bridge, and to the complex of junctions at Acton Town.

But just imagine an area of this extent and complexity worked entirely by programme machines, with no signalmen! South Kensington, Gloucester Road and High Street Kensington; Earls Court, and the whole of the Wimbledon line as far as Putney Bridge; the link-up between the Piccadilly and the District lines at Hammersmith; the junctions with the Southern at Turnham Green, and finally Acton Town, where the flexibility of programme machine working must have extended to something near its limit, by the occasional interposition of *steam* hauled work trains in and out of the large carriage works at Acton. London Transport had indeed bought up a number of ex-Great Western 0-6-0 passenger tank engines that were used for yard shunting and general works both at Acton and Neasden; and many a time when we were deeply involved in the technicalities of preparation for the new Victoria Line it seemed an anachronism to see these little engines go puffing past the windows of Robert Dell's office at Acton getting, miraculously(!), a path provided by the programme machines amid the swarm of fast-stepping multiple-unit electric trains. One of my associates in those days dealing particularly with the braking techniques on the new trains, was an ex-steam man, whose railway career began at St. Rollox works, Glasgow. More than once I noticed his eyes straying to the windows, as one of the steam pannier tank engines went skipping past!

On the lines equipped for programme machine working the lineside signalling still remained standard. On the open sections of the District colour lights had gradually replaced the old electro-pneumatic semaphores, and the more modern type of automatic train stops replaced the original District Railway pattern. Although automation had advanced to a marked degree the time had not yet come for the signals to drive the trains—though London Transport was a surprisingly short time in arriving at that epoch-marking stage as is told in a later chapter of this book.

Automatic Fare Collection in London: a typical group of turnstiles.

Automatic Fare Collection: the ticket hall at Oxford Circus.

CHAPTER SEVENTEEN

Post War Europe: Rome—Paris—Milan

In 1938, in the high-noon of Fascist Italy, there were great preparations for a stupendous World Exhibition to be held on the outskirts of Rome. Those preparations included an underground railway from the city centre to the Porta Sao Paula, and then rising to the surface before reaching the station that was to serve the exhibition grounds. In the character of the *braggardocio* who then led the Italian nation—very much by the nose!—the Rome underground railway was to have been 'the last thing' in urban transport; but from 1939 onwards *Il Duce*, and his master in Berlin became entangled in other matters, and neither the World Exhibition nor the Rome Metro were completed. Many years later, when events had become more or less normal in Italy consideration was given once again to the partly finished underground railway in Rome, and it was appreciated that it would fulfil a very useful function, regardless of whether the project of a World Exhibition was revived, or not. The city terminus had been sited conveniently adjacent to the Central Station of the Italian State Railways, and it was to run beneath the Via Cavour to the Colosseum, and thence south westwards to the Porta Sao Paula. The line as actually constructed extended for $6\frac{1}{2}$ miles, to a terminus in the suburb of Laurentina. It was brought into service in February 1955.

The purely underground section, which is $3\frac{3}{4}$ miles long, is constructed somewhat on the Parisian model with double line tunnels throughout. Technically, it is operated on 1500 volts, direct current, with overhead line, of a seemingly very light and inconspicuous appearance. When first introduced, the service of six trains per hour was operated mostly with 2-car sets. Unlike the majority of underground railway systems nearly all the coaches are motored. When I travelled on the line recently the rolling stock consisted of 40 motor coaches, but only 8 trailers. The running is smart, and the scheduled time for the journey of $6\frac{1}{2}$ miles is 15 minutes, with 7 intermediate stops. The cars are pleasantly styled, in light blue, with a streamlined effect produced by introduction of dark blue 'waves' at the front end; and the travelling is smooth and quiet. But I must admit I found the general atmosphere of the 'Metropolitana di Roma' somewhat clinical and chilling. It was certainly pleasant at first to descend from the glare of the sun and from the hot streets into the cool stations below; but very quickly the effect of that unrelievedly grey *décor* tended to strike a chill in one. A plethora of garish advertisements on the walls of an underground station can irritate, as well as amuse; but underground at 'Colosseo' station, where we had evidently just missed a train, in that nigh-ten minute wait one missed also the gay London advertisements of theatres and films, and the admonitions—indirectly expressed, of course!—to drink

The Rome Metro: a typical station and train.

more beer. There was not even the homely odour of garlic! Then, of course, we never had occasion to use the Rome Metro in the rush hours. If commuting Italians talk as much as they do in long-distance main line trains then I can well imagine there would be an abundance of vitality, and noise, to off-set the igloo-like atmosphere of the stations themselves.

In the same decade when Rome was inaugurating its first underground railway, that in Paris was still being extended, and a very interesting development was included on Line 11. This runs from the Place du Chatelet to Maria des Lilas. It was a time when to combat the loss of traffic due to the vast upsurge in private motoring railway managements in all the advanced countries of the world were looking to means of making railway travel more attractive. There were studies towards the provision of greater amenities, and these studies extended not only to smoother riding, more pleasing interior *décor* and comfortable seating, but to reduction of noise. The Continental underground railways were behind London in these respects; and in Paris the noise of the Metro trains running on the open viaduct sections could always be heard above the clangour of steam operation in the Gare du Nord. It is even more pronounced since the Nord has changed to electric operation. It is the same where Metro trains climb out of the bowels of the earth, and cross the Seine by the Austerlitz bridge. Part of this is undoubtedly due to the reverberation from the viaducts themselves; but the trains seem inherently noisy—at least the older ones do!

For Line 11 the Metro authorities decided to use trains running on pneumatic tyres. Each coach has two 2-axle bogies. In the ordinary way one talks of 4-*wheeled* bogies, but these cars have such a multiplicity of wheels that the running gear cannot be so simply described. The bogies themselves are entirely welded, and rest on their axles through a primary rubber suspension. There is a secondary suspension consisting of helical springs. The normal running wheels have pneumatic tyres, similar to those used

202

on large lorries, and these run on wooden rails, made of a special timber known as Azobe. On the same axle are two railway-type wheels that are normally idle. These are brought into contact with steel rails only in cases of emergency, as if one got a puncture in one of the pneumatic tyres. The steel rails, and the so-called safety wheels are much lighter than would be used for normal railway running. In addition to this system of dual wheels there are also guide wheels, which press sideways against vertical guide rails fixed on both sides of the track. All this certainly seems a very elaborate arrangement to reduce noise; but various other advantages are claimed for this novelty. The fundamental point is the character of the cars themselves was changed from that of a railway to that of a road vehicle.

It is not generally appreciated how essentially different the two forms of vehicle must be. Travelling smoothly in a fast express train may seem very similar, to the passenger, to travel in one of the most up-to-date road coaches, on a well-built motorway. But between the passenger himself and the surface over which he is travelling there is a wealth of vastly different mechanical engineering design. Passengers apart, engineers found this out the hard way when an attempt was made to use standard road-vehicle components in some of the earliest diesel locomotives and railcars. To the astonishment of certain well-known diesel manufacturers the components rattled themselves to bits in record time. They then came to appreciate that steel wheels on a steel rail are not quite the same thing as pneumatic tyres on a concrete or macadamised road surface. Appreciating however that road vehicle construction was somewhat lighter the engineers of the Paris Metro decided to try putting the process into reverse, and run some of their trains on pneumatic tyres, even though a number of complications would necessarily be involved. It was estimated that the cost of these would be outweighed by the savings made in the cost of the lighter vehicles, and in the improved performance. At the same time travellers on the tube trains of London Transport on the open sections of the line will be aware of some incidental effects of weight reduction in the stock, and how the coaches tend to bounce their way along when loaded into something short of a maximum complement of passengers.

On the Paris Metro some further advantages are claimed for the use of pneumatic tyres, namely that better adhesion between the wheel and rail enables more rapid acceleration to be achieved, and braking characteristics to approximate to those of an automobile. The rate of retardation was stated to be $4\frac{3}{4}$ft. per second. Now this will be an abstract figure to many readers; but in amplifying it to the extent of saying the maximum normal deceleration with electric trains is around 3ft. per second the implications of such a rapid slowing up must be considered far more than a matter of simple mathematics. Such a rate of deceleration would be nothing out of the ordinary in a road vehicle; the passengers in a motor coach, or in a private car would be seated, or protected to endure such a rapid stop, but it is another matter in a train. While a crowded Metro train has many points of similarity to a crowded bus, or street car, a deceleration of $4\frac{3}{4}$ft. per second, is a bit 'hot', and one would expect that it would only be resorted to in emergency. One could well imagine that after such an application most of the standing passengers would end in a heap at the leading end of the car! I shall have more to say about pneumatic tyred underground railways when I come to Montreal.

Reference to rush-hour traffic however brings me back to the standard train-consist on Line 11 of the Paris Metro. On this line the 4-car train sets are made up as follows:

Paris Metro: Train with pneumatic tyres.

Paris: a modern control cabin at one of the terminating points, the Porte d'Orleans
on Line 4. The arrangement of the tracks to provide run-round facilities can be seen on the
illuminated diagram.

one motor coach, second class, with driver's cab; one trailer, composite; one motor coach, second class; one motor coach, second class, with driver's cab. The coaches have a seating for a total of 214 first and second class passengers, but in the rush hour it is claimed that another 347 can be accommodated standing. While the seating arrangements in the first class are naturally more lavish, and provide for no more than 89 passengers, the total for a 4-car train, packed to its limit, is around 560 people! The tare weight of a 4-car train is only 81 tons, and with a packed compliment of passengers it would be necessary to add another 37 tons. This is surely a record increment of gross over tare weight for a railway carriage. On a main line express train, not of the super-luxury, but of the ordinary type one reckons an increase of 10 per cent over tare weight for a full complement of passengers, while in a crowded non-corridor suburban train the increase might be as much as 20 per cent; but in a really packed pneumatic-tyred train on Line 11 of the Paris Metro the increase could be 46 per cent.

A still further innovation for a Continental underground line was introduced with the inception of the Milan Metro in 1964. To appreciate the features of this interesting railway one must also be aware of the rapidly changing sociological conditions in most of the advanced countries of the world. There was a general shortage of labour; its cost was rising, and its standard of reliability certainly not increasing, while on the other hand technological advances were very much on the increase. It was, furthermore, the experience of all administrations dealing with mass transportation that 'fare-dodging' was very much on the increase. The difficulties in obtaining staff were inevitably resulting in a lessening of the degree of scrutiny that could be maintained over the crowds of passengers entering and leaving stations in the peak periods, with the natural outcome of much fraudulent travelling. This unwelcome trend of the times was

Paris: the centralised traffic control panel for Lines 3 and 4.

205

Milan: construction on the 'cut and cover' principle in the city streets.

experienced to an almost alarming degree in London, and the measures taken to meet it are discussed in some detail in the chapter dealing with the Victoria Line; but in the general conception of its equipment the new Milan underground was one of the first to put into service apparatus for automatic collection of fares.

This feature of underground management may not have the same appeal to those whose interest is principally in engineering matters, train operation, and in the simple pleasure of riding in trains. But railways are, after all, business concerns, and if circumstances develop that make increasingly difficult the collection of the revenue that is due to them, then all the ingenuity of engineers and the astuteness of management must be called into play to stop the leaks. The business of fare collection has, on certain railways, become as vital a task of the Signal Engineer's Department as the interlocking of points and signals. While one branch of the department is constantly engaged upon means to minimise any possible risk of trains colliding, another is equally exercised to ensure that passengers do not travel without a proper ticket. The movement of trains is being 'interlocked' with the aspects displayed by the signals; the movement of passengers is being 'interlocked', by means of automated barriers, with the functioning of automatic ticket machines.

In London new methods are gradually imposed upon old layouts, and the procedure is as much dictated by psychology as by engineering; but in Milan the entire railway was new, and the novel techniques of automation could be introduced from the very outset. From all accounts the new arrangements did not get away to a very good start. The Metro was going to employ so few people that the population—or that section of it most likely to use the new line—took a poor view of it; and while this attitude, which was expressed in countless utterings, both public and private, did not extend to the point of a complete boycott the utilisation was at first far below what was hoped for by those who had sponsored it. I visited the line about six months after its inauguration, and on what might have been expected to be a busy morning there were few people about. Traffic has however greatly increased since then, and a second line has been brought into service.

It is perhaps significant of the social changes that are now in progress that I have been discussing such features as automatic fare collection before coming to the railway itself. The original line, opened in November 1964, taken with the branch from it that was brought into service in April 1966, had a total length of 9 miles. It was built beneath the streets, partly by deep tunnelling by shields, and partly by 'cut and cover' methods. There was naturally some dislocation of road traffic while the latter process was in progress; but many of the streets concerned were wide enough to carry the normal traffic with little deceleration. Once the roof girders were put in the road surface could be restored, and excavation continued below to the full depth required. As in Paris and Rome the tunnels were mostly arranged to accommodate two lines of railway. Unlike the Paris and Rome underground systems the form of traction adopted was the same as that of London, with separate positive and negative current rails, and no overhead wires. The power supply is 750 volts, direct current. The use of a separate rail for the traction return simplifies the signalling arrangements, since the track circuiting is independent of all traction currents.

The smartly appointed carriages are evidently intended to convey a high proportion of standing passengers. Seating is confined to three places longitudinally beneath each window, giving a total of no more than 15 aside in each carriage. Then, in the very

Milan: construction by the shield method.

wide space between the seats there are numerous vertical rails, and suspended bars intended for the convenience of standing passengers. A really well-filled carriage could take at least four times as many standing as seated. The supports for the 'strap-hangers' are all solid; there are no flexible straps, as in the earlier underground trains in London. The trains were made up to five cars, when I visited the line, though the station platforms have been built long enough to accommodate much longer trains when these become necessary. An eight-car train, when fully loaded, could carry at least 1000 people. Every attention has been given to means of rapid loading and unloading when the service reaches maximum intensity, and each carriage has four pairs of sliding doors on each side. Internal decoration is very restrained, and advertisements and pictorial matter is confined to neatly framed panels above the windows.

Centralised control of the entire line and its one branch is exercised from the Tele-command Centre at San Babila. Normally it operates quite automatically; the reversal

Milan: typical train and station:
note the strip-lighting parallel to the
platform edge.

Milan: Interior of coach showing
provision for very many standing
passengers.

of trains at the terminal stations, and routeing movements at the junction of the branch, is regulated by process of sequential switching, according to timetable and to a pre-arranged programme of movement entrusted to a computer. This latter is located in the Controller's room at San Babila, and transmits the necessary tele-commands in sequence to apparatus at the furthest points on the line. There are crossovers between the two main tracks at every station on the line, but these are used only in emergency. The Controller at San Babila can interrupt the programme in course of fulfilment through the agency of the computer, and electrically authorise individual control at any station. When this is done all the appropriate safeguards to other traffic are applied, through the signalling arrangements described later in this chapter. Each station has its own signalling control panel, for use in 'out-of-course' conditions; but this is not normally used. The degree of automation at intermediate stations is quite astonishing, no more than a single man normally being needed for the entire working. He would remain in his control room for most of the time. The passengers obtain their tickets from automatic machines, and then they insert their tickets end-on into a machine that operates the turnstile and gives admission to the platforms. In the control room at each station there are closed-circuit television receivers that can be switched on as required, and which give a picture of what is happening on the station platforms. Duplicate instruments are provided in the central control room at San Babila, whereby the Controller there can switch in to any station on the line, and see exactly what is happening on any station platform.

It is appropriate to a railway so highly automated that very advanced security measures are installed for controlling the running of the trains. The colour light signals display the familiar red, yellow and green aspects, though under automatic working conditions these do not indicate the extent to which the line ahead is clear, as in normal practice, but instead the speed at which the train may be run, namely:

Green: speed not to exceed 53 m.p.h.
Yellow: speed not to exceed 31 m.p.h.
Red: speed not to exceed 9 m.p.h.

Special instructions cover the occasions when individual control of stations is in operation. Then a 'red' compels a dead stop, and to advise the driver when these conditions are in force an auxiliary light signal is provided adjacent to the main signal. When normal automatic operation is proceeding this auxiliary signal shows an illuminated purple letter 'P', indicating that if 'red' the signal may be passed at a speed not exceeding 9 m.p.h. If the letter 'P' is not shown the 'red' signal compels a dead stop. These arrangements, clear as they might appear, could be capable of misunderstanding in extenuating circumstances, and so superimposed upon the signalling itself are some interesting and important safeguards. The track circuits that control the aspects displayed by the lineside signals are of the coded type, as previously referred to in connection with the latest developments on the Madrid Metro, in Chapter Twelve; but in addition to the wayside signals the trains are equipped with continuously controlled light signals in the driver's cab. Apparatus is carried on the trains that enables the codes flowing in the track rails to be picked up and used to operate the cab signals. So that if a train enters upon a track circuit leading up to a yellow signal at the lineside that 'yellow' is immediately shown up in the cab, some little distance before the train reaches the actual signal.

The line is for the most part fairly straight and in the tunnels the drivers can usually

Milan: Tele-control at station: note the closed-circuit television viewers to enable the control to observe traffic on the platforms.

see the lineside signals some distance before coming level with them; but as well as providing an extra and immediate signal, the continuous cab signalling system gives the driver instant advice, at his elbow so to speak, of any change in the aspect of the signal ahead. He might, for example, be running under a yellow, at restricted speed; but then the train ahead running at normal speed increases the distance between the two trains, clears the section ahead and allows the signal to change to green. The driver of the following train does not need to sight the signal itself; his cab signal changes at once and he can begin to accelerate to normal speed. Just as the cab signals provide a useful additional aid to the driver in normal working, so special safety arrangements come into force if an emergency movement takes place at one of the intermediate stations, and the signals are put to red to protect a movement across the points. The 'P' light is extinguished, but that is not considered sufficient safeguard of the situation. Those signals equipped with a purple 'P', which when it is extinguished demand a dead stop if showing red, have associated with them a train stop working on a similar principle to those standard in London. When the signal is indicating a dead stop this inductive device is energised, and if a train should inadvertently run past such a signal the apparatus causes an emergency application of the train brake. Control is taken completely out of the driver's hands, and the train stopped in a very short distance.

Such are the leading features of the Milan Metro. The running arrangements, it will be appreciated differ considerably from those long standard in London, in the absence of any absolute stop requirement under automatic operation. In the circumstances the

211

superimposing of cab signalling upon the ordinary lineside signals is perhaps an essential feature. When I was in Milan last and saw the railway working the public seemed to have overcome its initial prejudice—or perhaps I should say, wariness—towards the highly automated features of the equipment, notably the automatically controlled turnstiles. Milan was certainly a milestone in the gradual evolution of underground railways, and the further extensions now planned provide evidence of its undoubted success.

In October 1970 the second line of the Milan Metro was opened. This runs from the central area into the eastern suburbs to an intermediate terminal point at Cascina Gobba, whence the Metro trains continue over an up-graded suburban line to Gorgonzola. In the central area the present terminus is at Piazza Caiazzo, which is some 300 yards from Milan Central Station, but a westward extension is already under construction that will provide an underground station beneath the great terminus of the Italian State Railways. The new route of the Metro, known as the 'Green Line',

Milan: Power-supply control panel at S. Babila station.

has a station at the heavily used main line junction of Lambrate, where certain international express trains for destinations beyond Milan make their stops, instead of entering the Central Station. The 'Green Line' differs from the first section of the Milan Metro (Red Line) in using a higher traction current of 1500 volts, direct current, and overhead wires, instead of third and fourth rail conductors. For this line an interesting design of light-weight coach has been introduced, and 81 vehicles have been built by various Italian manufacturers. They are designed for maximum carrying capacity as will be appreciated from the following specifications. Both types of car are 57·5ft. long.

Motor coach:

Tare weight	27·3 tons
Passengers seated	46
Passengers standing	154

Trailer coach:

Tare weight	16·2 tons
Passengers seated	46
Passengers standing	181

These vehicles have thus the very high loaded to tare weight ratio of 1·48 and 1·93—the trailers, being nearly twice the weight when fully loaded to when empty.

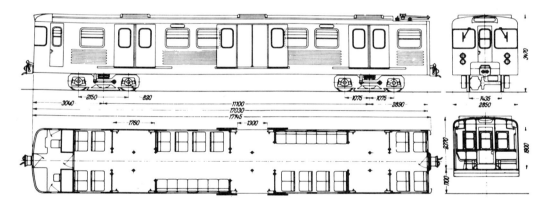

Milan new lightweight stock: ganeral arrangement of power cars; provision is made for 154 standing passengers in addition to 46 seated.

CHAPTER EIGHTEEN

Two Canadian Subways

The City of Toronto in common with all major centres of population in the world has experienced a large increase in its population in recent years, and in the period of post-war recovery the situation so far as metropolitan transport was concerned was causing acute congestion in the peak periods. Since the war many new industries had grown up; business had expanded in many directions, and the layout of the city centre generally aggravated the traffic problem. The city itself, lying on the northern shores of Lake Ontario, is roughly T-shaped in geographical plan. The head of the T lies along the waterfront, while the 'stroke' extends northwards to the suburb of Davisville and Eglinton. Until the 'subway' was projected transport had been provided by an extensive series of electric trams, working on a multiplicity of routes; but trams running on fixed tracks at street level are not conducive to the *relief* of traffic congestion in thoroughfares that were not particularly wide. Furthermore, the trams were only single-deckers. They were adequate enough when the tramway system was first installed; but by the end of World War II the population of Toronto was roughly *three times* what it had been in 1910: 950,000 against 368,500. Something had to be done about it, and the decision was taken to build a 'subway' down the very centre of that 'stroke' of the T, the main highway, Yonge Street, from the city centre right out to Eglinton.

It was to be a virtually straight line throughout, following, as with nearly all underground systems, the line of the roadway. Yonge Street is a highway barely as wide as Oxford Street in London, but it was nevertheless decided to adopt the 'cut and cover' method of construction rather than deep-level tunnelling. Although 'cut and cover' inevitably meant a complete interruption of road traffic in the meanwhile there were conditions in Toronto that made it less of a nuisance than might otherwise have been the case. First of all the road was 'up' only for the time necessary to insert temporary cross-girders, which would carry the full weight of the street traffic, including the trams. Then, the street layout of Toronto is built on a rectangular plan. Excavation work was done block by block, and while one section of Yonge Street was 'up' diversion of traffic was arranged round the block concerned. Once the temporary cross-girders were in place, and a road surface restored excavation could continue beneath, to the full depth required for the double-line tunnel of the 'subway'. The tunnels were constructed to the full width afforded by the roadway overhead where stations occurred, providing spacious platforms for inward-bound and outward-bound trains. The proximity of many tall buildings on both sides of Yonge Street made it necessary to use very careful excavation methods, and a good deal of underpinning was needed. This subway system

Toronto: Construction of Sheppard Station 60ft. below Yonge Street. Reinforcing rods are in position for the first concrete pour.

has no connection with any part of the Canadian main line railways, and the gauge is the unusual one of 4ft. $10\frac{7}{8}$in.—actually 1·5 metres exactly. The traction is 600 volts direct current, with third rail pick-up.

The Toronto 'subway' is interesting particularly in respect of its rolling stock and special equipment on the trains. In view of the nearness of the city to the United States border it was no more than natural that first considerations should have been towards American-built rolling stock. The original intention was, in fact, to have cars of similar design to the trams already operating in the streets of Toronto, adapted to underground operation; but the adaptation of the equipment on these trams to rapid transit working was found to be too expensive. Then consideration was given to the type of car used on the New York subway; but tenders from a number of countries were called for, and an English design, that of the Gloucester Railway Carriage and Wagon Company, was chosen, as being lighter and cheaper than the American product. An order for 104 cars was placed in 1953, ready for the opening of the line in March 1954. Although these cars were of relatively lightweight construction the majority were in steel; but to investigate the possible running economies from still lighter vehicles four cars of the order were built in aluminium. These were, of course, more expensive in first cost than the steel cars, but from their introduction a close monitoring of the performance, particularly in regard to current consumption, was made in the same running conditions as four steel cars. The trial was necessarily to be a long-term one, and no immediate results were expected to be forthcoming.

The surface tram routes were carrying a maximum of 14,000 passengers per hour in the peak periods, and the target set for the new subway was 40,000 per hour. Once the subway was fully operational it was intended to scrap the trams. The new trains

216

were arranged as two-car units, designed to be coupled, as traffic required, to make up a maximum length of eight cars. The car interiors were designed very much in the style of those on the London Underground, with some longitudinal and some cross-seats, with ample space for standing. They are much wider, and taller even than the District and Metropolitan stock in London, having a width over the doors of no less than 10ft. 4in. and a height of 12ft. There is seating for 62 passengers, and if Milanese standards of loading are anything to go by such spacious cars should be able to carry 200 standing, at a crush. Much care was taken in the design to provide a smooth and quiet ride. Sound deadening materials were used to insulate the interior of the body panels, and these proved very effective. The tare weight of the steel cars is 27·2 tons (English), and although the ratio of tare to loaded weight is not so startlingly small as in the lightweight Milanese cars on the Green Line it is good enough, with a loaded weight—assuming an average full complement of 200 per car—of 40 tons. More detailed reference is made later to the aluminium cars, when the time came for a long-term analysis of their performance. So far as the Toronto cars in general are concerned the interiors are quietly styled, and businesslike, with the amount of advertising material inside severely restrained.

From the viewpoint of British industry the securing of the contract for the cars was something of a triumph, because for many years the North American market had been generally considered as beyond the pale for manufacturers of railway equipment. And the supply of cars themselves opened other doors to that market. It is perhaps more than a little inappropriate that the first reference in this book to the Westinghouse electro-pneumatic brake should be made in connection with a Canadian railway, when it had been a standard feature of all new stock on the London Underground for nearly a quarter of a century. But in the equipment of rolling stock for our own underground lines one is apt to take the efficiency of the braking for granted, and perhaps to pass over the steady developments that have been taking place, as each successive batch of new coaches has been introduced. It has been a case of adding important features of refinement and sophistication to an already admirable system. In the earlier chapters of this book I referred to the work of Bernard H. Peter, when he was the youthful signal engineer of the Metropolitan District Railway. After joining the Westinghouse organisation he rose, first, to be Chief Engineer and General Manager, and later to be Managing Director. Although his early engineering experience had been in signalling, on assuming his extended responsibilities, from 1920 onwards, he took a keen interest in problems of braking, and their close relation to those of signalling, and it was he who invented the electro-pneumatic brake.

While both the Westinghouse and the automatic vacuum brake fulfilled the essential safety requirements for passenger train working both had a limitation, in speed of application and release, from the fact that control was by fluid pressure difference initiated from the driver's end of the train. To provide the safety feature demanded by the Board of Trade—a most fundamental requirement that any leak, or parting of the couplings in the train should cause an application of the brakes—both systems, Westinghouse and vacuum, worked by default, as it were. The Westinghouse was applied by the driver *reducing* the pressure of air that was maintained in the train pipe; similarly the vacuum was applied by admitting air to reduce partially, or totally, the degree of vacuum normally maintained. In both systems of braking when the driver operated his brake valve it took some time for the effect to travel down the full length of the

217

P

Toronto: a train at Warden Subway station.

Toronto: interior of one of the cars.

train. Consequently the brakes went on first at the front and the potential effect of the application was not realised until the pressure reduction had travelled the whole length of the train. This was sometimes evident from jerks and snatches, as a train slowed down; but with a well-maintained British main line express train, with all couplings tightly screwed up no ill-effects were usually felt. One did however lose stopping distance, because for the first few seconds of an application only a proportion of the train was being retarded by the brakes.

As traffic increased on the London underground railways, and the need arose to increase the capacity of every line Bernard Peter saw clearly that time could be saved if the stopping distances of trains could be reduced. Trains could be allowed to run at closer headways, and at higher speeds, and it became a matter of how to get the brakes on quicker throughout the length of the trains. On the Great Western Railway that genius of railway mechanical engineering G. J. Churchward, had introduced his 'Direct Admission Valves' for speeding up application of the vacuum brake. Instead of relying upon the entire admission of air to the system to be made through the driver's brake valve the admission was triggered off sequentially down the train: the 'D.A.' valve on each coach, causing a reduction in vacuum enough to operate the next, and so on. It made a considerable difference, and made the Great Western version of the automatic vacuum brake the fastest in the world. But still there was a time lag between front and rear of the train. Peter secured *instantaneous* application, by operating the brakes on every vehicle electrically. It might seem an obvious enough thing to do, but in this invention, effective though it proved, an additional safeguard had to be built in. In any system of braking for passenger trains the utmost precaution has to be taken against failure of any part of the equipment and what is termed a philosophy of 'fail-safe' is paramount in every designer's mind. With the ordinary types of automatic brake, Westinghouse and vacuum, a leakage in the system, or a failure of the apparatus for creating pressure or vacuum results in a full application of the brakes.

Now with the electro-pneumatic brake electrical power is used to *apply* the brake, or rather to initiate the action of the electro-magnetic valves that apply air to the brake cylinders. If no other equipment were included a failure of the electrical supply could leave the train without any brakes. So in addition to the electro-pneumatic brake there is also installed the standard Westinghouse automatic air brake, for use only in emergency. The electro-pneumatic brake is the fastest acting brake that could be devised; but like all other powerful tools it needs careful handling. In certain circumstances, or inexpert use the rate of deceleration could be unpleasantly fierce, and on the Toronto subway as on the latest London Underground stock of the day what are termed 'retardation controllers' are built into the equipment to ensure that the rate of slowing down for a station stop, or in face of an adverse signal was smooth and uniform. The retardation controller was an extremely simple device, consisting of nothing more than a mercury U-tube having electrical contacts that were made or broken by the backward and forward surge of the mercury, according to the retardation of the train. It was most effective.

I referred earlier to the experimental inclusion of four aluminium cars in the initial order for 104 placed with the Gloucester Railway Carriage and Wagon Company in 1952. The number of aluminium cars was later increased to six. These, and the steel cars were built to identical design requirements, and incorporated the same traction, lighting, ventilation and brake gear. The interior *décor* was also identical. The only

Toronto: the signal control room, focal point of subway operations.

Toronto: central control room. The operation of the Communications and Subway Signal Control rooms is under the direct supervision of a Controller.

difference was that the steel cars were painted in the standard red livery of the Toronto Transit Commission, whereas the aluminium cars had a bare metal unpainted finish. In this respect their introduction, in 1954, anticipated by three years the introduction of unpainted aluminium-alloy coaches on the London Underground—in the latter case breaking the traditional red that had prevailed for so very many years. But external liveries apart the aluminium cars on the Toronto Subway were the subject of very careful and continuous scrutiny. The measurements made on these six cars, and on the six steel cars set aside for comparative working in strictly comparable conditions, covered energy consumption, wear in axle bearings, brake shoes, and tyres, and maintenance costs on the body shell. The cars themselves were roughly $4\frac{1}{2}$ tons lighter than the steel ones, turning the scale at $22\frac{1}{2}$ tons each, tare.

The results of the investigation were given in a paper read at a Conference of the American Institute of Electrical Engineers, held in Montreal in June 1957, and thus represented the statistics gained from three years of running experience. Every single factor measured showed considerable savings over the steel cars, but the particular interest of this paper was that the savings were given in cash, and have value in the return on investment they represent for the higher capital cost of the aluminium. They had an added interest in that they were published just at the time when London Transport was introducing its first trains with aluminium-panelled bodies. In quoting the figures of financial savings for the all-aluminium Toronto cars the particularities of service must be borne in mind, because precisely similar results might not be realised in different running conditions elsewhere. The scheduled speed on the one line then in operation was $15\frac{1}{2}$ m.p.h., including turnround time. The saving in respect of all operating and running costs amounted to 465 Canadian dollars per year, for each car, with another estimated 66 dollars per year on body maintenance. The cars have an expected life of 30 years, and the annual saving capitalised at 5 per cent over this period amounted to some £3000 at the rate of exchange then prevailing in 1957. This was certainly an impressive figure, and far outweighed the extra initial cost of the aluminium cars.

Since the original line was put into commission the Toronto Subway has been notably extended, by the construction of an east-west line intersecting with the original line, but at lower level, at Bloor station, and having a total length of just over 14 miles. The original line was 4·6 miles long, and subsequently lengthened by a northward loop from its previous terminus at Union Station—beneath the joint main line station of the Canadian Pacific and Canadian National Railways—to make a second exchange point with the east-west line at St. George station. I was able to ride both east-west, and north-south routes during a visit to Toronto in the late summer of 1971 and was most impressed with the smartness of the working, and the spaciousness of the trains. Although I did not travel at a business rush-hour it was certainly a rush-hour of a different kind. Yonge Street could be described as the Oxford Street of Toronto, and on a Saturday morning 'all the world and his wife' were descending upon it for weekend shopping. The trains were extremely busy, and the exits from the stations so conveniently arranged for shoppers that on alighting from one station and making my way towards an exit I found myself on the basement floor of a large department store. The train working is extremely 'slick', and despite the numbers of passengers I timed one station stop as brief as 7 seconds.

I have referred to the interest of the Toronto Transit Commission in lightweight

221

Toronto: where the 'subway' comes to the surface between Rosedale and Bloor stations.

Toronto: the repair and maintenance yard, located on the surface at Greenwood.

cars at the time the original line was built. By the time the decision was taken to construct the extensions new designs had been developed, in cooperation with interested car-builders, and these took advantage of new advances in the production of aluminium alloys and extrusions. The first order, for 36 cars of the new design, was placed in readiness for the extension of the original line from Union station to St. George, which was then nearing completion. They are readily distinguishable from the original red cars, by having an exterior in unpainted, brushed aluminium, fluted beneath the windows. They were the first 'subway' cars ever built in Canada, and were constructed by the Montreal Locomotive Works Ltd., who had built many of the most famous Canadian steam locomotives in the past. For the new east-west line an order for 164 of these aluminium cars was placed with the Canadian Car Fort William Division of Hawker Siddeley (Canada) Ltd. The new cars have a very rapid rate of acceleration, and give a most comfortable ride. Unlike many underground lines there is an opportunity for passengers to have a view of the line ahead. The motorman is located in a small compartment at the leading end extending to no more than half the width of the car, and the remaining half, on the left hand side has a seat with a view of the track from a head-end window. At shopping time, with children accompanying their parents, I noticed considerable competition for this front seat! The fare structure is simplicity itself. You pay 30 cents to enter the Subway property, and then you can travel up and down all day, if so desired, exchanging from one line to the other, or from north-south to east-west at will.

One cannot travel far in the world without coming across examples of friendly rivalry between relatively adjacent cities that takes the form of trying to do everything 'differently'. In Great Britain itself one has the cases of Liverpool and Manchester as one instance, and of Edinburgh and Glasgow as another. Both pairs are so relatively near, and yet as different as the proverbial chalk from cheese. In Australia the cities of Sydney and Melbourne reflect the stout individualism of the States of which they are the capitals, while Canada provides yet another example in Toronto and Montreal. In this latter case one has the difference of language in addition, for while Toronto is in 'English' Canada, Montreal, in the very spelling of its name, is undisguisedly French. So far as underground railways were concerned Toronto got in first, and the influences were strongly English, and towards London practice in particular. The Montreal metro was authorised in November 1961, and by complete contrast was modelled on that of Paris. Its interesting features were to some extent less publicised than they might otherwise have been, because at the time of its opening, in 1966, most attention was being concentrated on preparations for the great exhibition EXPO 67 staged to mark the Centenary of the Dominion of Canada.

Then at the time of EXPO 67 itself the thunder of the newly opened Metro was somewhat stolen by the equipment of the special electric railway 'Expo Express' which was built to provide access within the exhibition itself. This was a welcome facility, because the site extended from the mainland over two hitherto barren islands lying off-shore in the River St. Lawrence. In connection with the 'Expo Express', entirely *above* ground, it may be mentioned that automatic driving of the trains was used, anticipating by about a year the opening of the Victoria Line in London. The system of control was however different, and the 'Expo Express' line was dismantled after the end of the Exhibition. Most visitors to Montreal in the summer of 1967 will probably have taken the Metro for granted. It provided the kind of rapid-transit urban facility

223

Montreal: open cut work, prior to building of tunnel sections.

one might expect to find in a modern city, but actually it is deserving of special mention, quite apart from the similarity of its rolling stock to some of the latest in use on the Paris Metro, in its use of pneumatic tyres throughout. The general principles of the bogie design are similar to those described in Chapter Twelve, dealing with the latest development in Paris; but certain features of the running gear of the Montreal trains require a special mention.

Before turning to the details of equipment however the general scheme and geographical layout of this Metro must be described. The situation of Montreal, alongside the River St. Lawrence, is not unlike that of Toronto on the shores of Lake Ontario, in that the city extends along the waterfront, and outwards at right angles to it. But there, in such general terms the similarity ends. For one thing, Montreal is larger. It is in fact the sixth largest city in North America, and the second largest French speaking city in the whole world. It stretches out away from the St. Lawrence on both sides around the base of what the citizens call 'the mountain'—Mont Royal—and it is therefore not surprising that the Metro should have a two-pronged westward exit from the city centre as well as lines running parallel to the waterfront, and an extension crossing the islands of EXPO 67. Unlike the Toronto Subway, and unlike most 'underground' railways in other parts of the world the Montreal Metro is wholly underground, except where the service line comes to the surface to enter the Youville car sheds. The track is standard gauge, for the very good reason that one projected line is to use an existing track of the Canadian National Railways. Away from the city centre the land is hilly, and although entirely underground the Metro includes some stiff gradients. This in turn has led to the adoption of one of the latest and most sophisticated forms of electrical control of the running.

The pneumatic-tyred Metro cars run on concrete rails 10in. square in section, in pre-cast lengths of 18ft. Although the affiliation, so far as the general conception of the design is French the dimensions are in English units. The concrete sections are set down on a fibre-glass base, with spikes set in a special concrete with a very high crushing strength. Between the concrete 'rails' is the standard gauge track, as on the Paris Metro. In normal running the convertible flanged wheels are 1in. above the steel rails; but the wheels have specially deep flanges 3in. below the tread, and so these dip down 2in. below rail level. These deep flanges are used primarily for guiding over points; but of course they act as a safeguard in the event of flat tyres. The use of the standard gauge is also of value as enabling rolling stock for the Metro to be delivered from the manufacturers over the ordinary railways—at least for the major part of the distance. In ordinary running in passenger service the guiding of the trains is by horizontal wheels bearing on vertical sided 'rails', as in Paris. Each car bogie has, therefore, twelve wheels: four pneumatic-tyred running wheels; four steel wheels, for emergencies; and the four horizontal guiding wheels.

The trains usually consist of nine cars, of which six are powered. As in Toronto the interior arrangements provide for a high proportion of standing passengers, but with motors having a total horsepower of 3600 per train ample power is available, and the speed rises to around 50 m.p.h. between stops. Much of the system is in deep tunnel, in fact the maximum depth of 150ft., is deeper than the London tubes. Access to the islands of EXPO 67 was by tunnel under the narrow channels of the St. Lawrence between the islands and the mainland. The gradients, and the relatively high speeds of running led to the adoption of one of the most advanced systems of braking to be found anywhere in the world. This is a wholly-British development by the Westinghouse Brake and Signal Company, and includes an ingenious blend, by electronic circuit control, of dynamic and friction braking, while taking fully into account the varying weights of the passenger cars when they are lightly loaded at off-peak periods, and when they are packed to repletion in the rush hours. Finally from the driver's viewpoint, in this, the Westcode system, there is only one instrument in the cab, to provide control of the train acceleration, and braking, by the operation of a single handle. Something must, however, first be said about the principle of dynamic braking. In quite early days of electric traction on railways its great advantage in operating heavy trains over mountain gradients were readily appreciated; while it was one thing to haul such trains up the gradients it was another matter to control them safely on the equally steep descents. Such trains were of course fitted with continuous automatic brakes throughout; but continual pressure of the blocks upon the wheels naturally gave rise to heating, inordinate wear, and to the disturbing phenomenon referred to as 'brake fade'. It was

Montreal: tunnel construction in progress after the open-cut channel had been made.

Montreal: a partly-finished tunnel junction.

in these circumstances that the idea developed of securing additional brake power, and reducing that produced purely by friction, by so arranging the electrical controls of the locomotive motors that on the long descending gradients their function was reversed. Instead of taking power from the overhead line, or the conductor rail, to drive the motors and so provide tractive power to haul the train the connections were reversed. The motors themselves, driven by the downhill progress of the train under the action of gravity, were changed to act as generators, and to pump back electrical power into the overhead line. This action provided a very powerful additional brake, but until the development of the Westcode system its application had been almost entirely in the field of main line railways, on mountain gradients descended at moderate speeds. It is very effectively used with the international express trains operating on the Trans-Alpine routes of the Swiss Federal Railways.

The introduction of electronic methods into the control system of the Westcode brake ensures a virtually instantaneous response to varying running conditions. The braking 'command', as initiated by the operation of the driver's control handle, is met by a continuous blending of dynamic and friction braking. The scheme of control is designed to use dynamic braking wherever possible—as being the most economical in power, and mechanical wear and tear; but any inadequacy in dynamic braking at high speed, or under maximum loading conditions is automatically and instantaneously made good by a friction brake supplement.

A very important feature is the load-sensing device, which is electronically sensitive to the number of passengers actually travelling in any one car. In several previous chapters of this book I have mentioned the considerable difference in modern light-weight underground cars between their tare weights, and that when packed with passengers. This can have a most important effect on the braking characteristics. If the brake power is too high in relation to the weight the wheels will lock, and skidding conditions arise. If the car is under-braked the retardation will be too slow for traffic conditions. With freight trains it has become the practice to fit 'empty load' changeover valves, which can be set by hand before the commencement of a journey; but with a freight vehicle it can generally be regarded as 'empty' or 'full', particularly with heavy traffics such as coal, or iron ore, with which the wagon is entirely completely full, or empty. The changeover valve alters the degree of braking that will be applied. With a passenger car, particularly on a commuter service, there can be no strict line of demarcation between 'empty' and 'loaded', and in the Westcode system an air suspension pressure system selects one of 7 different settings covering the range of loading between 'empty' and maximum 'packing' in the peak hours. The result is a very smooth retardation, with each car braked according to the extent it is filled. One could certainly not apply a standard degree of braking to the entire train, because even in the busiest hours certain parts of every train—particularly those nearest to the station exits—inevitably become more crowded than others.

The surface entries to the Metro are quite unobtrusive—in fact so unobtrusive that a visitor sometimes finds difficulty in locating them. Once the small entrance at street level has been found the descent to platform level is spacious enough, though I found the underground passages and escalator tunnels rather clinical in their severity of finish and almost complete absence of colourful advertisements. The general treatment is a cold grey, relieved only by a very limited use of stainless steel. The tunnels are double-tracked, and at the stations the enlargement is generous to

Montreal: excavation for Metro station in the city centre.

Montreal: heavy constructional work, in rock formation.

provide notably wide platforms, and quite a large concourse, with bookstalls and such like on both platforms. At Berri de Montigny, which is the general interchange station between all routes, the underground layout is such that the various tracks are not hidden from each other, as at London interchange tube stations; but there are open galleries from which one can look down to trains on a line at a lower level, and the interchange between the different levels is provided by short, and conveniently sited escalators. The *décor* here is in places startling in its originality and colour. Above the tunnel entrance on one line is a huge 'stained glass window' designed in the most dramatic colouring of modern art, and lighted from behind to give the impression of sunshine. Other panels in the station are scarcely less colourful.

For an ultra-modern Metro, on which so much money has obviously been spent, the trains themselves seem rather narrow, and strongly reminiscent of the older coaching stock of the Paris Metro in its cross-sectional area at any rate. The seating is a little austere. It is evident that the passenger is not intended to 'settle down' to a comfortable journey in the main line style, that is if he or she gets a seat in the rush hour. The outside and inside finish of the trains is very smart, with a pleasant external colour-scheme of pale blue-and-white. Travelling, on the pneumatic tyres, is reminiscent,

Montreal: one of the pneumatic-tyred trains.

229

as one would expect, of riding over a hard concrete highway, with the occasional bumps one experiences in such travel. It is true that my journeys were made at quiet periods, when the cars were lightly loaded. The riding would probably be more like that of a limousine, when fully loaded. The Metro has become very popular with those commuters who drive in from outlying districts and park their cars near a Metro station to avoid the congestion in the city centre: as a Montreal man expressed it to me, "It's the best 30 cents' worth in town."

I have, perhaps, devoted an undue amount of attention to the technical features of these two Canadian underground systems; but as with all rapid-transit networks safety of operation, far more than station adornment and interior of cars, is the backbone of such mass-transportation. In Toronto, with the use of electro-pneumatic brakes with retardation control, and in Montreal with the Westcode, the science of safety in working has been still further advanced in North America. It is of particular interest that the further lines of the Toronto Subway have been equipped with trains having the West-code type of brake. In view of the developments to be chronicled in the concluding chapters of this book it is not inappropriate to add that the Westcode system was from the outset designed to be actuated either by an operator in the cab, by use of the one-handle traction and brake controller, or for the train to be automatically driven by 'commands' detected by inductive equipment from coded track circuits.

CHAPTER NINETEEN

The Victoria Line

It needs little more than a glance at the map of the underground railways of London to see that the network existing prior to the 1960s left some appreciable gaps. These would not have been considered unduly serious at the time when the 'Ashfield' extensions of the late 1930s were planned, largely because the marked shift of business activity and increased density of population, if foreseen in the long term, was not imminent enough as to present an immediate problem. The areas mainly concerned were north-east and south-west of the central complex, in the districts lying between the Cockfosters and Epping lines on the one hand, and between the Morden and Wimbledon lines on the other. Quite apart from the need for commuter services into these two areas, all the existing tube lines running from north to south across the central complex were being worked up to their limit in the peak periods. Nothing new had been built in this area since the Yerkes enterprises constructed the Bakerloo, Hampstead and Piccadilly tubes. Furthermore, there was Victoria, one of the busiest of London's main line terminal stations, and the only one with no direct connection to the tube railway network. The position of a traveller, and a relative stranger to London, in attempting to cross from Victoria to Euston or Kings Cross was certainly unenviable. Unless he or she chose to make the lengthy perambulation of the Inner Circle, and pay more for the ride(!), he would have to take the District line to Charing Cross, and change. Amid the hurly-burly there would then always be the chance of his getting on to the *wrong* tube line, and finding himself speeding to Paddington instead of Euston, while if St. Pancras or Kings Cross was his immediate destination there would be a further change at Leicester Square.

A line connecting Kings Cross and Victoria had been a long-desired traffic facility in Central London, but in the economic situation prevailing after World War II, the capital cost of such a project seemed prohibitive. But such a railway of the future was no mere pipe-dream. The engineers of London Transport were actively investigating the latest methods of tunnelling. As will be evident from the immediately preceding chapters of this book the construction of underground railways was proceeding in many countries of the world; and while the problems of those enterprising such lines for the first time were inevitably tunnelling to some extent into the unknown their tasks were in other respects easier. In London the very existence of the complicated underground network from the Yerkes era, presented some formidable problems, particularly as any new line that was to provide the fullest traffic facilities would necessarily have to make possible easy exchange with existing lines at a maximum number of stations. Again,

Victoria Line: the new line in pre-cast concrete tunnel near Finsbury Park.

although a wealth of experience had been gained in the construction and development of tube railways in the years before World War II, the boring of tunnels, even with all the most modern instruments and heavy machinery usually has some surprises in store for the engineers.

There was one major development in tunnel constructional technique however that held out such promises of economies in capital cost as virtually to turn the scale, and enable Government sanction to be given to the building of the new line. This was the use of pre-cast concrete linings for the running tunnels. Authority to go ahead was given in August 1962 for construction of 10½ miles of entirely new tube railway between Walthamstow and Victoria—the first railway of this kind to be built under Central London for nearly 60 years. The southerly extension to Brixton was authorised in August 1967. The line was planned to come in through the north-eastern suburbs, with stations at Black Horse Road, Tottenham Hale, Seven Sisters, Finsbury Park, Highbury and Islington, and so to Kings Cross. After that its route lay along the track so often desired by Londoners, serving Euston, Warren Street, Oxford Circus, Green Park and so to Victoria. It was programmed to be brought into service in three stages: Walthamstow to Islington; Islington to Warren Street; and finally Warren Street to Victoria. Almost every station from Finsbury Park southwards was an exchange point with existing underground lines, and at Kings Cross, Euston and Oxford Circus the civil engineering work was extremely complicated. Those who had recently built new underground lines in Madrid, Rome, Milan and elsewhere had nothing remotely to compare, for example, with the situation at Kings Cross where there were two existing deep level tube railways, the full-sized tunnels of the Inner Circle, the main line tunnel connections to the Eastern and London Midland systems, to say nothing of the Fleet Sewer!

A whole book would be necessary to describe in any detail the intricate operations involved at these exchange stations where traffic requirements for the new line sometimes involved diversions of existing tunnels to bring tracks adjacent and convenient for interchange purposes. A very interesting and difficult case occurred between Euston and Kings Cross, where the new line was to run parallel to the City Branch of the Northern Line—the old City and South London. For interchange purposes at Euston it was desired to have the tracks of the Victoria line between those of the Northern, so that the order of lines in the new station, from north to south, would be Northbound City, Southbound Victoria, Northbound Victoria, Southbound City. This involved a considerable diversion of the Northbound City line in order to straddle the new lines at Euston station. The plan on page 234 which is reproduced by courtesy of the Council of the Institution of Civil Engineers, shows that this diversion begins at the precise point where the Northern (City Branch) tunnels pass beneath Somers Town Goods Station. This was laid out when the Midland Railway constructed their London Extension line, and opened St. Pancras passenger station in 1868. The goods station

London: Victoria Line, 'drum digger' being skidded through station tunnel at Green Park.

233

Q

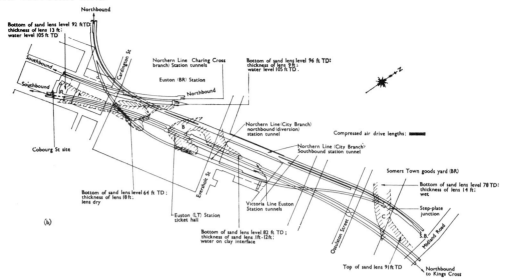

Constructing the Victoria Line: Silt-Sand Lenses of Woolwich and Reading Beds in vicinity of (a) Euston and (b) Warren Street Stations.

which was massively constructed with a number of large girders supported on vertical columns, had twice previously been subject to tube railway tunnelling far beneath it. There was an awkward strata of wet sand near to the level of the railway, and it was known that there had been some subsidences of the columns when the original Euston extension of the City and South London Railway was bored, and when it was subsequently enlarged to standard cross section. A careful investigation showed that the maximum amount of subsidence had been 2¾in., immediately above the tunnels. This had not caused damage to the structure, which was of a nature that could accommodate such a settlement. In fact the disturbance caused by the earlier tunnelling, when surveyed over the area in which it had occurred, was of much value to the engineers setting out upon the diversion necessary to fit in with the required location of the Victoria Line at Euston.

Of the 75 columns supporting the first floor of the goods station more than half that number had been virtually unaffected, and only 14 showed a settlement of 2in. or more. The new diversion line was planned to leave the route of the existing tunnel by what is known as a 'step-plate' junction. This term refers solely to the construction methods used in the excavation, and it required the insertion of two working chambers, one 25ft. in diameter and the other 30ft. These embraced the existing northbound tunnel and provided a working chamber to one side of it from which the new diversion line could be bored. One had, therefore, a standard 'tube' in which the trains continued to run, inside a much larger tube. The excavations to 25ft. and 30ft. diameter, even though of relatively short length came immediately beneath the goods station, and with the record of subsidence of the columns during the previous tunnelling available, and with the known existence of that layer of wet sand at a depth near to the line of the tunnel it was considered necessary to apply chemical treatment to the ground to provide some consolidation. The initial injections were carried out from the surface

234

using clay-cement grout. This caused a small amount of upward 'heave'; but the columns were very carefully scrutinised during the progress of this work, and although a maximum of 2½in. of upward movement was at one time noted this caused no ill effects, and when all the tunnelling work was completed below the final settlement of the columns brought the levels of the goods station back remarkably close to those that had existed when the station was built 100 years earlier.

The conditions in the vicinity of Euston were extremely difficult. At various places in this book I have referred to the advantages engineers boring the underground railways beneath London had from the stable and homogenous nature of the London clay. There were however many areas where less favourable strata are encountered and beneath Euston the thickness of the London Clay is only about 30ft. Earlier tube tunnels had been driven through layers of sand and silt known to geologists as the Reading and Woolwich beds. Previous experience in this area was enough to counsel

Victoria Line: 'drum digger' in southbound shield chamber at Netherton Road.

Oxford Circus Station: erection of 'umbrella' to carry traffic while station reconstruction progressed immediately below: Phase one, the area closed to road traffic.

Oxford Circus Umbrella: night work in progress, August 1963.

236

the utmost caution in driving the tunnels. It was necessary constantly to probe ahead of the working faces, because the 'lenses', as they are termed, are fully charged with water. In some locations, beneath Euston, it was possible to counteract the effects of water by the well-known expedient of putting the workings under compressed air, the incidental effects of which I described in the chapter dealing with the expansion of the Central London line eastwards from Liverpool Street. It was not however possible to use compressed air in all these wet locations. Beneath Euston the lenses of sand and silt are very extensive, and they are mostly surrounded by clay. The water in the sand is thought to enter through small fissures in the surrounding clay, and when the working face of the tunnel was put under compressed air, this gradually permeated the whole strata of sand and silt; the whole area eventually became charged with compressed air at the same pressure as that in the working air locks at the face, and water could thereafter enter without hindrance.

A remarkable instance of the hazards involved in the boring of the Victoria Line, even with all the experience previously gained in tunnelling beneath Central London, occurred at the western end of the Euston Area, this time from strata of sand or ballast that did not contain water. These strata had been water bearing until a few years previously, but pumping in the neighbourhood had lowered the underground level and drawn air down through some 100ft. of the clay, losing its oxygen on the way, leaving an 'air' almost entirely consisting of nitrogen. Working was in progress in a tunnel at normal pressure—a 'free air' tunnel—and no danger was suspected, until one Monday morning the gang entered the workings, and those going in first were immediately overcome. Fortunately those coming later realised something was seriously wrong, and although suffering to a lesser degree were able to extricate all the others. The 'air' was found to be highly short of oxygen. The reason why the trouble was not always present was found to be that the nitrogen remained in the dry sand pockets at average barometric pressure, but seeped out when the pressure was low. During a weekend when the 'glass' was very low, in bad squally weather on the surface, the nitrogen had escaped into the working, when there was no one there to suspect any danger. When the men went to resume work on that Monday morning the tunnel was highly charged and it was fortunate there were no fatalities.

In view of all the past experience of tunnelling beneath London, and the fact that no new tube railways or extensions had been built for nearly 30 years, it is most interesting to find that so much of the Victoria Line, and particularly its extension to Brixton was built with the Greathead type of shield, with hand excavation. In the intervening years a mechanical type of excavator shield had been developed; and naturally every consideration was given to the possibility of using these. They not only offered the chance of making much more rapid progress, but also, of course, of using a smaller labour force. The type of men having the skill and stamina to undertake mining work by hand, in a Greathead shield, are neither numerous nor cheap to employ. It is generally considered that in comparable conditions of working the rate of progress with a hand shield will be about 50 yards per week, whereas a mechanical excavator can advance from 70 to 90 yards in the same time. On the other hand the use of a mechanical digger is not possible in bad ground. The preliminary surveys indicated the areas where these could be safely used, but beneath London you never know for certain! Of course one can always stop the digger and probe ahead if trouble is expected, but in the experience of those on the job it was then usually too late. On the original section of the line,

237

Oxford Circus: the umbrella deck completed and traffic flowing, Sept. 1966.

between Walthamstow and Victoria, about one third of the running tunnels, and those of all the stations, were driven with the old-type Greathead shield. On the southward extension to Brixton no mechanical shields at all had been used, because there is so great a variation in the strata experienced.

One feature of the construction of the Victoria Line, of which I have the most lively personal recollections, was the very close scheduling of the various contracts. This, of course, applied in very great measure to the civil engineering work, on which everything depended, and which led London Transport to take certain 'short cuts' which were not altogether to the liking of some consulting engineers, and contractors. One point brought out subsequently was the practice adopted in carrying out such prior negotiations with property owners along the route without any consultation with parties that were likely to be involved in the construction, and who would have been in the position to advise of likely difficulties, and suggest alternatives. But when it is realised that between Victoria and Walthamstow no fewer than 3300 properties were referenced, within the limits of deviation, there is necessarily a limit to the amount of consultation that can take place. In actual fact there were only 26 petitions against the Parliamentary Bill presented for authorisation of the line, and these were all satisfactorily settled. This was remarkable in view of the very large number of properties likely to be affected by the construction of an underground railway beneath the very heart of the West End of London.

Victoria Line: Diversion of westbound Piccadilly line at Finsbury Park. The last westbound train passes just after midnight on October 2, 1965. Note the difference in level of the tunnels. Steel stool supports are numbered ready for dismantling.

Diversion at Finsbury Park: the animated scene during reconstruction work in the early hours of October 3, 1965. This was a striking example of the major operations involved in connecting up 'tube' railways.

On the Brixton extension there was naturally much difficult work on the section where it passed under the river Thames. As it so happened the tunnels ran continuously in stiff blue-grey fissured clay, with a minimum depth of 24ft. below the bed of the river; and although these tunnels were driven under compressed air at a pressure of 9 lb. per square in., as a precaution, no trouble was experienced. It was a different matter on the south bank. Under Vauxhall Park a buried channel of gravel required compressed air working at the unusually high pressure of 35 lb. per square in. for short lengths, and at Stockwell, where the route of the Brixton line intersects with the Old City and South London, there was some very intricate work. Although there is no physical connection the Victoria Line tracks are arranged to straddle those of the City Line at Stockwell to give cross-platform interchange, and the new tunnels passed under the old with only 6ft. of cover between the two. The ground was brown silty sand with flints and gravels overlying the mottled clay of the Reading beds—a most difficult place for tunnelling. Mention of the minimum 'cover' between tunnels brings me back once again to the multiplicity of tunnels in the neighbourhood of Kings Cross where the crown of the new station tunnel on the Victoria Line is so close to the junction of the Midland and Eastern Region connections to the City Widened Lines, known respectively as the 'Midland Curve' and 'Hotel Curve', that during the constructional period the 'squeal' of carriage or wagon wheels on the rails in the standard-sized tunnels above could be distinctly heard from the Victoria Line tunnel.

The civil engineers were not the only parties faced with difficult and unusual tasks in the construction of the Victoria Line. Reference has been made earlier in this book to the difficulties in obtaining staff for manning the underground railways of London, both in train crews and station staff, and from an early date it had been decided that a maximum degree of automation should be applied to the whole line. The outstanding decision, of course, was to instal automatic driving of the trains. In this, as in so many other features of underground railway working, London has once again scored 'a world-first'. Once again, as with many previous innovations this latest and epoch-marking development was the result of close collaboration between the engineers of London Transport and the Westinghouse Brake and Signal Company. Even before the Victoria Line was sanctioned in August 1962, equipment development was well under way. Robert Dell, Chief Signal Engineer of London Transport, had formulated his ideas, in collaboration with A. W. Manser, the Chief Mechanical Engineer, and in December 1962, only 4 months after the passing of the Act authorising construction of the line work had advanced sufficiently for the first automatic train trials to be made between Acton Town and South Ealing. These trials were made with empty coaches, but early in the following year a passenger train was put into service fitted with proto-type equipment, and was automatically driven between Ravenscourt Park and Stamford Brook stations on the District Line. The target date for the completion of the Victoria Line was given as the year 1968, and an immense amount of work had to be done in the meantime. In such a development it was not likely that the prototype equipment would be satisfactory in all respects. It was a case of collaboration, closer than ever before, between design of signalling and of brake equipment, and in April 1964 a complete service of automatically driven trains was put into operation between Woodford and Hainault, at the country end of the easterly extension of the Central London line.

At this stage it is important for me to make clear exactly what is meant by an 'auto-

Victoria Line: constructional work in progress outside Victoria main line station.

matic' train. In all the developments that preceded it, and on the Victoria Line itself the principle has been that the train should be started from a station by some very simple movement, such as the pressing of a push button, and it would then run without any further human attention, or intervention, until it was at rest at the correct position in the platform of the next station. The automatic driving equipment should provide adequate safeguards in the event of one train tending to close in upon the preceding one, and would ensure the correct observances of any speed restrictions temporary or permanent, that might be imposed because of engineering conditions on the line. Technically it would be possible, in fulfilling such requirements, for the train to be started from the station platform, and to proceed to the next station without driver or guard; but from the general operating point of view it was considered desirable to have an attendant on the train, since automation of this kind cannot cope with the human side of any incident that might arise from emergency, or delay. For this reason it was decreed that the train attendant should be able to communicate with the passengers by loudspeaker. In normal working the only *action* required from the attendant would be to press the starting button, when the 'right-away' was given by the platform staff at each station. By this method of working the number of men on each train was halved, from two to one, and those of us with memories of much earlier days on the London

241

tubes could well reflect upon the profound change since the era when there was a man on the platform between each pair of coaches, and the 'right-away' was signalled sequentially from rear to front of the train, as each gangway was cleared and the gates closed. It is important to emphasise however that the one man on the Victoria Line trains is a fully experienced motorman who, in the unlikely event of a breakdown of the automatic equipment would drive the train by hand controls of a type similar to those on previous tube railways.

The completely automatic driving of the trains is actually a dual system, of which one part is based on the traditional safety methods of railway signal engineering used on the London Underground since the first days of the District and Metropolitan line electrification, and which, through the agency of the lineside train-stop made an emergency application of the brakes if a train should inadvertently over-run a signal at danger. This principle is maintained through highly sophisticated modern equipment on the track and trains of the Victoria Line. But while this safety equipment is a fundamental necessity to ensure the correct response of automatically driven trains to adverse signals, for an overwhelming proportion of the working hours of the railway the trains are running in their correct timetable paths and under clear signals. Then their progress must be controlled so that they accelerate swiftly from station stops, and come in smoothly to stop at the correct position on the station platforms. Another requirement is that if a train should be stopped intermediately by signal it shall restart again automatically when the signal clears. Officially the two parts of the dual system are referred to as the 'safety' and the 'non-safety' systems. This is not to suggest that there is anything unsafe about that part of the system that controls the accurate stopping of the train in the station platforms; it is a method of distinguishing between the 'vital' and the 'non-vital' part of the controls.

There is an analogy here between the remote control principles developed by Robert Dell for junction operation, and described in Chapter Sixteen of this book, and the principles of automatic train operation on the Victoria. The 'safety' or 'vital' system is the equivalent of the basic signalling interlocking between points and signals that positively prevents the setting up of a route that could result in a collision. The 'non-safety', or non-vital system is the equivalent of the remote control, by telephone type of apparatus, which, if in telephone parlance rang up a wrong number could have no ill-effects, because the safety system, in the form of the basic interlocking, would prevent any dangerous condition being set up. On the Victoria Line one has always the automatic braking system, based upon the signal indications, to act as the ultimate safeguard. Although the trains are normally running under automatic driving controls it was considered essential to provide colour light signals at the appropriate locations in the tunnels to aid the train attendant if he had at any time to take over and drive the train manually. There are however no train stops of the previous standard type. The interconnection between the latter and the braking equipment on the trains was simplicity itself. If the signal was at danger, and the train stop arm raised, this arm struck a pendant lever at the leading end of the train, and the movement of this lever made a full emergency application of the brakes.

On the Victoria Line the train brakes had to be designed to respond to a multiplicity of 'signals' from the track, and anything so simple as a plain mechanical contact between a raised train stop arm and a pendant lever was out of the question. It will be convenient to consider how the 'safety' part of the system works, in providing the

Victoria Line: equipment in the experimental train operated on the Woodford—Hainault loop line.

Victoria Line: a train of the new rolling stock.

straight equivalent of the old train stop control. The track circuits are fed with pulsating, rather than continuous current, and the number of pulses per minute are an indication of the state of the line ahead. This governs the speed at which a train is allowed to run. The code flows in the running rails, as with steady current track circuits, but while the trains cut off the flow of current when their wheels enter upon a track circuit they each carry, at each end, four pick-up coils, mounted ahead of the first pair of wheels. These coils detect the codes that are flowing in the rails ahead of the train. Two coils one each side of the train, are used for the safety system, and the other two control the automatic driving equipment. Different conditions initiate four different codes in the rails, these are all 'low-frequency' produced by robust, well-proved electro-mechanical equipment, and provide, as appropriate to track conditions, 420 pulses per minute, 270, 180 and 120. The '420' code permits full-speed running, but the 270 and 180 codes permit a maximum speed of no more than 22 m.p.h. The '120' code is not detected by the train apparatus, and compels a dead stop. There is a difference between the 270 and 180 codes, both of which are of a cautionary nature. Receiving the 270 code a train is permitted to motor, if keeping within the 22 m.p.h. speed limit, and this code permits the restarting of a train after a signal stop. But if when running under either a 270 or an 180 code the speed should exceed 22 m.p.h. the brakes would be applied and the train stopped. For a train to proceed at all under automatic operating conditions it must always be receiving one of the safety low-frequency codes from the track—either 420, 270 or 180; if this should cease the brakes would be automatically applied and the train brought to rest.

Superimposed upon this fundamental safety system is the automatic driving, the purpose of which is to give 'instructions' to the train to stop at required positions. In the approach to each station there are what are termed 'command spots'; these are 10ft. lengths of one running rail, positioned so as to provide a smooth rate of deceleration for a train coming into stop at a station. The trains have standard patterns of deceleration, under the action of the brakes if being operated manually, and at each command spot the speed of a stopping train is specified. In a typical instance there could be 12 command spots from the outer approach to the station and the position near the head of the platform where the front of the train is required to stop. Under the action of the first four command spots a train could emerge from the tube and enter the platform at about 30 m.p.h. and then, under the action of 7 command spots along the length of the platform come accurately to rest at the far end. As distinct from the safety codes used in the track circuits the command spots are fed with high frequency signals, chosen so that 100 cycles per second equals one mile per hour. The high frequency 'signals' applied to the command spots are detected by the second pair of pick-up coils on the leading end of each train, and after suitable amplification applied to the 'auto-driver'. This, by appropriate application of the brakes eases the speed down as required, and gives a remarkably smooth stop.

I have not attempted to describe in any degree of detail the brilliantly ingenious circuits and apparatus by which these principles have been made to operate so successfully. As a contractor's engineer I first became associated with the equipment for the Victoria Line when it was passing beyond the stage of experimentation, and research, and plans were being made for large scale production of the many items of equipment required. By that time, the late autumn of 1964, the automatic train service with passenger trains, between Woodford and Hainault had been in service for just over six months and its success and reliability enabled the engineers of London Transport to go ahead in full confidence towards the equipment of the Victoria Line. It was a strange and fascinating experience to travel in the cab of an automatically driven train. After the driver had pressed the starting buttons one could almost imagine him saying: 'Look, no hands!', because he sat back and allowed the train to proceed. On the stretch of line between Woodford and Hainault there are three intermediate stations, at all of which precisely accurate stops were made, while the section included one sharply curved junction over which a permanent speed restriction is enforced. On one occasion when I was in the cab there was a stop in mid-section from an adverse signal.

When it came to the application of the principles and apparatus so convincingly vindicated in the Woodford–Hainault trials the engineers of London Transport felt that a number of detail improvements could be made as a result of the trial experience, to increase further the safety, reliability, and long-service potential of the equipment. This involved considerable new design work, and the installation in the manufacturers' works of special equipment for testing the apparatus. In contrast to the earlier 'non-vital' systems installed by London Transport, in which telephone type electro-magnetic relays were used for switching between the various circuits, the Victoria Line equipment is entirely of what is termed the 'solid state' type, using transistors and similar items. These function like relays, but have no moving parts, and for that reason were expected to have greater reliability, and require less maintenance. At the same time however these tiny units had not previously been used to any great extent in railway

Victoria Line: the Royal opening.
Her Majesty the Queen in the
cab with Mr. F. G. Maxwell,
Chief Operating Manager.

245

signalling work, and although a failure could result in nothing worse than a 'wrong number', any failure on a railway leads to delay while it is being rectified. I need not elaborate upon the consequences of even the slightest hold-up on the London Underground in the peak hours; it usually produces banner headlines in the evening newspapers. So in deciding to use transistors and their kind for the Victoria Line very careful selection of available makes had to be made. They were then operated at no more than 50 per cent of the makers' recommendations.

During the course of our many meetings it was once said that a transistor was a device that worked perfectly as long as you were watching it, and then failed inexplicably the moment you turned your back! But apart from all this the advantages to be gained from their large-scale use were so great that the most thoroughgoing measures were taken to ensure the maximum reliability. They were first tested, then given a period of heat-soak in an oven at constant temperature, and then subjected to a severe vibration test. Then they were retested to make sure no change had taken place. Only when this second test had been satisfactorily concluded were they assembled in the equipment. It is of interest to put on record that of the makes finally selected only 6 in every thousand failed to pass the final test. The first section of the Victoria Line was opened in September 1968, and the final section in March 1969. From those beginnings until March 1970 there had been no more than 39 failures of solid state equipment—a good record seeing that the total number of such devices on the whole line amounts to 196,000.

In Chapter Sixteen of this book I described the development of the programme machines on London Transport, used for the working of junctions and routeing of trains in the daily timetable. On the Victoria Line the programme machines provide for the complete running of the trains from the moment they leave the depot at Northumberland Park until they return. No signalmen are required at all. In the depot the trains are marshalled by a shunter working on a control panel in an elevated tower, but he gets his instructions as to which trains are required first from a programme machine! He arranges for the required train to move on to a reception road, and from there again it is a case of 'look, no hands'. Not all the trains work over the whole length of the line between Walthamstow and Victoria. A number terminate at Kings Cross, and the programme machines arrange for the necessary shunting and reversal. A very complete system of closed circuit television has been installed. There are cameras at each end of every station platform, and one at the lower circulating area of the escalators. The camera at the rear end of the platform operates a large-screen monitor where it can be seen by the train operator. On this screen he can see the passengers entering at the rear end of the train, and it helps him to know when to close the doors. The central traffic controller of the line, in the control room at Coburg Street, near Euston, can switch his own minitor screen to any station on the line, to observe traffic conditions as and when required.

A very important feature of the automation applied to general traffic conditions on the Victoria Line is the automatic collection of fares. For many years previously automatic ticket-issuing machines have been a familiar feature of the London Underground, and their use has now been extended by the introduction of increasingly ingenious types that print the ticket as required, and give change. But the most important development, which it is intended will eventually eliminate the use of human ticket collectors at the barriers, has been the introduction of magnetically-encoded tickets for use in the automatic barrier gates at the stations. Most of the stations on the Victoria Line are equipped

The Brixton Extension: construction of Vauxhall station.

with a four-door type of gate operated by compressed air. The passenger inserts his ticket in the appropriate slot. The magnetic coding on the ticket itself checks that the ticket is a valid one. If it is the gate is operated; if not the ticket is rejected. Photo-electric cells detect the movement of the passenger through the gate, and ensure that more than one passenger does not get through on one ticket by smartly reclosing the gate in his or her rear. The ingenuity of certain members of the public in 'fooling' any type of automatic machine has certainly met its match in the ingenuity built into the apparatus for automatic fare collection on the Victoria Line, and many amusing tales have been told of the fate of would-be cheats, but also that of hapless travellers who were a little slow off the mark in passing through the gates.

On March 7, 1969, Her Majesty Queen Elizabeth II opened the final section of the Victoria Line to its first southern terminus at Victoria itself. It was the first time ever that a reigning Monarch had opened one of the London Underground railways, though her great-grandfather, King Edward VII, when Prince of Wales, had opened both the City and South London, and the Central London Railways, as recorded earlier in this book. In its finished form, in the style and *décor* of the stations, it follows the general practice of London Transport, with numerous detailed improvements, but without any of the grandiose ostentation that has characterised some of the underground railway systems abroad. The general atmosphere is very pleasant, but it is designed for use

247

rather than prestige effects. The trains themselves are most efficient in their swift and silent running, though the civil engineers of London Transport have expressed themselves as disappointed that a greater degree of quietness has not been achieved. In transport within London the new line has proved an inestimable boom. Before this book is completed the Brixton extension will be opened, and the new terminus there, as well as providing a convenient interchange with several routes on the electrified system of the Southern Region of British Railways, will be invaluable as a suburban railhead for bus routes from many districts in South London. Then the heavy commuter traffic entering Central London from these areas will be able to go underground, relieving some of the pressure in the streets.

CHAPTER TWENTY

Sub-Aqua in Rotterdam

Bitterly cold weather, with occasional snow, greeted me in Brussels when I arrived by the Night Ferry from London one morning in February 1968. After business lasting the best part of the day, and getting from place to place in the snow and slush, I caught a late train to Rotterdam, to await there the arrival next morning of a party of friends from England. It was colder than ever in Holland, with a tearing east wind, and while it howled around the hotel where I was staying I thought with some concern of my friends who were crossing the sea that night, from Harwich to the Hook of Holland! Next day we were to be conducted on a technical inspection of the new Rotterdam · Metro, on which public service had begun only two weeks earlier, and as this includes some elevated sections, in an extremely exposed part of the city, it seemed that we were in for a rather strenuous airing. In this book I am, of course, primarily concerned with the underground section, although as I have indicated in the chapter heading it should more strictly be called an 'underwater' section.

The city of Rotterdam, while experiencing all the problems of increasing traffic congestion that are common all over the world today, has its own peculiarities, not only in the wide, and heavily used waterway of the River Maas dividing the city, but in the geological conditions that prevail. It has been rightly said that if someone were to dig a hole anywhere in Rotterdam's centre he would find water after going down to a depth of just three feet! There were already bridges across the Maas, but these were congested with tramlines and all kinds of vehicles—not to mention the swarms of bicycles that one sees in Dutch cities. The extent of the traffic problem that existed before the construction of the Metro may be judged from the facts that out of a population of three-quarters of a million some 160 million journeys were made each year, and with 14 tram and 27 bus routes nearly 60 per cent of all journeys were made by tram. Any question of building more bridges across the Maas would have been complicated by the need for making new tramway junctions at each end, and in any case bridges are not the most convenient way of crossing waterways in the midst of a port with the activity of Rotterdam. In the ordinary way tunnels would seem the obvious solution, but the physical conditions hardly favoured the deep level method of construction by shield and possible use of compressed air. A most ingenious and successful precedent had been set in the construction of the road traffic tunnel under the Nieuwe Maas river, completed in 1941, whereby a series of pre-cast rectangular sections were made in a special 'dry-dock', and then floated, towed out to the site and sunk into position. When the Rotterdam City Council took the decision to build a 'Metro' railway, in

1959, this same method of construction was decided upon.

There is no question of boring. A trench is dug in the river bed deep enough to accommodate the tunnel sections and allow for some cover, so that the original depth of the waterway is not impaired. A constructional basin was dredged, and excavated in the neighbourhood of the tunnel site, and this was kept dry during the pre-casting process. The depth of the basin, or dry-dock, had to be so arranged that the completed tunnel elements could be floated, and then towed out. It was a colossal task. The twelve sections embodied in the tunnel passing under the river were built in a special dry dock, constructed on an island in the river east of Rotterdam, Van Brienenoord. This dry dock was constituted as an inlet in the river. In its depths two sections of tunnel were built simultaneously side by side, each section being extended gradually by additions of sub-sections 49ft. long. Watertight sealing was made between adjacent sub-sections and the composite 'sections' extended until they consisted of 5 or 6 sub-sections, thus varying in size from 240 to 290ft. long. The average time for building a pair of tunnel sections in the Van Brienenoord dry dock was five months, and then units weighing some 5000 tons each were ready to be floated.

When the units were completed temporary watertight bulkheads were erected at each end, water was let into the dry dock, and the tunnel sections, each 19ft. deep were floated out, with their roofs about 4in. above water level. Special barges equipped with

Rotterdam: a high level view showing what appears to be a canal, but which is actually the track of the Metro. In this watery cutting were laid the 'tubes' for the railways.

Rotterdam: a close-up of the girder work covering the channels in which the railway was laid.

winches and sights were coupled up, and the slow haul by tugs commenced. As these tunnel sections each had the displacement of a large cross-channel packet steamer their haulage and manoeuvring was a problem in itself. The sub-soil beneath the river bed gave rise to some special problems. In some instances where the submerged trench system of construction was used the ground in the river bed was sufficiently stable to allow the pre-cast elements to be based on a gravel bed; but this was not so at Rotterdam. Deep piling had to be driven into the river bed, to get a stable foundation, and to these piles were connected cross-beams and side supports. The sinking of the tunnel sections on to the piles was an operation that had to be minutely controlled. Generally it was done at weekends in order to cause minimum interference to the heavy river-borne traffic constantly flowing. Resting the sections on the piles was not a simple matter either. The depth to which these had to be driven could not be gauged with precision, and so they were all built with adjustable heads that could be set finally when the tunnel sections were actually in position.

The first station on the north bank of the Maas is at Leuvehaven, and from there to the terminus at the Central Station the Metro runs entirely below ground. Beneath the city centre there is a layer of water-logged peat and clay that extends downwards to a depth of 60ft. In trying to construct a railway tunnel the advantages and disadvantages of the so-called 'wet' and 'dry' methods had to be considered. As in London and elsewhere the tunnels for the Metro were to be carried underneath the streets, but in Rotterdam there was the all-pervading existence of water. The normal 'cut and cover' methods were impossible. To use the 'dry' method would have required constant pumping to keep the water back; heavy piling would have been necessary on both sides,

251

foundations of buildings would have been jeopardised, and substantial shoring up would have been needed. Instead the 'wet' method was adopted.

As the channel was dug, extending in many cases to the full width of the street, it was allowed to fill with water. The sides were reinforced with steel coffer-dams, and the pressure of the water in the channel was enough to resist any tendency for the water-logged soil on either side to cause a collapse of the steel reinforcement. Construction started towards the end of the year 1960, and the open water-filled channels in the streets along the route provided a spectacular feature of interest in the city centre for several years. It was a slow job, but throughout the constructional period it was a never-failing source of interest for those who, in every city, seemed to have time to stand and stare. As on the section under the river Maas the tunnel sections were to rest on deep-driven piles with adjustable heads, and when the pile-drivers got to work the curiosity of many onlookers knew no bounds. The piles had to be driven to a depth 30 to 35ft. below the bottom level of the tunnel sections. The pre-cast sections had to be constructed as near as possible to where they would eventually be sunk. There was no question in these cases of building them in a dry-dock out in the River Maas. Certain streets were set aside specially and dry-docks were dug in the Weena and Blaak thoroughfares. The same procedure was adopted as in the great dry-dock on Van Brienenoord island, and sections floated and towed into their final resting places. The pre-casting of the sections was rendered more difficult in certain locations where the line was on a fairly sharp curve.

Taken all round, it was a remarkable project, and except for two short sections the entire 'underground' portion of the Metro was built by pre-casting the tunnel sections, and sinking them into the water. The arrangements for sealing the joints between adjacent sections was very successful, and no leakage of water into the tunnels has been experienced. It was nevertheless a measure of the magnitude of the task that it took a

Rotterdam: steel skeletons on which the concrete 'tubes' were constructed.

full eight years to build the 1·3 miles of 'underground' line. On the south bank of the river the line changes from an 'underground' to an 'elevated'. The latter is naturally much easier and cheaper to construct, and with less density of building there was plenty of room for it. All the four stations on the north bank are underground, namely Central Station, Stadhuis, Beurs, and Leuvehaven, while all three on the south bank are elevated—Rijnhaven, Maashaven, and Zuidplein. The line climbs out of the tunnel under the river on a gradient of 1 in 26, and I shall not forget for many a day the positively Arctic weather that greeted us on that February day when our train climbed out of the tunnel, and we got out on the elevated platforms of Rijnhaven station!

The line has been equipped in the most modern style. The track is laid to the European standard gauge of 4ft. 8½in., with rails continuously welded throughout. There are no sleepers as such. The rails are carried on longitudinal concrete supports, resting on resilient pads that have a high sound-absorbing character. The tunnel sections are so designed to provide space for a footpath at carriage floor level running throughout. The system of traction is 750 volts direct current, from a 'third rail', which is carried at the lineside, on the opposite of the tunnel to the footpath. The Metro was designed to carry 40,000 passengers per hour, with trains running at a 1½ minute headway, and as a result of an exacting specification a most interesting design of articulated car was produced, having an overall length of 95ft. and running on three four-wheeled bogies. In the off-peak hours a 'train' will consist of just one of these twin-units, but in the rush hours as many as four units are coupled in multiple. The first order was for 27 of these twin-units. The accompanying diagram shows the general layout.

It will be noticed at once that in contrast to practically all recent designs of coaches for rapid-transit metropolitan railways *all* seats are arranged transversely, and in such a way as to provide ample circulating space around the sliding doors. The gang-wayed connection between the two halves of the articulation, over the central bogie makes practicable a central block of 16 seats spaced almost identically to those in the main bodies of the cars. With seating for 80 passengers in each twin-articulated unit the Dutch authorities have also worked out the standing capacity on the basis of 4·8 persons to the square yard. This might seem a curious basis of computation, and it does not resolve itself into a round number even when converted into metric units. It then becomes 5·75 per square metre. Whether reckoning Imperially or metrically however, 4·8 to the square yard is not pushing them in too tightly; but even so the space available provides for another 210 persons per twin unit. On this basis a fully loaded four-unit train could carry 1160 passengers, and at 15 to the ton the gross weight of such a train would be 240 tons. The tare weight of a twin-unit is 39·7 tons.

Every one of the six axles in an articulated unit is powered, and the total power available continuously is 450 horsepower. With a total of 1800 horsepower available for a 4-car train weighing 240 tons maximum it is not surprising that acceleration is rapid; in fact, a speed of 15 m.p.h. is attained in 23 yards from rest, and the maximum permissible speed is 50 m.p.h. The braking system is the British-designed 'Westcode', as described in Chapter Eighteen. The electro-dynamic feature of the brake is used normally from 50 down to 7 m.p.h., and for the last stages of the stop from 7 down to zero the braking is electro-pneumatic. These trains can stop from 30 m.p.h. in about 80 yards. Apart from specialised items of equipment, such as the English-made brakes these cars were built entirely in Holland, and were the first venture of the Dutch carriage-building industry into 'underground' stock. The seats are covered in red plastic, designed to give good wearing qualities, and to be easy to clean, while the blue-grey external livery gives them a distinctive appearance. The heating is electrical, and I must say I found it very efficient on that icy winter's day when I first travelled on the line. They were not cheap. In a brochure issued by the Public Works Department of Rotterdam it is stated that the 27-twin-articulated units cost a total of £2 million—£74,000 each.

The stations are simply, but attractively designed with a single chain of strip lights continuously along the length of every platform, mounted on the ceiling about a foot back from the platform edge. This gives very effective illumination for anyone entering and leaving the cars. All the stations have one main concourse from which passengers proceed to the platforms, and at each station, both on the underground and elevated sections the concourse is a shopping centre in itself, with a total of 26 shops. Among many other things they sell snacks, smokers' requirements, jewellery, and photographic supplies; there is a savings bank, a repair shop for ladies shoes, and agents that furnish temporary typists and other office help—all in the Metro station concourses! Another modern facility is the provision of many slot-machine lockers for passengers' luggage. The Metro has been designed for operation with a minimum of staff. Platform announcements are all made by loudspeaker from the central control, and in contrast to many such installations the spoken word is very clear. Particular attention has been given to providing good reception and accoustical roof panelling is used throughout the areas concerned. Close circuit television is installed so that the situation on the platforms at any station is under constant surveillance from central control. At the moment, of course, the Metro is a simple line to operate, with trains shuttling back and forth on the one route; but as will be mentioned later some considerable extensions are planned.

From what I have written so far it will be appreciated that the Rotterdam Metro has some remarkable, if not unique features, in the placing of the pre-cast concrete tunnel sections in the watery channels, and in the unusual and very effective design of the trains themselves; but the most striking degree of automation is to be seen in the actual operation of the traffic. On the elevated section at Hilledijk, where there is an exchange siding with the main line of the Netherlands State Railway from Rotterdam towards Eindhoven, are to be seen the car sheds, and maintenance depots. There is also a car washing plant. But quite apart from these car-servicing facilities there is an elevated

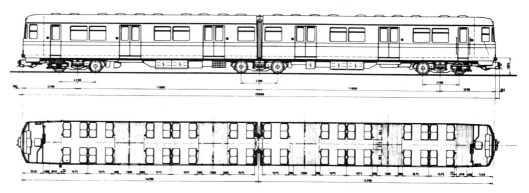

1 m is 3.281 feet

Rotterdam Metro: twin unit railcars.

signal cabin with a control panel from which the entire Metro system can be operated. I have used the words 'can be', rather than 'is', because that over-riding control is used only in emergency. In normal circumstances no signalmen at all are needed, because the entire service works automatically. The man on the signalling control panel is normally concerned with regulating trains into and out of the depot. Once out on to the main line automation becomes complete. At the present time no more than 15 men are required to operate the service at maximum peak hours density—13 train drivers and 2 traffic regulators. But the Rotterdam authorities have publicly announced that their intention is to dispense entirely with drivers, and that the present aim is to control all train running from the Hilledijk panel.

The Dutch have already carried the process of automation further, in one respect, than anyone else has so far ventured, on passenger railways. In writing of the Victoria Line in London, and the automatic operation of the trains I commented that wayside signals were no longer necessary, since the inductive control of the train, by the coded track circuits ensured complete safety and maintained the requisite distance between succeeding trains. In Rotterdam, with a system of automatic train *control* they have dispensed entirely with the wayside signals. In London some consideration was also given to this, but it was felt desirable to retain those in the approaches and leaving points at the stations to guide drivers who might have to resort to manual driving in the case of a disabled train. In Rotterdam the equivalent of the lineside signals is given to the driver on a console in the cab of the train. On this console are displayed visual signals indicating what is required in the way of running speed and braking. At the present time, while the system is novel—but nevertheless thoroughly proved and efficient—the trains are being manually driven, yet under a system of automatic train control. The driver has a time-lag of two seconds to act upon the visual signals given on the console in his cab. If he is slow to do so, or fails to act upon the indications displayed control of the train is taken out of his hands. As this control applies from end to end of the line it will be realised that there is nothing technically to prevent the removal of the driver entirely, as on the Victoria Line in London.

The presence of the driver on the train is however not entirely a matter of psychology, and the presence of a railway employee present could well be a matter of saving a great deal of time in the case of even a minor and quite harmless breakdown. But one does not have to look very far ahead to envisage a time when there will be driverless passenger trains on many rapid transit systems. Certainly the City of Rotterdam has gone farther than other administrations in stating categorically that their aim is to dispense with the drivers. How soon this will become an actuality remains to be seen. One thing is quite certain; the present Metro line, no more than 3·65 miles long, is only a beginning. Already studies are in hand towards extending the existing line, southwards from the present terminus at Zuidplein to Hoogbliet. A further most important project is to construct an East-West line connecting with the existing Metro at Exchange ('Beurs') station. This is part of a huge development scheme to build a satellite town at Alexanderpolder, to house some 200,000 people. The plans for this satellite of Rotterdam include provision for the Metro. At Beurs station, where interchange facilities are projected, the contract for the original station included excavations for the East-West line. This will run at a different level from the present line, and to avoid the general upheaval that would be inevitable if no preliminary preparations were made the authorities decided to get the lower level tunnel built at the same time as the first, just for the length of the interchange station and just beyond the area that would cause disturbance to the present railway when construction of the second started.

It is of particular interest that Rotterdam has made public not only the total cost of the Metro, as first opened, but details of the various sections of railway itself, and its fixed equipment. These costs have been converted into English pounds at the rate of exchange prevailing in 1968, when the line was first opened, thus:

Tunnels, elevated permanent way	£17,150,000
Pedestrian tunnel, Civil Defence spaces, bus-station	£2,500,000
Rolling Stock, 27 cars plus auxiliaries	£2,000,000
Tracks, including those in Hilledijk Yard	£2,450,000
Signalling, wiring, telephones, station lighting	£760,000
TOTAL	£24,860,000

Cost aside, the city of Rotterdam has one of the most interesting of all recent metropolitan railways, in its unusual location and in the automatic control of its train movements.

Rotterdam: motorman's view of the line ahead in a tunnel section.

CHAPTER TWENTY-ONE

Many New Schemes

This book is being written at a time when a plethora of schemes for underground railways are being projected in many parts of the world. In Mexico, in East Berlin, in Japan and elsewhere, lines are in hand, many following the patterns long established in London, or in Paris, and some including features peculiar to their own localities. But everywhere there is the over-riding aim to reduce congestion, and when it is not to reduce congestion in the streets it is to reduce congestion on well-established underground railways that are already being worked to capacity. On one or two of the older networks the pattern of development is significantly changing, and nowhere more strikingly than in Paris. In Chapter Six of this book I told of the extreme controversy that developed between the Government of the day and the City Council over the form the first Paris Metro should take, and how the Council won the day, and kept the underground a completely self-contained system, with no physical connection with the main line railways. Until two years ago it remained so, but in December 1969 the first stage of a striking development was brought into service.

With the gradual extension of the City, building a large number of dormitory suburbs, and no less the need to provide rapid transit to and from the major airports the Paris Transport Authority decided upon a new scheme altogether, by taking over a number of suburban branch lines of the S.N.C.F. and linking them with new deep-level underground lines cutting beneath the heart of the city. This was a revival of the authorised, but still-born 'Deep Level District' scheme in London, in which the new lines would be essentially express routes, with comparatively few stations. Furthermore, the new Parisian scheme did what the old Metro had never attempted to do, namely to provide ready interchange with the large main line terminal stations. The Metro itself has remained, to an overwhelming extent, contained within the line of the old city walls, whereas the Paris Transport Authority in following the Ashfield policy of probing out in the surrounding suburbs is avoiding the overloading of the purely central-metropolitan lines, by the construction of these new deep-level 'express' lines. By them it is hoped that congestion will be relieved at very busy main line terminal stations like the Gare du Nord, and St. Lazare, by diverting a good deal of the commuter traffic to the deep-level underground direct from the suburban lines. The case is somewhat analogous to the Eastern Region connections to the Central Line tube in London, made by the cross-platform exchange at Stratford except that the Parisians will go underground on a new 'express' line, instead of a standard tube already worked to capacity.

At the present time three express lines beneath Paris are projected. The western and eastern extremities of one line, connecting in each case with S.N.C.F. branches are already under construction, and by the time this book is printed it is anticipated that the branch line of the old Etat system, from Nanterre to St. Germain en Laye will be connected to a deep level express route running beneath the line of the existing Metro from La Defense through Etoile to what will be a grand central junction at Auber. It is proposed that this line will be continued, deep underground, beneath the very heart of the city to the Gare de Lyon to link up with a line already in operation, at deep level, from the Place de la Nation to beyond the city fortifications just short of Vincennes. There it comes to the surface to pick up a former Est branch running to Boissy St. Leger. No timetable has yet been set for the completion of the deep level portion between Auber and 'Nation', but the significance of the project, and the likeness, in its effect, to Ashfield schemes like Epping to West Ruislip, via the Central Line in London will be appreciated from the accompanying map. The country sections at both ends of this underground artery are planned to bifurcate, to provide high speed electric services to Montesson, in the west, and to Lagny and Meaux, in the east.

The other two routes projected at present run from north to south, and roughly parallel to each other, as can be seen from the map. In the meantime the two sections of the Regional Express Metro that are already opened to the public represent some of the most finely executed underground railway construction to be seen anywhere in the

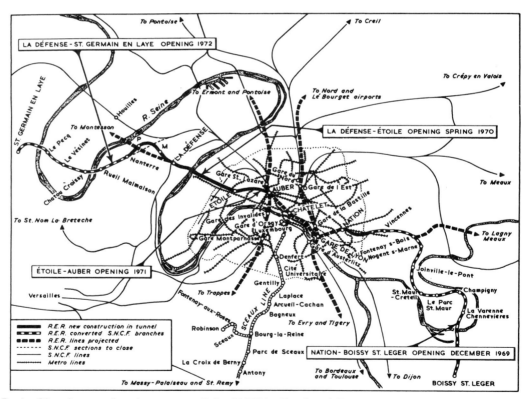

Paris: Sketch map showing routes of the 'RER'—Regional Express Metro.

258

world. The civil engineering has been exceedingly difficult. The cross-sectional drawing of the station Auber shows at a glance the exceedingly ambitious and comprehensive layout of the line, in comparison to that of the old Metro, while the photographs reproduced speak for themselves in conveying the spacious air, and atmosphere totally unlike that of an ordinary 'underground' station. The system of traction is 1500 volts direct current, the same as that of the Orleans, and P.L.M. main lines, and the liberal structure gauge clearances permit of the running of main line express locomotives through the tunnels. The stations, Nation, Etoile, La Defense, savour more of modern main line standards than of an underground line, with cafeteria, bookstalls, and even platform cafes with seats and tables, while each station has a large underground circu-lating area on a mezzazine, above platform level. Provision has been made for an immense carrying capacity, both in the trains and in the multiplicity of escalators, ticket barriers, and platform space. At the stations platform width has been varied as between one line and another, because the anticipated number of passengers in the peak periods are not uniformly heavy in both directions of travel.

Between the stations Etoile and La Defense the new deep-level line passes under the river Seine. It is carried in a double-track tunnel of 28ft. diameter from La Defense towards the city centre, and there was some difficult ground, necessitating working under an unusually high pressure of compressed air as the river bank was neared. The actual river crossing was made by the submerged tube method, as at Rotterdam, except that the sections were much heavier in cross-section. As at Rotterdam the sections were pre-cast on an island in the Seine adjacent to the Pont Neuilly, and then floated into a position for lowering into a deep trench excavated in the river bed. As with the old Metro the routes were chosen to pass, for the most part, beneath main thoroughfares, so that in many locations one has the deep level Regional Express Metro immediately beneath the modest tunnels of the old Metro. But at the crossing of the Seine it was thought advisable to make a divergence from the straight line of the Avenue du General de Gaulle so as to avoid tunnelling immediately beneath the Pont de Neuilly, with the risk of disturbing the foundations of the bridge. In general, the civil engineering works on the line must be some of the most extensive ever built on a deep level railway. The arched roofs in the Auber and Etoile stations have a clear span of nearly 70ft., with rail level nearly 100ft. below the surface of the road above. The station La Defense, with no old-style Metro line above it, is constructed nearer to the surface, and the huge and elaborate reinforced concrete structure was built in an open excavation.

It goes almost without saying in such an ultra-modern installation that a high degree of automation is included in the signalling, train control, and in the regulation of passenger movements. In recent years certain of the old Metro routes have been com-pletely re-equipped so far as signalling is concerned, installing a centralised form of control for all train movement, and it is the experience of this that has determined the form of control on the Regional Express Metro. When the intervening underground section between Auber and Nation is completed the entire line between St. Germain en Laye and Boissy St. Leger will be controlled from one signal box, located at Vin-cennes. At present, the spectacular control room shown in the photograph reproduced on page 260, covers only the eastern section of the line, from Nation to Boissy St. Leger. The system of working, known as Systeme de Commande Automatique, or S.C.A., manufactured by the Jeumont-Schneider company, is, in over-all effect similar to the programme machine operation on the Victoria Line, in London, but the technical

Paris: The Regional Express Metro. This view of the station "Nation" gives a fine impression of the spaciousness and elegance of the new underground railway.

Paris: The Regional Express Metro; the control centre at Vincennes.

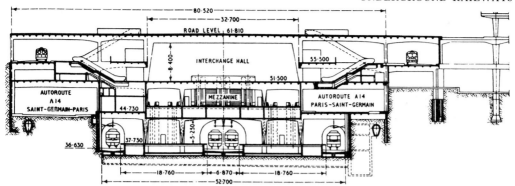

Paris—'RER': A section through La Défense Station. This massive structure contains four platforms to cater for a future divergence of routes to the west, although only that to St Germain is under construction.

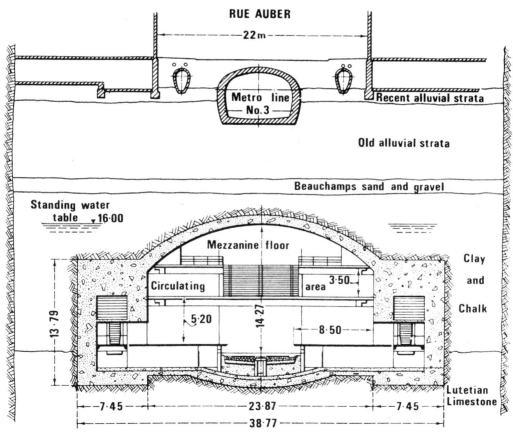

Paris—'RER': the deep level Auber station in relation to the existing Metro line.

details and principles involved are different. The 'programme' for each train is initiated when the crew takes over at the depot. They 'clock-in', so to speak, by setting up an eight-digit number in the cab of the train, and this pin-points the particular train, and depot, and transmits accordingly to the S.C.A. apparatus. The time of departure from the depot is checked automatically, and if that time is imminent the route is set, and the train signalled. Its progress is subsequently monitored through the day's running, and the attention of the regulator at Vincennes drawn to any irregularity, or divergence from schedule.

The S.C.A. is a very comprehensive computerised form of control, and is capable of being extended to fulfil functions in addition to signalling, and provision has been made for the automatic operation of the trains, as on the Victoria Line, at some future time. A very important feature is the facility available to the Regulator, at Vincennes, to intervene, or make emergency movements, while another feature of the operation is that on the surface extensions over what were previously steam worked branch lines of the S.N.C.F. some freight trains will still require to be worked at infrequent intervals. These do not have identification code transmitters, whereby they could 'clock in' on the S.C.A. system; but their approach to the Regional Metro Express route concerned is detected by an electronic track circuit, and information transmitted to the S.C.A. apparatus at Vincennes. In the daily programme of fast electric trains there are what the French term 'ghost paths'. In British railway operation such timetabled workings are usually referred to as 'conditional paths', or noted that a train at that particular time 'runs when required'. On the Regional Metro Express system the Regulator at Vincennes, on receiving advice of the approach of an S.N.C.F. freight train allocates to it, in the S.C.A. programme, the first convenient 'ghost' path. When the appropriate time comes up on the programme the route is set, and the train signalled through.

The trains are naturally larger and more commodious than on the in-town Metro, with a higher proportion of space allocated to seats. Even so, standing in the peak periods appears to be regarded as a foregone conclusion. The express Metro trains consist of a number of three-car sets, with a trailer car including accommodation for both first and second class passengers sandwiched between two motor coaches. These latter are second class only. The total seating accommodation of a three-car set is for 40 first class, and 160 second class passengers. But it is officially reckoned that these three-car units provide standing room for 658 passengers. According to traffic requirements trains are made up to one, two or three units, and the latter, if carrying a maximum complement would convey 2574 passengers. The maximum speed in ordinary service is 62 m.p.h., but these fine trains are capable of a maximum speed of 78 m.p.h. The section between Auber and Defense was opened to the public on November 18, 1971 and some very fast running is now scheduled. The distance between these two stations is 4·55 miles, and the time allowed is a mere $6\frac{1}{2}$ minutes—inclusive of a 20-second stop intermediately at Etoile! This gives an average speed, inclusive of the one intermediate stop of 42 m.p.h.

This, it will be realised, is something far away from the kind of running ordinarily associated with underground railways. It is, of course, the outcome of having no more than a few widely spaced stations, and a track and rolling stock fully up to main line standards.

The Stockholm 'Tunnelbana' is another fine example of modern underground railway construction and working. As in many great cities it arose from the steady

Stockholm: In the driver's cab, showing telephone and cab signal equipment.

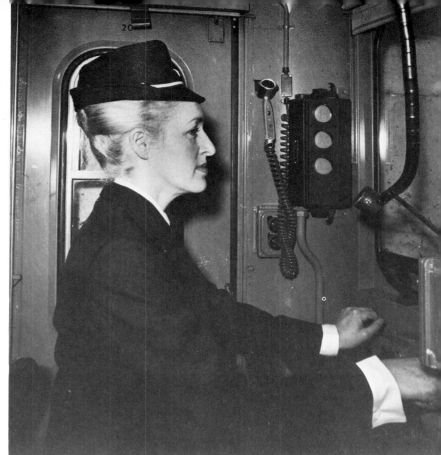

Stockholm: The Central Control Office, at Tunnel-Centralen

worsening of traffic conditions in the streets, which were complicated in that so much depended upon the various tram routes. The decision to build an underground railway system was taken in 1941. The geographical situation has some points of similarity to that of Rotterdam, in the many waterways that intersect some of the busiest and most congested areas; and as in Rotterdam the 'underground' was planned to include both tunnel and surface sections as most suitable for the varying conditions. In certain cases the existing tram routes were converted to railways, but some of the most difficult and expensive work was involved in connecting the two arms of this system running north and south of the main waterway. This involved tunnelling, and a four-track underwater section. Practically the whole of the old city centre was demolished, and the tunnel built in the bottom of the excavation. This section, which included a mile of underwater tunnel cost approximately £4000 *per yard*.

The system of electrification is 700 volts d.c. with third rail pick-up, and a handsome and commodious design of lightweight car is in general use. The stations, especially those in the central underground area are handsomely styled, with wide platforms and brilliant lighting, that effectively dispels any impression there might be of tunnel conditions. The picture of Odenplan, one of the principal stations in the central area conveys vividly the light and airy atmosphere that has been created. The operating nerve-centre is at Tunnel-Centrallen, in the heart of the city, where the control room contains an illuminated track diagram of the entire Tunnelbana system, and control panels from which all train movements can be regulated. Colour light signals and automatic train control are installed, and telephones are mounted at intervals of 220 yards along the lines by which the motormen of trains may communicate with the central control at Tunnel-Centralen. To keep constant surveillance over the flow of passengers closed circuit television is installed at stations whereby the situation may at all times be seen at operation headquarters.

Another new project that is interesting because of the many new features that are involved, is the underground loop authorised in Melbourne. The capital city of Victoria, with a population of more than two million persons, has until now been dependent upon the Victorian Railways for a large proportion of its commuter traffic. The majority of the suburban lines are electrified, and operated at a high density of service, but so far as purely city traffic is concerned it is all handled at two large stations, Spencer Street, and Flinders Street. The latter is claimed to be one of the busiest stations in the world. To stand on the steps of St. Pauls Cathedral, just opposite, and see the commuters pouring out of Flinders Street station at the start of the working day is one of the most astonishing sights I have ever seen. London has nothing to compare with it, because at great terminal stations like Waterloo, London Bridge, and Liverpool Street a high proportion of arriving passengers transfer at once to one or another of the underground lines, and never appear on the streets. And that is just the point that has been so concerning the Victorian Government in recent years. Flinders Street station is being worked to capacity, and no ordinary scheme of modernisation would provide the extra that will undoubtedly be needed to cope with the meteoric rise in population of the city that is now in full flood. By the year 1985 it is expected that the population will have reached 3·7 million, and that the metropolitan area will have expanded from something less than 500 square miles to around 700!

The Metropolitan Transport Committee set up by the Victorian Government based its proposals upon a development of existing transport facilities rather than the estab-

Stockholm: Odenplan a busy station in the central area

Stockholm: Television supervision of underground stations.

265

blishment of entirely new ones, and in the underground railway plan, with which I am concerned, is conceived entirely within the framework of the Victorian Railways network. It is unique in this respect. While the original Metropolitan Railway in London had connections to certain of the existing main line railways it was independent of them all, and with some of them not always on the friendliest of terms! To appreciate the Melbourne underground concept some reference to the existing railway facilities must be made. This can be done most graphically by referring to the aerial photograph of the city centre, reproduced on this page, and on which the proposed route of the underground loop is superimposed. The enormous volume of suburban traffic arriving at Flinders Street comes from both left and right of the map, with a not-inconsiderable 'extra' crossing the bridge across the river Yarra, beneath the word 'Underground' in the bottom left hand corner of the map. But while Flinders Street, as can be seen, is a through station an overwhelming proportion of the traffic either terminates, or originates there. Under the words 'Northern Connection' and 'Sandringham Connection', towards the bottom right hand corner, is an enormous nest of carriage sidings, and while these are very skilfully arranged so that empty stock movements to and from the station can be carried out with a minimum of interference to other traffic, the process of handling a train is much slower than if a single through movement was involved. A train has to draw in, unload its tremendous complement of passengers, and then reverse into one of the appropriate sidings.

A study of train and personnel movement indicated that the maximum frequency of service that could be expected at existing platforms in Flinders Street is about 10 trains per hour, at each platform. This in itself is extremely good amounting to a train leaving

Melbourne: aerial view of the City Centre, with the route of the projected underground rail loop superimposed.

every six minutes. If on the other hand the trains did not terminate at Flinders Street, but could unload, and proceed in the same direction it is estimated that with modern colour light signalling each platform could deal with 24 trains every hour. But if they did not terminate at Flinders Street, and were subsequently pushed in the carriage sidings outside, where on earth could they go to? There is certainly no parking space at the other large station, Spencer Street, which is concerned with long distance express passenger work, and has a very large freight marshalling yard adjacent and taking up practically all the space for sidings. It was then that the concept of the underground loop railway took shape. If there was a loop making a circuit of the central business district of the city it would serve two major functions: it would avoid the necessity of many suburban trains terminating at Flinders Street, and by the provision of new underground stations would distribute the commuter traffic more evenly around the central area, instead of having almost all the clientele swamping Flinders Street twice a day. Arriving trains would call at Flinders Street and then proceed round the loop, either terminating in the present sidings, or continuing to one of the country termini. The underground loop, as now authorised, will form a part of the Victorian Railways, with its operation fully integrated with the existing suburban and main line network.

The accompanying diagrammatic track plan shows that the underground loop will be quadruple tracked, with the most comprehensive connections to the existing surface lines between North Melbourne and Spencer Street, on the one hand, and to the Flinders Street–Richmond complex on the other. An additional two running lines are to be added on the 'viaduct' section between Flinders Street and Spencer Street to accommodate the through running of many trains that now terminate at one or other of the existing large city stations. So far as the surrounding streets are concerned the 'viaduct' section is an 'elevated', though not in the style of American cities. The aerial photograph shows that the streets are beside, and not beneath the railway tracks; and although it is not strictly within the subject of underground railways—rather the reverse!—these streets give splendid views of the magnificent arrays of old-time semaphore signals on the viaduct lines, which will disappear with modernisation. The quadruple tracked underground loop will run beneath existing streets, and to keep within the width thus prescribed the tunnels will be double tiered. There will be two tracks abreast of each other at one level, and two more at a lower level. Much preliminary work had already been done in sinking shafts and bores to examine the rock formation; but the complexity of the connections to existing lines, with the numerous burrowing junctions will provide a rare task for the civil engineers and their contractors, not least in the steep gradients that will be involved in transferring tracks from the high elevation of the viaduct lines to the lower level of the underground loop. No doubt a large amount of intermediate stage work will be necessary; but having been associated with those who carried out the extremely complicated stage work involved in the new Melbourne marshalling yard, just to the north of Spencer Street station, I can well believe the engineers of the Victorian Railways will take the 'Underground Loop' in their stride.

And so, finally in this chapter dealing with new developments, I come back to the *alma mater* of all underground railway systems—London. It is fascinating to see how the problems of London have echoed round the great cities of the world; how those who have journeyed to England, and studied the working of the railways of the London

Transport Board, have set out to resolve their own problems. In London itself the stultifying effect of World War II cannot be over-emphasised, in its halting of the development at the eastern end of the Central Line, and through financial stringency bringing development in line construction to a complete halt after the Woodford and Epping extensions were eventually completed. It is always interesting to contemplate the 'might have beens', and to try and imagine how development would have gone forward had the years from 1939 onwards been 'normal' and Lord Ashfield had been able to continue his established policies. But there is no doubt that the central areas, represented by the three Yerkes tubes, the Central London, and the City and South London would have become seriously overloaded; and it is possible that the Victoria Line would have come much earlier.

Despite the great success of the Victoria Line it has relieved the pressure in the central area only on one directional flow of traffic, and urgent consideration has been given to giving some relief to one of the hardest pressed tube lines of all, the Bakerloo. The Northern line has its central relief in the alternative routes between Camden Town and Kennington, via Charing Cross and the Bank, respectively, while the Victoria Line has undoubtedly relieved pressure on the Piccadilly, and to some extent on the Inner Circle. But the Bakerloo, with two long and popular country extensions, has two streams of crowded trains funnelling into one pair of tunnels at Baker Street. The proposed relief is the Fleet Line, which has long passed beyond the stage of an 'idea', and is now, at the time of writing, a fully worked out scheme awaiting Government approval of the expenditure. The management of the London Transport Board has never ceased to stress the immense advantages in cost that would accrue if it were possible to start work on this new line as soon as the Brixton extension of the Victoria Line was completed. All the specialised equipment, and experienced labour force

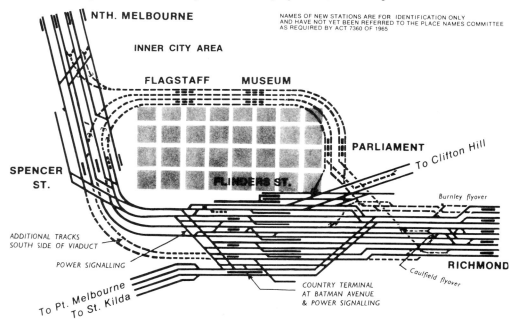

Melbourne: Diagram showing track layout of new underground loop.

London: for reconstruction of Cannon Street station (Inner Circle Line) in 1969 the 'umbrella' form of construction was used to carry the road traffic while modernisation was effected beneath. Phase One: getting the girders into position.

Cannon Street reconstruction: traffic flowing on both 'umbrella' bridges.

269

could be immediately available, whereas if a hiatus was allowed to develop between the completion of one and the starting of the other project, a great deal of additional expense would be involved. At the moment of proof-correction it is gratifying to be able to record that authority to go ahead has now been given.

In the meantime, in the light of the experience so far gained, it can be said that the Fleet Line looks like another absolute winner. Its starting point will be at Baker Street, where it will absorb the whole of the existing Bakerloo traffic from the Metropolitan Line extension routes. Henceforth the present services from the Watford (L.N.W.R.) line will be the only ones passing over the inner London section of the Bakerloo, from Baker Street to the Elephant and Castle; the whole of the traffic from the Metropolitan extensions of the Bakerloo will pass henceforth over the Fleet Line. This is planned to run via Bond Street and Green Park to Trafalgar Square, Ludgate Hill, Cannon Street, to Fenchurch Street, thus providing an immensely valuable relief for purely local traffic on the Charing Cross–Aldgate section of the Inner Circle. Beyond Fenchurch Street the line would pass under the Thames and enter an area of South-East London so far served only by the Metropolitan Line, by the somewhat roundabout route through the existing Thames Tunnel, via Wapping, and of course by the Southern Region of British Railways. A bifurcation is planned so as to provide interchange with both the Brighton and the South Eastern sections of the Southern at New Cross Gate and New Cross respectively. The latter line is planned to continue to Lewisham, and one can well imagine that will not prove the ultimate extent of the line.

The second very important project on London Transport, now fully authorised, is the extension of the Piccadilly Line westwards from Hounslow to Heathrow Airport. As a first thought it may seem slightly incongruous to associate underground railways with inter-continental and trans-oceanic air travel; but there is a growing consciousness of the need for integration of all forms of sophisticated travel in this present age, and

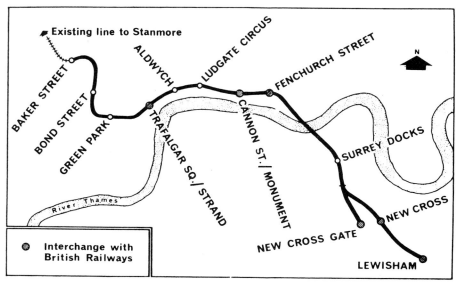

London: route diagram of the Fleet Line which will be constructed in three stages from the Baker Street end to Strand, Fenchurch Street and finally to Lewisham.

270

just as one finds the Paris Regional Express Metro including a future service to Le Bourget Airport in its plans, so also is London now embracing Heathrow in the 'underground' network. At the time of writing this chapter news of the decision to site the third London airport at Foulness has been received. It is to be hoped that the fullest consideration will be given to the provision of speedy railway communication with Central London. If the arrangements presently in hand for Heathrow can be taken as a prototype a branch of the Fleet Line continuing on the north bank of the Thames. from Fenchurch Street could be a possibility. So far as Heathrow is concerned the point, in relation to the present book, is that the extension from Hounslow will be mainly an underground line. The new mileage is about $3\frac{1}{2}$, of which 2 will be constructed by 'cut and cover' methods and on the surface, and the remaining $1\frac{1}{2}$ miles will be in relatively deep-level tube.

The new line is expected to provide a greatly accelerated service of public transport between the airport and Central London, and a journey time of 35 minutes has been quoted between Heathrow and Hyde Park Corner. While travel by 'underground' may not appeal to the more affluent of airline passengers the enormous growth of long distance air travel, in recent years must be taken into account, and there is the question of daily transport for the ever increasing staff constantly on duty at Heathrow. This is now well in excess of 45,000, and is expected to reach about 65,000 by the year 1980. Traffic studies made prior to the authorisation of the construction of this new underground railway give the following conservative estimates for likely traffic in 1981:

Airline passengers	7·6 million
Airport staff	5·0 million
Sightseers	0·9 million
Additional London commuters	0·4 million

It is certainly significant of the public interest taken in aircraft that London Transport anticipated conveying upwards of a million sightseers in a year over the new line. The additional commuters are expected to come from the one intermediate station between Heathrow and Hounslow, which is at present designated Hatton Cross.

While it is true that the majority of airline passengers today are travelling fairly 'light', in view of the restrictions on weight of luggage that may be taken free, an ordinary tube train is hardly an ideal means of transport, especially if one's journey happened to coincide with the London peak commuter period! Accordingly it is intended that the trains running to Heathrow will have special luggage compartments in every car. As it is proposed that all trains at present terminating at Hounslow West will be extended to Heathrow this will entail the construction of much stock of a modified style. The present estimates of traffic anticipate the operation of a 5-minute service to and from Heathrow, on Monday to Fridays, increased to 4 minutes in the commuter peak periods. At weekends the interval is expected to be $7\frac{1}{2}$ minutes. It is nevertheless a remarkable facility that will be provided, of a train at never more than $7\frac{1}{2}$-minute intervals from Heathrow into Central London.

Of course, airline passengers will always run the risk of getting entangled in the rush-hour traffic, and for those making for Heathrow at such times it could mean standing for part of the journey, after having manoeuvred maximum weight of luggage on and off the escalators at stations like Piccadily Circus, Holborn, or Kings Cross. On the other hand the evening commuter peak does not in general, coincide with the outgoing airline peak. Lovers of statistics will be intrigued to know that it has been estimated that of the total time spent by all airline passengers on the Piccadilly line only about $1\frac{1}{4}$ per cent will be spent standing—a comforting thought, except if one happened to be one of those involved, and enjoying this pleasure as the first lap of a journey to Australia! Many years ago the story used to be told of two passengers on a Southern Railway express from Waterloo. In the fashion of most English travellers neither spoke until the train was drawing into Southampton; then one of them, gathering up a few items of hand luggage remarked: 'Well, that's the worst part of the journey over.'

'Oh', replied his companion, 'How far are you going?'

'Singapore!'

This is not to deprecate in advance a new London Transport service to which I know a great deal of market research has been devoted. To the vast majority of travellers who have to use public transport of some kind or another, to and from Heathrow, it will be an inestimable boon, particularly as the underground station is planned to be located centrally among the various airport terminals, and no doubt connected liberally with escalators, luggage conveyors and such like. But one does wonder how long it will be before real 'express' connections will be demanded, not only from Heathrow, but also from Foulness and airports of the future, with limited stop underground trains feeding into some deep level terminal, or exchange station in central London, adequately equipped with all facilities for dealing with 'long distance' travel. In the meantime it is evident that the present extension to Heathrow is a straight continuation of the Ashfield policy, of feeding more and more traffic into the existing central 'tube' area.

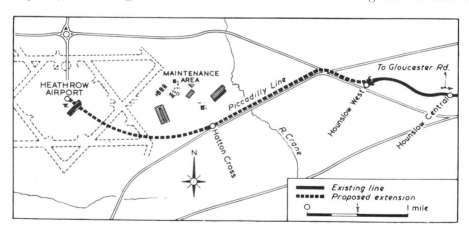

London: the Heathrow extension of the Piccadilly line, on which work is now in progress.

CHAPTER TWENTY-TWO

San Francisco: Bay Area Rapid Transit

There is nothing like long distance air travel to confuse any sense of direction, or 'bump of locality' that one might possess. One may fly for thousands of miles on the direct course of a terrestial Great Circle and then at journey's end comes the frequent circling round an airport, and manoeuvring to take which of the various run-ways is appropriate to the direction of the wind. I found this confusion nowhere more so than at San Francisco. That unique and beautiful city was to be no more than a staging point for my wife and me on the long journey to Australia. Our 48-hour stop-over could be a pure bonus. We had no sight-seeing planned; we would, as the modern saying goes, 'play it as it came'. For the same reason I had done little in the way of preliminary reading; after all, there is nothing so frustrating as planning a programme of sight-seeing and then to be baulked by bad weather, or other circumstances. So it was that I was little prepared for the remarkable geography of San Francisco; and arriving at dusk and driving straight from airport to hotel I was conscious of no more than stretches of wide waterway where I least expected it. As it turned out our two days were favoured with glorious weather, and in the short time we were able to see a good deal of the city and its surroundings.

An acquaintance with the geographical layout is necessary to an understanding of the importance of the Bay Area Rapid Transit system—BART for short—and one of the most remarkable urban, or inter-urban electric railway systems built in recent years. It was under construction at the time of our visit, but the first section will probably be in operation before this book is in print. Bay Area: to English minds the term 'bay' conjures up a stretch of coast line like that of Torbay, or going further afield, to the Bay of Naples, or Table Bay on which the City of Capetown sits so graciously. But San Francisco Bay is like none of these. It is an almost completely land-locked lagoon, in geographical plan like those lonely and fascinating *etangs* along the Mediterranean coast of France to the west of Marseille, but alike, nevertheless, in nothing else. San Francisco Bay is surrounded by low rocky hills and a host of teeming suburbs, in addition to the twin-cities of Oakland and San Francisco itself, and entrance to the 'lagoon' is through the far-famed Golden Gate. San Francisco, though built on the relatively narrow strip of land between the 'bay' and the sea turns its back, as it were, upon the Pacific Ocean and clusters in an extraordinarily picturesque array of sky-scrapers where two sections of the 'bay' are separated by a channel only 5 miles wide. 'Only 5 miles'; indeed the bay both north and south of San Francisco City is some 15 miles wide, and in the haze of a hot summer's day there are times when the visitor looking

273

towards the mainland might well imagine he was looking out to sea!

The greatest residential development has taken place on the eastern shores of the bay. The immediate environs of San Francisco are rocky, barren, and inhospitable, and it is natural that the Oakland side has proved more attractive, particularly with the provision of the Oakland Bridge connecting the two. But one supreme facility breeds the need for another. We crossed the Oakland bridge in a motor-coach in mid-afternoon, and even at what would undoubtedly be considered an off-peak hour the traffic was tremendous—six lines, and every one well occupied and all moving at maximum speed. If ever an urban complex called for railway communication this was it. The main line railways of the U.S.A. naturally serve both San Francisco and Oakland, but there has hitherto been no connection between the two, and it was for construction of the Bay Area Rapid Transit system that funds were made available in 1962. This is no purely urban project, but an extraordinarily comprehensive scheme that involved the construction of no less than 75 route miles of double-tracked railway. Of the entire BART system 23 miles are in tunnel, 27 miles are on ground level, and 25 miles on viaduct. Much of the tunnelling has been done by 'cut and cover' methods, with the inevitable

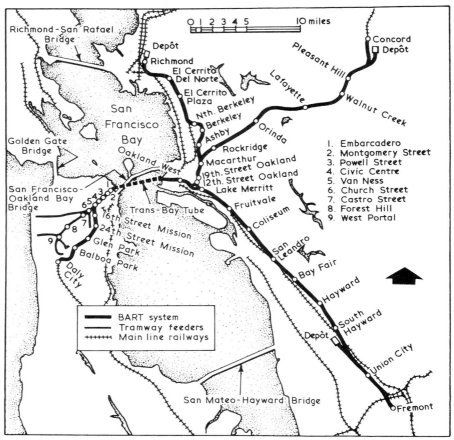

San Francisco: The 75 mile BART System as it will be in 1972 on completion of the initial construction phase; several extensions are planned.

disturbance of street traffic during the constructional period. This has been particularly the case in Market Street, San Francisco's main business artery.

A glance at the accompanying sketch map shows that by far the greatest extent of BART is on the Oakland side, with three lengthy branches leading to Richmond, Concord and Fremont respectively. The critical section from the operating point of view is that between MacArthur and 12th Street Oakland, with the Richmond and Concord routes converging at the north end, and the Trans-Bay tube, and the Fremont lines converging at the south end. On the San Francisco side, after tunnelling under the length of Market Street, a single route leads out to a terminus at Daly City. This limited extent certainly highlights the difference in residential and other development between the San Francisco and the Oakland sides of the bay. BART, when completed, will present a number of quite outstanding features in urban transport that clearly reflect the extent to which the existing systems in many parts of the world have been studied. A specification has been laid down that 30,000 passengers an hour were to be conveyed on each running line, *all seated*, and this has involved the provision for 10-coach trains, each carrying 720 passengers, at $1\frac{1}{2}$ minute headway. Including station stops of 20 seconds duration the average speed demanded is 45 to 50 m.p.h. with maximum speeds of 80 m.p.h. As the stations in suburban territory are about $2\frac{1}{2}$ miles apart the acceleration from rest will need to be pretty fierce. The system of traction is 1000 volts direct current, with third rail pick-up.

BART has been aimed particularly at competition with the private car. At present commuters in their tens of thousands stream across Oakland bridge, morning and evening, with all the frustration of heavy traffic, and the problems of parking near to one's place of work. The new trains contemplate no standing. The 72 seats in each side of the 10-car trains are upholstered with foam rubber covered by woven and smooth vinyl fabric; the floors have fitted carpets throughout, and a full system of air-conditioning is installed, with temperature varied automatically as the outside air temperature varies. No steps that could lead to the comfort of passengers during the journey have been neglected, though with no more than 20-second station stops, the general tempo of passenger movement will necessarily have to be in the style of the London Underground. The doors are of the double-leaf type, opened and closed automatically to conform with instructions from the central computer, though how this may preclude more passengers surging in than there are seats available is not clear. Presumably some standing will be inevitable at times; but the significant point is that in calculating the carrying capacity of the line *no* standing passengers have been allowed for. This, of course, is in the strongest contrast to the situations in London, Paris, Milan, Rotterdam and elsewhere, as already noticed in this book.

In any rapid-transit urban system however comfort is a secondary consideration in comparison to speed and reliability of service, together with the utmost safety in operation, and the system of signalling and automatic train control is accordingly one of the most highly-sophisticated the world has yet seen. It goes almost without saying that the whole 75 miles of line will be regulated from a single control centre located at the Oakland 'funnel' section. It has been stated that successful operation of the high-speed, $1\frac{1}{2}$ miles headway service requires consistent operation to within 5 seconds—*five seconds*! —of scheduled time, and as this was considered to be completely beyond the capabilities of human drivers it has been arranged for all train movements to be continuously monitored by a central computer, at Oakland, and their progress directly controlled by the programme installed in that computer. The principle of automatic train operation established on the Victoria Line in London is carried a stage further on BART, in that the central computer will close the doors after a 20-second interval, and initiate the starting of the train. As in London an attendant will travel in the front of each train, but in normal working he will have nothing to do. He is there to answer passengers' queries, and has the power to stop the train in emergency, and similarly to open and close the doors. In an emergency he can drive the train, at low speed.

It is a marvellous, and, to an engineer of an older generation, an almost frightening conception of the capacity of modern computerised techniques that a railway of 75 route miles could have as many as 105 ten-car trains in operation at the same time, each running up to 80 m.p.h. between stops, and all be controlled by a single 'machine' at headquarters. It is, in some ways, the consumation of the whole history of urban

San Francisco: the control centre of the entire BART system, from which as many as 105 trains will be controlled at once.

railway transport, as outlined in the history of underground railway development in this book. The rate of progress has been incredible seeing that within my own lifetime we have advanced from ordinary block signalling, with mechanical full-sized levers, a signal box at each station, and the 'right-away' given to the driver by a chain of attendants travelling on the open platforms between each pair of coaches! But with all the intense sophistication of BART provision has to be made for the eventuality of things going wrong. The mischance against which precautions have definitely been taken is that of a train not running up to standard performance, which by its dilatoriness could delay and slow down a large part of the intense service. The continuous monitoring of the running of all trains would quickly detect any such sluggard, and the aim would be to take it out of service and substitute a good train as soon as possible. There are train storage sidings at the terminal points of each line, and the regulating Officer at Oakland Control would use his facility to intervene in the programme set by the master computer to make such substitution, which can be done by altering the programme rather than through any need to resort to individual point switching, or signal operation.

The control centre at Oakland is far more than a glorified power signal box, as now becoming familiar on railways in most advanced countries of the world. The system of facets, to give an approximately radial appearance, covers three distinct aspects of the overall control organisation. Each of these aspects has its own control console, and the normal staff on duty comprises one supervisor at each console—three men in all. The first section deals with train operation, and has a track diagram covering the entire 75 miles of the system. As it is anticipated that there may be 105 trains in motion at the same time the track occupancy is not normally indicated. The running is continuously monitored by the computer and the supervisor at the control console wants to know only when anything is not going according to plan. He can switch on to any section of line, to observe the actual running conditions, or to any particular junction or interlocking. He can speak to any individual train, by radio, or make announcements at any passenger station. The diagram opposite shows the layout of the tracks in the critical central area and of the four routes leading into that area. It will be seen that there are numerous cross-over facilities between the two running lines, though these would be used only in emergency.

The second control console, with its associated section on the huge panel diagram, covers what could be termed the supporting facilities. In such a highly automated system as BART all the essential ancillary equipment, such as ventilation, water pumps, communication systems other than train control, is continuously monitored and its performance regulated by computer. The display panel includes provision for instant advice of any emergency such as fire, or the interruption of communications. The highest degree of precaution has been taken with the working through the tube section of line beneath San Francisco Bay. The length that is under water is approximately $3\frac{1}{2}$ miles long, and this section of the Oakland display panel shows continuously the occupancy of this underwater section. This is the one part of the BART system on which continuous indication of train movement is provided; the underwater section is divided, for indication, into 1000ft. lengths, and the occupancy or otherwise of these lengths displayed. There are, in addition, emergency telephones located at frequent intervals throughout the underground sections of the line. It has however not apparently been considered necessary to adopt the standard practice of the London tubes, whereby

San Francisco: BART'S advance publicity: an artist's rendering of the control centre situated on the lower plaza of the Lake Merritt station.

San Francisco: one of the striking and original high-speed trains for the BART system.

telephone wires are run continuously through the tunnels, and a motorman using his own handset can, in emergency, 'clip in' on the tunnel wires at any point and speak to Control. In Oakland the third console, and section of the central display panel covers the electric traction supply, and works in connection with the continuous monitoring of the various supply voltages, and of voltages in the conductor rails at all sections of the line.

Without attempting to go into the technical details of the automatic train control equipment it can be said that in the broadest outline the overall strategy of operation has some points of similarity to that of the Victoria Line in London. In BART the central computer sets the pattern of speed, and train frequency required to provide the timetabled service; but there are 34 local control units that supervise all functions relative to train safety, observation of speed limits, and the interlocking of points at junctions. The line is track-circuited throughout, and the occupancy or otherwise of sections ahead determines the speed of trains. The central computer in its function of overall line regulation lays down the desired speeds for all trains at all times of the day; but the central computer cannot over-ride the safety provisions afforded by the local controls, which are at all times based on the actual occupancy of the tracks. The only thing that can over-ride the local controls, and then in conditions of the utmost safety, is the manual takeover of the train attendant, in cases of emergency. It is important to appreciate however that he can drive the train only within the safety provisions of the track circuit control, and could therefore not proceed to the point of entering a dangerous condition.

Some very careful consideration had to be given to the design of the carriages. They are all independent powered units, so that it is possible to run anything from a one-car to a 10-car train by coupling in multiple unit. A number of novel technical features are being incorporated in the design of the electrical controls and in the method of suspension of the cars from the bogies, but it is in relation to the passenger accommodation that the interest of visitors and regular travellers will undoubtedly centre. The cars are as wide as they are high—10ft. 6in. in each direction. It needs no more than a reference to the dimensions of British main line coaches, 9ft. wide by 12ft. 6in. high, to emphasise the striking difference. BART is completely separate from the main line railways running into San Francisco and Oakland, and so to afford greater stability in high speed running the gauge was made 5ft. 6in. instead of the standard 4ft. 8½in. But while the uniform height and width of the cars was ideally suited to the Trans-Bay tube section of the line, on which the tunnels are circular in cross-section, there was another cogent reason for adopting so low a profile. This was influenced by the 52 miles of route that will be at ground level, or on viaducts, and thus subject to the high winds that often prevail in the Bay Area. The low profile will do much to reduce air resistance at the high rates of acceleration and maximum speed that will be a characteristic feature of the service. Each car will be no less than 70ft. long, but by the use of aluminium alloy for the body construction the tare weight of the cars will be only 32 English tons, a very moderate figure seeing that each car has four 150 horsepower traction motors. Passengers will account for another 4½ to 5 tons in a car with every seat taken, and with 600 horsepower for about 37 tons total load, there should be ample power for acceleration. As in all other things so with coaching stock, BART is not doing things by halves!

In the foregoing paragraph I mentioned the Trans-Bay tube. This has been constructed by what is generally termed the 'Submerged Tunnelling' system, as used for

San Francisco: a model of BART'S Mac Arthur station in which the central steel canopy will cover four running lines.

the Rotterdam Metro, and for the crossing of the Seine in Paris by the new Regional Express Metro. Over the years however, American methods of submerged tunnelling have differed considerably from those commonly adopted in Europe, and the Trans-Bay tube has a number of features of special interest. Considerable experience has been gained during the past 40 years on the eastern side of the U.S.A. with sunken tunnels for road traffic, mostly built to provide two-lane roadway within an octagonal-shaped concrete jacket. Where more than two lanes of traffic had to be provided for additional tunnels were installed, running side by side. These tunnels usually had a cylindrical steel shell to ensure water-tightness, and an inner reinforced concrete cylinder, for strength. The techniques adopted in nearly all these 'east coast' installations were derived largely from shipbuilding practice; but when it came to the provision of certain submerged tunnels on the west coast of the U.S.A., the practice described in connection with the Rotterdam Metro, of building the tunnels in sections, in a dry-dock was adopted. Actually the prototype American tunnel of this kind preceded the first Dutch example by ten years, and was laid under a part of San Francisco Bay in 1928 between Oakland and Alameda, for road traffic. The BART tunnel is however of a highly specialised form of construction, first used in the Baytown Tunnel at Galveston, Texas, in 1953.

The cross-section can be likened to that of a pair of binoculars, with two circular 'tube' tunnels, one for each running line, contained within a single steel shell. The form

280

is shown in the picture on page 282. Within the outer shell there is a thick inner shell of reinforced concrete, while the base of the unit is flat. Whereas tunnel sections used on the east coast of the U.S.A. were actually built on the slipways of established shipyards the Trans-Bay tubes were built in the 'west-coast' style in dry dock. The line of the tunnel is marked by a trench dredged in the sea-bed, and this is made somewhat deeper than will actually be required for the finished tunnel. In practically every case it would be impossible to make the bottom of the trench of a sufficiently correct slope, by simple dredging methods, and the usual practice is to wait until the tunnel element is ready, or nearly ready for sinking, and then to put a layer of coarse sand throughout the length of the trench. The upper surface of this layer of sand is then 'planed' to the precise level required for the base of the tunnel section. This needs quite an elaborate apparatus, that could be likened to a floating travelling crane. Instead of running on rails along factory walls the transverse carriage carrying the 'planing' apparatus runs on girders supported by two massive barges. The girders are shaped in accordance with the profile of the tunnel base required, and the planer, or 'screed' as it is termed is suspended from the travelling carriage and provides a smooth and accurate base for the tunnel segments to rest upon. These latter are sunk into position as soon as possible after the planing is completed, so as to eliminate the chance of any disturbance of the profile by under water currents.

Reference to the cross-section of the tunnel binocular, and noting that the outside consists of steel plating, $\frac{3}{8}$in. thick, might suggest that submersion in muddy water, especially salt water, would lead to rapid corrosion, and raise the question as to why the outside were not protected by an outer shell of concrete. It has been found from long experience that however effectively a metallic surface be covered with paint, or other protective coating there will inevitably be points—admittedly very small ones— where defects or damage to the coating will lead to the bare metal being exposed, and there of course corrosion will start. It was a trouble encountered with buried oil pipe lines, and it has been successfully overcome by a process known as 'cathodic protection'. Corrosion is something of an electrical process, rather like the dissolving away of the zinc terminal in a primary battery, in which current flows from the zinc to the copper through the acid of the battery. The principle of cathodic protection involves the passing of a counter-acting current in the reverse direction, of such a strength as to neutralise the current tending to cause corrosion; and what is being applied to oil pipe lines in the deserts of the Middle East is equally being applied to the steel shell surrounding the 'binocular' tunnel of BART between Oakland and San Francisco.

From what I have written it will be seen that BART is not primarily an underground railway, though it exemplifies the co-ordination that is needed between all forms of railway in the provision of a modern rapid transit service. It is, like the great majority of railways featured in this book a purely passenger line, and the present 75-mile network is intended to be expanded later into a much larger system extending to a route mileage of 385, covering all the nine counties that surround the San Francisco Bay. The area at present served contains a population of some $2\frac{1}{2}$ million people, and is still growing rapidly, and the first section that will be completely in operation by 1972 has cost them about £420 million. In finally surveying its many outstanding features one inevitably makes comparisons with the latest practices in London and elsewhere. Its General Manager, Mr. B. R. Stokes, has said that in its profound impact on the economic, social and public improvement aspects of life in the San Francisco Bay Area, it

San Francisco: an artist's impression from sea-bed level, of how the tubes were lowered into position.

could well prove as significant as the trans-continental railways of a century ago. Speed and comfort is the essence of BART's philosophy, together with mass transportation on a scale equal to that of the busiest underground lines in London and Paris.

From the San Francisco bay area one looks to city commuter travel the world over, and everywhere one finds the same problem of extreme street congestion with private cars of the men who prize independence of movement, at any time of the day, because public transport is crowded and often inconvenient. While in the majority of cases there is little difference in speed, unless ones points of origin and destination lie on a direct route, the ordinary commuter, as well as the senior business executive prefers the morning and evening 'tooth and claw' progress on the roads to the 'squashed microbe' atmosphere of the underground. In this respect BART could well be making a major breakthrough, and one looks back somewhat wistfully to the vision of that genial old buccaneer, James Staats Forbes, with his 'deep level District' express line from Earls Court to Charing Cross! If only Charles Tyson Yerkes had been a railwayman as well as a financier the pattern on London Underground might have been very different. In the event the majority of cities have followed the London formula, though as the preceding chapter showed the conception of a much faster deep level line has come to fruition in Paris in the form of the Regional Express Metro. One of the most recent manifestations of the problem of commuter travel into large cities, though not with underground railways, comes from Perth, Western Australia, where a most interesting development over the existing surface lines of the Western Australian Government Railways has taken place. Perth would not be reckoned among either the largest or most congested of cities in the world; but an exchange station has been established at Midland, 10 miles from the city centre, where extensive car parking and bus terminal facilities have been provided, and from whence a frequent service of non-stop trains is operated into the central city station.

The suburban traffic problem is not likely to grow less in any of the large centres of population in the world, and the San Francisco venture will be watched with the greatest interest. It is by any standards an expensive job, but already it is evident that trade and housing developments are following the line of the railway. A remarkable example is afforded by the city of Fremont, at the present terminus of what is called the Southern Alameda line of BART. Fremont is roughly 30 miles from Oakland, and 35 from downtown San Francisco, and yet around the still unfinished terminus a new civic centre is rapidly taking shape; the value of land is increasing up to ten times its former value, and a core of large commercial and industrial enterprises are being established. This follows the pattern of the country extensions of London's Underground, but on a very much more comprehensive scale, which were usually developed only to the extent of becoming dormitory suburbs. In San Francisco and the Bay Area, the whole project has involved such a huge capital investment that there is naturally concern as to what extent it will pay off. The General Manager, Mr. B. R. Stokes, has this to say:

'We at BART have learned considerably from our experiences in the areas of economic boom, sociological impact and public development as our system grows. And we expect that other cities just now embarking upon rapid transit systems can learn from our experience.

'I think it is necessary to keep three things firmly in mind. First, a rapid transit network can be an effective development tool, but it must be used. Affected cities, through master planning, zoning and land-use changes, must determine early in the game what they want their cities to become.

'Secondly, the rapid transit agency must launch and sustain a far-reaching educational programme aimed at private and public decision-makers to make them aware of just how much the system can change the face of their particular region.

'Lastly, a system such as BART's can be a strong catalyst in sociological change. It is up to the people who plan, build, ride and pay for such systems to see that this catalytic energy is harnessed for the maximum benefit to all.'

Pondering upon these words, uttered when BART is on the threshold of opening its turnstiles to the commuting public of the Bay Area, one can see in the underground railway of the future a function altogether wider and more important sociologically than we, in Great Britain, for example, have seen up to now. Imagine for instance the impact of an outer ring of, say, five underground express terminals around London, each equipped with lavish car-parking, from which a frequent service of really fast trains, of maximum comfort, would follow deep level, independent routes to a relatively few central exchange stations. The capital cost would be astronomical, but so would be the savings in time, petrol, wear and tear on cars, and in relief of congestion in the central area streets. Meanwhile the story of underground railways is one of never-ending variety and development. It would be a venturesome thing to try and predict, for example, what the next steps in automation are likely to be!

San Francisco: interior of one of the high-speed tubes.

INDEX